Anna Becker
Identity, Power, and Prestige in Switzerland

Pedagogy

Anna Becker, Ph.D., is a postdoctoral scholar in the Department of Education Sciences at the University of Fribourg, Switzerland, where she conducts research and teaches seminars on multilingualism, second language learning, language and power, and migration and mobility.

Anna Becker

Identity, Power, and Prestige in Switzerland's Multilingual Education

[transcript]

Dissertation zur Erlangung der Doktorwürde an der Philosophischen Fakultät der Universität Freiburg (Schweiz). Genehmigt von der Philosophischen Fakultät auf Antrag von Prof. Dr. Cathryn Magno (1. Gutachterin), Prof. Dr. Kara Brown (2. Gutachterin) und Prof. Dr. Elena Makarova (3. Gutachterin). Freiburg, den 5. Mai 2022. Prof. Dr. Dominik Schöbi, Dekan.

Original title of the dissertation: "English in Multilingual Switzerland - Mediator or Troublemaker? An Analysis of Lived Experiences of Language, Perspectives on Multilingualism, and Language Education Policy in Swiss Upper Secondary Schools."

Published with the support of the Swiss National Science Foundation.

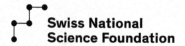

Bibliographic information published by the Deutsche Nationalbibliothek
The Deutsche Nationalbibliothek lists this publication in the Deutsche Nationalbibliografie; detailed bibliographic data are available in the Internet at http://dnb.dnb.de

This work is licensed under the Creative Commons Attribution 4.0 (BY) license, which means that the text may be remixed, transformed and built upon and be copied and redistributed in any medium or format even commercially, provided credit is given to the author.
Creative Commons license terms for re-use do not apply to any content (such as graphs, figures, photos, excerpts, etc.) not original to the Open Access publication and further permission may be required from the rights holder. The obligation to research and clear permission lies solely with the party re-using the material.

First published in 2023 by transcript Verlag, Bielefeld
© Anna Becker

Cover layout: Maria Arndt, Bielefeld

https://doi.org/10.14361/9783839466193
Print-ISBN 978-3-8376-6619-9
PDF-ISBN 978-3-8394-6619-3
ISSN of series: 2703-1047
eISSN of series: 2703-1055

Meinen Eltern

Contents

Acknowledgements 11

Abstract 13

List of Figures 15

List of Tables 17

List of Abbreviations 19

Introduction 21
1.1 The Study's Setting 24
1.2 The Study's Purpose 26
1.3 Language, Ideologies, and Hierarchies within Linguascapes 28
1.4 Lived Experiences of Language 31

Education, Languages, and Power 33
2.1 Introduction 33
2.2 Education and Power 34
2.3 Language, Education, and Power 38
    2.3.1 Gramsci's Linguistic Hegemony 39
        2.3.1.1 Spontaneous Grammar 41
        2.3.1.2 Normative Grammar 43
    2.3.2 Bourdieu's Symbolic Power 47
    2.3.3 Delpit's Culture of Power 51
2.4 (Unequal) Englishes 55
    2.4.1 (Unequal) Englishes – Concepts and Definitions 56
    2.4.2 English as a Lingua Franca 58
    2.4.3 The Economic Nature of (Unequal) Englishes 61
2.5 Critical Multiculturalism 64

2.6 Plurilingual Identities, Heteroglossic Linguistic Repertoires,
    and Multilingual Educational Approaches 68
    2.6.1 The Multilingual Turn 69
    2.6.2 Linguistic Identities and Repertoires 72
          2.6.2.1 Linguistic Identities 72
          2.6.2.2 Linguistic Repertoires 74
    2.6.3 Heteroglossia 77
    2.6.4 Translanguaging 79
          2.6.4.1 Definitions and Conceptualization 80
          2.6.4.2 Translanguaging as Empowerment 80
          2.6.4.3 Toward Equitable Language Teaching 82
    2.6.5 Content and Language Integrated Learning 83
          2.6.5.1 Definitions and Conceptualization 83
          2.6.5.2 Student-Centered and Future-Oriented Language Teaching 84
          2.6.5.3 CLIL and Empirical Studies 86

Methodology 89
3.1 Relevant Research in Phenomenology/Multilingualism 90
3.2 Research Questions 92
3.3 Research Design 93
3.4 Protection of Human Subjects 97
3.5 Researcher Bias 97
3.6 Data Collection 99
    3.6.1 Research Setting 99
    3.6.2 Site Selection 100
    3.6.3 Questionnaires 101
          3.6.3.1 The Instrument 102
          3.6.3.2 Sample 103
          3.6.3.3 Procedure 105
    3.6.4 Interviews 105
          3.6.4.1 Students' Interviews 106
          3.6.4.2 Teachers' Interviews 107
    3.6.5 Data Collection Procedures: Gaining Entry 108
3.7 Data Analysis 110
    3.7.1 Transcription 110
    3.7.2 Questionnaires 111
    3.7.3 Interviews 111
    3.7.4 Emerging Themes 112
3.8 Pilot Study 113
3.9 Data Collection/Analysis Issues 114
3.10 Translation 114

3.11 Limitations of the Study 115

Findings 117
4.1 Plurilingual Identities within Restrictive Linguistic Diversity 117
    4.1.1 Students in Grisons 118
    4.1.2 Teachers in Grisons 121
    4.1.3 Students in Zurich 123
    4.1.4 Teachers in Zurich 126
    4.1.5 Students in Fribourg 128
    4.1.6 Teachers in Fribourg 129
4.2 'Monolingual Habitus' in the Education System 130
    4.2.1 Comparison of Student Data 130
    4.2.2 Students in Grisons 135
    4.2.3 Teachers in Grisons 140
    4.2.4 Students in Zurich 144
    4.2.5 Teachers in Zurich 148
    4.2.6 Students in Fribourg 155
    4.2.7 Teachers in Fribourg 156
4.3 Language Hierarchies 161
    4.3.1 Students in Grisons 162
    4.3.2 Teachers in Grisons 165
    4.3.3 Students in Zurich 168
    4.3.4 Teachers in Zurich 171
    4.3.5 Students in Fribourg 174
    4.3.6 Teachers in Fribourg 176
4.4 'Native-Speaker' and 'Standard-Speech' Ideologies 178
    4.4.1 Students in Grisons 178
    4.4.2 Teachers in Grisons 181
    4.4.3 Students in Zurich 182
    4.4.4 Teachers in Zurich 183
    4.4.5 Teachers in Fribourg 185
4.5 Symbolic Violence 186
    4.5.1 Students in Grisons 186
    4.5.2 Teachers in Grisons 188
    4.5.3 Students in Zurich 188
    4.5.4 Teachers in Zurich 190
    4.5.5 Teachers in Fribourg 191

Discussion 193
5.1 Sameness and Difference in Identity Expression through Language 193
5.2 Pressure toward Monolingualism 197

5.3 Language Hierarchies within the Hegemonic *Willensnation* 204
5.4 Symbolic Power and Legitimacy in the 'Native-Speaker' and 'Standard-Speech Ideology' 211

Conclusion 219
6.1 The Language Learning Debate as Starting Point 220
6.2 Linguistic Repertoires, Lived Experiences of Language, and Identity Expression through Language in Restrictive Multilingual Contexts 221
6.3 The Reproduction of the 'Monolingual Habitus' in Swiss Upper Secondary Schools 222
6.4 Language Hierarchies 224
6.5 Symbolic Power and Legitimacy in the 'Native-Speaker' and 'Standard-Speech' Ideologies 226
6.6 Theoretical Implications 228
6.7 Implications for Policy, Curricula, and Practice 230
6.8 Future Research and Conclusion 233

References 235

Appendix A 257
Questionnaire "Multilingual Switzerland" 257
    Your personal information 257
    Languages and country of origin 257
    Languages at school 258
    Language use 258
    Language preferences 259
    Semi-structured interview guide for students 260
    Semi-structured interview guide for teachers 261

Appendix B 263
Transcription 263

Appendix C 265
Descriptive statistics 265

Appendix D 267

Acknowledgements

This dissertation is also the work and achievement of many family members, friends, and colleagues who supported me and to whom I owe special thanks.

- First, I would like to thank my parents, Sigrid and Christoph, and my brother, Yannic, for your incredible love, support, and wisdom throughout my life and for your perseverance and positivity, even in the most difficult circumstances.
- This work would not have been possible without you, Mikaël, MF1. Thank you for always being there, for impressing and surprising me, and for helping me to pursue my dreams.
- To my family, Oma, Oma, Opa, Godie, Christoph, Pat, Isa, Kalli, Lenny, Marianne, Franco, and Denise: Thank you to all of you for believing in me. You have been so loving, supportive, and understanding. I am so very grateful that I can always count on you.
- I owe tremendous thanks to you, Professor Cathryn Magno, not only for your invaluable guidance and comments on the numerous drafts preceding this dissertation, but (and perhaps more importantly) also for helping me see the true purpose of academia and of education. Your relentless commitment to social justice in international and comparative education has shaped my way of thinking and has shown me the kind of scholar I wish to be.
- Thank you very much, Professors Kara Brown and Elena Makarova, for reviewing the manuscript and for providing your expertise as external advisors.
- I would also like to thank my colleagues and friends at the Department of Educational Sciences at the University of Fribourg: Alex, Doris, Edgar, Fabienne, Madeleine, Michael, Patrick, Patricia, Sonja, and Veronika, for your support, encouragement, and for our inspiring discussions. Special thanks should also go to my students, in particular those who participated in the pilot study, for your critical questions and thoughts on the dissertation's topic.
- Thank you so much Aurélie, Cristiana, Emily, Hanna, Katharina, Patrick, Pierre-Pascal, Richard, Tarun, Timon, and Valérie for accompanying me on this adventurous journey and for providing fun, distraction, and inspiration.

- I would also like to express my gratitude to Sean O'Dubhghaill for his meticulous proofreading of the manuscript and his interesting ideas on the topic as a minority language speaker.
- Many thanks are also due to the Swiss National Science Foundation for generously providing funding to publish this book open access for everyone to read and use.
- Finally, thank you – grazia – merci – danke – хвала – gracias – ありがとうございました – hvala – teşekkürler – e dupe – obrigada – köszönöm – asante – cảm ơn bạn – Ви благодарам – 唔該 – شكرا to all of the students and teachers who participated in this study! It is thanks to each and every one of you that this dissertation exists today.

Abstract

Multilingualism has played a major role in Swiss society, enshrined historically in its four national languages policy (French, German, Italian, and Romansh). Laws protect each language region's historical 'homogenous' composition and seek to guarantee mutual understanding and social cohesion at a national level. However, the extant legal/policy framework does not account for the plethora of local varieties (notably in German), the influx of heritage languages such as Portuguese, and the international and intra-national *lingua franca* English which increasingly shapes Switzerland's linguistic landscape. The study analyzes the interplay among the neoliberal forces that led to a growing popularity and (perceived) necessity of English, the romantic, traditionalist view on national languages, and the social justice perspective of including heritage languages. This work is embedded in on-going sociopolitical debates in Swiss education language policies and is framed in critical theories of language, education, power, and multiculturalism. This work also draws on concepts of plurilingual identities, heteroglossia, and translanguaging to examine individuals' linguistic repertoires, lived experiences of language, perspectives on Switzerland's multilingualism and multilingual education, and language (sub-)hierarchies. It strives to ameliorate linguistic and educational practices and to increase equity and social justice for minoritized speakers by elucidating underlying (obfuscated) power, hegemonic, and ideological mechanisms. This study contributes to innovative, non-hierarchical approaches to language learning and to bottom-up policy decision-making processes by showcasing students' and teachers' perspectives on languages, language learning, and the aforementioned policies. The study draws on 94 student questionnaires and 34 interviews with students and teachers from the cantons of (French-speaking) Fribourg, (Romansh-speaking) Grisons, and (German-speaking) Zurich by adopting a phenomenological research design that zooms in on individuals' perspectives and practices within their multilingual lifeworlds. The data analysis reveals that Switzerland's multilingualism is restricted to official and prestigious languages, but that this is detrimental to plurilingual identity expression and does not mirror the society's linguistic diversity accurately. This situation is exacerbated within an education system that continues to impose a 'monolingual habitus' or, at best, a 'bilingual habitus' despite the increasing heterogeneity of its students. The data also showed that language hierarchies are legitimized and reproduced within education systems and structures, thereby attributing prestige and power not only to certain languages, but also to their speakers. Ideological influences also legitimize and reproduce sub-hierarchies based on speakers' 'deviance' from the native-speaker yardstick or from local varieties' resemblance to standard-speech norms. The study found that linguistic prejudices and discrimination result in a symbolic violence that negatively affects speakers' linguistic repertoires, well-being, self-confidence, and language teaching in schools. Finally, the study advocates for the (institutional/official) recognition of each individual's linguistic repertoire, the 'normalization' of linguistic and cultural diversity, and for a critical awareness of the interdependency of language, education, and power among all actors in the education sphere.

List of Figures

Figure 1: Geographical distribution of Switzerland's languages 24
Figure 2: The permanent resident population's main languages, 1970–2019 (FSO, 2021a) ... 25
Figure 3: The 15 most common non-national languages among Swiss permanent resident population (in %, in 2019) (FSO, 2021b) 26
Figure 4: Cycle of spontaneous and normative grammars 44
Figure 5: Three Concentric Circles of English, adapted from Kachru (1985) 58
Figure 6: Languages and idioms spoken in the canton of Grisons 101
Figure 7: Students' satisfaction with language teaching 131
Figure 8: Prioritization of English in school 131
Figure 9: Prioritization of English in the curriculum 132
Figure 10: Including students' heritage languages in the classroom 133
Figure 11: Self-evaluations in non-L1 national languages and in English 134
Figure 12: Grades in non-L1 national languages and in English 134
Figure 13: Liking non-L1 national language versus English 161
Figure 14: Ranking the most significant language in their personal lives – GR 162
Figure 15: Ranking the most significant language in their professional lives – GR 163
Figure 16: Ranking the most significant language in their personal lives – ZH 168
Figure 17: Ranking the most significant language in their professional lives – ZH 169
Figure 18: Ranking the most significant language in their personal lives – FR 174
Figure 19: Ranking the most significant language in their professional lives – FR 175

List of Tables

Table 1: Common reasons for introducing CLIL 85
Table 2: Questionnaire sample 104

List of Abbreviations

AL:	Additional language
CAE:	Cambridge Certificate in Advanced English
CEFR:	Common European Framework of Reference for Languages
CLIL:	Content and Language Integrated Learning
CoE:	Council of Europe
EDK:	Schweizerische Konferenz der kantonalen Erziehungsdirektoren (The Swiss Conference of Cantonal Ministers of Education)
EFL:	English as a foreign language
ELF:	English as a *lingua franca*
FL:	Foreign language
FSO:	Swiss Federal Statistical Office
GFL:	German as a foreign language
HL:	Heritage language
L1, L2:	First language, second language
LangA:	Languages Act
LEP:	Language education policy
LPP:	Language policy and planning
RG:	Rumantsch Grischun

Introduction

There is a saying by Ludwig Wittgenstein that could be used to summarize the underlying message of this study: *Die Grenzen meiner Sprache bedeuten die Grenzen meiner Welt*, which is commonly translated into English as *the limits of my language mean the limits of my world*. Languages and language hierarchies develop out of ideologies that connect individuals, languages, and culture within a social space. People are judged according to their linguistic skills and the 'market value' that a certain language variety, or the one they speak, has within this space or 'field' (Bourdieu, 1991). Some varieties are considered to be more prestigious than others so that speakers of a variety situated at the lower end of a particular language hierarchy can be limited in terms of their personal and professional development. Speakers of prestigious varieties, conversely, typically benefit from the high status of their first language(s) (L1(s)), the seemingly unrestricted access to opportunities, and their ability to accumulate 'linguistic capital' effortlessly (Bourdieu, 1991). A central question facing scholars in the field of language and education, therefore, is: "what [language] resources are assigned what value, by whom, how, why and with what consequences?" (Heller, 2008a, p. 517). Almost ten years later, Heller and McElhinny (2017, p. xv) still see the need to investigate the "question of what language has to do with social difference and social inequality" further. They call for a better "understand[ing of] the relationship between language and social order through linking the value and meaning of language to the value and meaning of the rest of the resources that count in society, and so to the basic working of the economic and political order" (Heller & McElhinny, 2017, p. xv). The present study's intention is to make a meaningful contribution to this field of research by elucidating not only the relationship between languages and social (in)equality,[1] but also between languages and social (in)equity more generally.[2]

English is typically considered a highly prestigious language, one learned and used by individuals from all over the world for inter- and intra-national communication, (social) media, internet, technology, business, education, science, and for other uses. English functions as a *mediator* among individuals with different L1s and cultural backgrounds in most of these contexts and vies to achieve a common communicative goal and to engage in mutual meaning-making. This can involve simple interactions such as a student participating in an exchange in a foreign country or a mandatory working language in big international companies with multinational employees. In both situations, English is defined as a *lingua franca* (ELF) (Seidlhofer, 2011). English functions as a key to opening doors to new opportunities socially, culturally, and economically by vastly enlarging the amount of people with whom one can communicate and connect, and by rendering more spaces accessible. It appears to be a 'good' that people should, and do, wish to obtain in order to enhance their private and professional life in an ever-changing globalized world (Brutt-Griffler, 2002; Graddol, 2006; Blommaert, 2010).

Contrarily, people's chances of personal and/or economic improvement are drastically diminished without this 'linguistic capital', and they risk an enormous lack of competitiveness compared to those who are proficient users of this highly valued language (Grin 2001; 2006; Grin & Korth, 2005; Gal & Woolard, 2001; Heller & Duchêne, 2012; Tupas & Rudby, 2015). In contrast to knowing English, which seemingly easily opens doors to new opportunities, insufficient linguistic skills symbolize a key that locks doors from the inside and restricts access for those who do not fulfill the necessary (or expected) requirements. Thus, English has become a medium that simultaneously creates barriers and inequality as well as promotes and facilitates the cooperation and inclusion of culturally diverse people in an interconnected, dynamic, and diverse world in which there is ever more transnational interaction and integration among people. Language, then, is not *only* a medium of communication for individuals intra- and inter-culturally; language also expresses, embodies, and symbolizes cultural and political prestige, belonging, identity, and power (Kramsch, 1998). As Brown, Koreinik, and Siiner (2017) put it succinctly: "The voluntary and

---

1   In the case of Switzerland, the Swiss Federal Constitution "ensure[s] that [the Confederation] treats the four national Swiss languages equally" (LangA, Art. 3, a, 2017). According to the Cambridge Dictionary, 'equality' means "the right of different groups of people to have a similar social position and receive the same treatment," for the purpose of this study, based on their linguistic repertoire.

2   Despite the *equal* legal basis of Switzerland's four national languages, this study promotes an *equity* perspective since a (restrictive) *de jure* linguistic equality does not automatically lead to a situation of linguistic equity in which individual speakers and their linguistic repertoires are treated fairly, never mind equally (Stewart, 2013).

forced transnational mobility of people, ideas, and money generate new, sometimes hybrid ideas of belonging, identity, and possibility, while shaping language choice, need, affiliation, and understanding" (p. 6).

The seeming paradox of English's omnipresence and usefulness, and its related problem of unequal access, are critical challenges for the education system because it serves as the main provider of modern societies' language teaching. Language education policies dictate who will learn what, when, how, and to what degree. This challenge is heavily intensified when decisions about language instruction in schools are made within officially multilingual countries. Countries with more than one official language typically provide language teaching in a second or third national language in order to establish, and potentially to ameliorate the social cohesion, cooperation, and understanding of different language groups within the same country (Coray, 2001). This is the case in Switzerland where language laws guarantee and strengthen the equal status of the national languages – French, German,[3] Italian and – to a more restricted extent – Romansh – for the sake of internal cohesion, linguistic equality, as well as for the sake of individual and institutional linguistic development. Furthermore, language instruction in public schools has traditionally focused on fostering linguistic and cultural competences in the two dominant national languages – French and German – and on navigating the corresponding, different characteristics between the Roman and Germanic cultures respectively. English takes on a more complex role in Switzerland, given that it is an internationally popular and important foreign language. Whereas the teaching of national languages can be said to follow the romantic idea of expressing one's identity in one's own language and valuing diverse cultures (Geeraerts, 2003; see also the concept of 'pride' in Heller & Duchêne, 2012), the teaching of English has rationalist underpinnings. It symbolizes emancipation and participation on the one hand, as well as academic and economic opportunities on the other (Geeraerts, 2003; see also the concept of 'profit' in Heller & Duchêne, 2012). By speaking English with a certain competency, individuals are granted access to transnational spaces that provide opportunities to participate and to engage in emancipatory and liberatory activities. Such instrumental value is

---

3   This study considers the following distinctions to be important regarding German: Different German varieties exist in Switzerland and terminology is not always used coherently. In this study, the following definitions are adopted: Swiss Standard German (SSG) is used in official contexts, such as educational institutions, written communication, and the law. It is the official language in German-speaking Switzerland by law. SSG differs from Standard German (SG) which is typically associated with Germany in terms of vocabulary, orthography, and other grammatical characteristics, which are called 'helvetisms' (Dürscheid & Sutter, 2014). Swiss German, conversely, according to the Federal Department of Foreign Affairs (2021a, n.p.) "...is a collection of distinct Alemannic dialects" which exist in many different local or regional varieties and is the *de facto* language spoken in German-speaking Switzerland on a daily basis (for more details see 1.4.2).

highlighted when students who seek to acquire a highly prestigious language, such as English, do so merely for their academic and socioeconomic benefits. At the same time, this acquisition endangers multilingual societies' linguistic diversity in terms of languages that may not have the same status and prestige as English (inter)nationally (Skutnabb-Kangas, 2000; Phillipson, 1992; 2003).

1.1 The Study's Setting

Switzerland can be considered an outlier among its neighboring countries and within the European context *tout court*. Heavily influenced by nation-building efforts in the 18th century, Switzerland's neighbors emphasized their unity by determining and by codifying one national language, such as German, Italian, or French. Interestingly, Switzerland has defied the *one nation – one language* ideology (Bauman & Briggs, 2000) and has integrated all three neighboring languages, plus Romansh, as its national languages. The preservation of these languages is protected by laws, such as the Languages Act and (educational) policies that introduce a second national language mandatorily in primary and/or secondary schooling. Further regulated by the territoriality principle, Switzerland's national languages are distributed geographically and serve to divide its linguistic landscape into 17 monolingual German-speaking cantons, four monolingual French-speaking ones, three bilingual (French/German) ones, one trilingual (Romansh/German/Italian), and one monolingual Italian-speaking one (see Figure 1 below).

Figure 1: Geographical distribution of Switzerland's languages

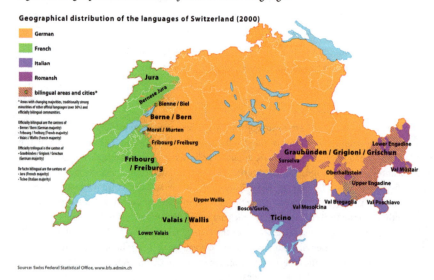

In addition to its already *de jure* multilingual landscape, Switzerland is home to a plethora of heritage languages (HLs), which have increased significantly over the past decades without any concomitant changes being made to the language policy framework. According to Polinsky (2018, p. 9), HL speakers are "simultaneous or sequential (successive) bilingual[s] whose weaker language is the dominant language of that society." While speakers of other languages than the four national ones made up 3.7% of the population in 1970, they accounted for 22.7% in 2019 (FSO, 2021a). The development is captured in the graph below.

Figure 2: The permanent resident population's main languages, 1970–2019 (FSO, 2021a)

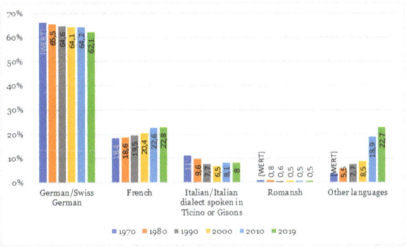

The 15 most common ones among these heritage languages for Switzerland's permanent resident population have been visualized in the graph below.

Figure 3: The 15 most common non-national languages among Swiss permanent resident population (in %, in 2019) (FSO, 2021b)

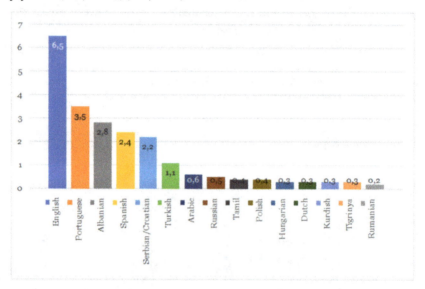

Thus, despite its multilingual landscape and the importance allocated in the education system, the average Swiss person is often not bi- or even plurilingual; that said, and interestingly, most Swiss people speak English to a very high level, thereby supporting its *lingua franca* function in the country (Durham, 2014).

1.2   The Study's Purpose

This study is situated in the intersections of applied linguistics and upper secondary education research in multilingual Switzerland; this is a setting particularly under-researched, but that remains relevant due to ongoing policy reforms that were expected to be implemented in 2023. Swiss upper secondary schools need to be defined, given national education systems' specificities; they represent the post-compulsory part of secondary education and can be further divided into three different programs in Switzerland: general education, vocational education, and training programs. The latter two offer trainings for adolescents to learn a profession and in which the majority of Swiss students enroll after lower secondary education. In the former, adolescents are prepared for tertiary level education programs in Baccalaureate schools and this accounts for 20–30% of the students enrolled in post-compulsory education. This study uses *upper secondary schools* to refer to the Baccalaureate schools, which students complete at the age of 18/19 (Swiss Education, 2020; Swissinfo, n.d.). According to the FSO (2020), 91% of upper secondary students are Swiss nationals.

This study's interest emerges out of societal debates concerning the power and politics of language teaching and draws on several examples in Switzerland in which English represents exactly both sides – a *mediator* and a *troublemaker*. It focuses on the lived experiences of local agents of Swiss language policies and on their implementation, namely students and teachers. These areas are becoming increasingly important in a globally interconnected 21st century education system shaped by neo-capitalism and migration: Students (are forced to) move, to complete their education in very different places with different local languages, and to adapt to the rapidly changing requirements for their entry into the job market. Teachers are increasingly challenged to cope with heterogeneous classrooms and with the discrepancy among their real-life teaching concerns, curricula, and the textbooks they have to hand. The study will, therefore, analyze the interplay among the neoliberal forces that led to an increase in English's popularity and necessity in Switzerland, the romantic, traditionalist view of its four national languages, and the social justice perspective on including students' heritage languages by asking:

1. How are students' and teachers' linguistic repertoires constituted and how are they employed so as to position individuals and groups within (restrictive) linguascapes?
2. What are students' and teachers' lived experiences of language?
3. What are students' and teachers' perspectives on Switzerland's multilingualism and its multilingual education?
4. How do students and teachers (de)construct and legitimize (existing) language hierarchies?
5. How do they (de)construct and legitimize (existing) sub-hierarchies within certain languages?

These questions address real, sociopolitical issues in Swiss education's language policies that have caused emotionally charged public debates and have raised difficult questions that have not been entirely answered to date. In answering the aforementioned research questions, this study sheds light on the underlying power and hegemonic mechanisms that can obscure and hinder the equitable integration of individuals' voices into a pluralistic learning space. It contributes to more innovative, non-hierarchical approaches to language learning and to bottom-up policy decision-making processes. The study makes apparent that the educational and linguistic choices made by these actors are often based on social and political factors and that this implies the need for an interdisciplinary sociolinguistic and educational investigation and input. *Language*, *ideologies*, and *hierarchies* as well as *lived experiences of language* are briefly outlined in the sections that follow in order to clarify the terminology used in the research questions.

1.3 Language, Ideologies, and Hierarchies within Linguascapes

This study adopts Heller's (2007) distinction between language as a static system and as a dynamic one, as "linguistic resources which are organized in ways that make sense under specific social conditions (or, to use a Foucauldian approach, within specific discursive regimes)" (Heller, 2007, p. 1). Although this study advocates the latter, the common understanding of language as a system was established historically through modernist nation-state ideologies (Heller, 2006; Hobsbawm, 2012) intending to construct national identity by following the *one language – one culture – one nation* paradigm (Pujolar, 2007). Consequently, these ideologies continue to impact upon individuals' (and even researchers') opinions, beliefs, and understandings of language, similarly to other crucial markers of social structurization such as gender, race, and class (Orelus, 2012). In this study, *language* is defined "as a set of resources which circulate in unequal ways in social networks and discursive spaces, and whose meaning and value are socially constructed within the constraints of social organizational processes, under specific historical conditions" (Heller, 2007, p. 2). Furthermore, viewing language "as a fundamentally *social* phenomenon…it also reflexively constructs our analyses as a form of social action, and situates our disciplines…within the modes of regulation and discursive regimes of our times" (Heller, 2007, p. 2 [emphasis in original]). This study examines language ideologies by adopting "a critical social perspective…combining practice, ideology and political economy," (Heller, 2007, p. 2) and investigates how they, materialized in hierarchies, have felt and material consequences for certain groups of speakers in specific and for Switzerland's multilingual society more generally.

Language hierarchies are to be understood – in this study – as an artificially constructed social phenomenon based on language ideologies, in which languages are ranked according to their perceived prestige and value within the linguistic market (Bourdieu, 1991; Kroskrity, 2000). Importantly, they "are not inherently linguistic, but rather social and political; language is but one terrain for the construction of relations of social difference and social inequality" (Heller, 2007, p. 2). Thus, language issues are *mobilized* in order to gloss over sociopolitical or economic interests or discourses (Pujolar, 2007). Hierarchies are never fixed, since languages are constantly revaluated depending on financial, economic, military, and other geopolitical factors. *Language ideologies*[4] or *linguistic differentiation*, as defined by Irvine and Gal (2000), are "the ideas with which participants and observers frame their understanding of linguistic varieties and map those understandings onto people, events, and activities that are significant to them" (p. 35). They go on to explain that researchers focusing on these linguistic ideologies are as biased as the speakers that they are analyzing; they also argue that it is often the linguists and other language experts who define, set standards, and separate varieties from others. In so doing, they attribute a certain value to a specific variety, thereby providing the necessary requirement for it to become an official language.[5] This is an important point to keep in mind throughout this study. Irvine and Gal (2000) further state that:

> ...linguistic features are seen as reflecting and expressing broader cultural images of people and activities. Participants' ideologies about language locate linguistic phenomena as part of, and evidence for, what they believe to be systematic behavioral, aesthetic, affective, and moral contrasts among the social groups indexed. That is, people have, and act in relation to, ideologically constructed representations of linguistic differences. (p. 37)

These linguistic/cultural images and ideologies typically incorporate power dynamics and transmit sociopolitical meaning (Blommaert, 1999). As Bucholtz and Hall (2004, p. 379) summarize: "ideology organizes and enables all cultural beliefs and practices as well as the power relations that result from these." They are localized within a given space, such as a nation-state, in which *de facto* or *de jure* language policies dictate how inhabitants of this space must speak. I use the term *linguascape* by drawing on Appadurai (1996), who coined the concept of *scapes*, which describe "deeply perspectival constructs, inflected by the historical, linguistic, and political situatedness of different sorts of actors" (p. 33). The analogy here refers to those speakers (actors) who position themselves based on their linguistic skills within an increasingly more complex and diversified space that is shaped by historical, political, and social factors (Blommaert, 2008). The term *linguascape* is employed – in this study – to describe a (virtual) space in which subjects position themselves through language, construct their own identities, and experience recognition or devaluation based on their linguistic repertoires' market value. Although Liebscher and Dailey-O'Cain (2013) do not characterize the linguascape as a physical space *per se*, they do

---

4   The term is also sometimes used in the singular. In line with Kroskrity (2004), I prefer the plural term since it is not a final product, but is rather a fluid organization of different layers and dimensions such as identity, morality, aesthetics, society, norms, and beliefs. For a broader overview on language ideologies see Woolard & Schieffelin (1994).

5   A saying that is commonly used in linguistics to emphasize the language's embeddedness in a sociopolitical reality, and the arbitrariness of the definition of what a language really is, goes as follows: "A language is simply a dialect that has an army and a navy" (author unknown, quoted in Irvine & Gal (2000, p. 35), most often attributed to Max Weinreich).

argue that the term emphasizes "the way the languages of a space form part of that space's environment and are as ever-present a part of that space as its physical landscape" (p. 35).

Focusing more on sociopolitical embeddedness, Otheguy, García, and Reid (2015) add that "like a named national cuisine, a named language is defined by the social, political or ethnic affiliation of its speakers...a named language cannot be defined linguistically, it is not, strictly speaking, a linguistic object" (p. 286). The authors contend that so-called languages are social or sociopolitical phenomena, which are constructed and regulated by the state, by deconstructing languages as actually existing entities. The state, thus, has the authority to make the *arbitrary* difference between languages, dialects, and other ways of speaking legally binding and, more importantly, can appropriate official status to the variety preferred by a small group of elites. They go on to argue that a focus on the individual's linguistic repertoire and the deconstruction of languages, as named entities, is necessary wherever appropriate in order to do away with language ideologies. Makoni and Pennycook (2007) and Pennycook (2010) have pushed for a 'decategorization' or 'disinvention' of named languages in order to reduce discrimination and social inequity based on linguistic differences; the implementation has proven rather difficult, however.[6] In line with Otheguy, García, and Reid (2015), this study adopts the perspective of recognizing a certain utility and necessity within these categories. In order to research the topic of multilingual education, one is faced with the reality that languages are (still) taught separately in schools, even though attempts have been made to foster integrative language teaching. Basing language teaching strategies on the Common European Framework of Reference for Languages (CEFR), students are expected to achieve a mastery in the medium of instruction as well as in at least two foreign languages. Entering the professional world, applicants are often asked to provide language certificates in a certain, required language that sometimes does not have a direct relevance to the job. Furthermore, a distinction of named languages is needed in order to examine language hierarchies. Languages and their attributed values need to be investigated in order to possibly entangle or even to do away with these different positions. This can only be achieved if (for now) named entities continue to be (critically) used as a categorical framework. Speakers of minority languages will continue to make use of the language concept in order to visualize the perceived and felt discrepancies between their language(s) and other (more) prestigious ones. Thus, it is not (yet) conceivable to simply abandon these categories when talking about educational/professional or advocacy settings. The difference between being a native English or Albanian speaker have physical,

---

6   Romaine (1994), for instance, hypothesizes that the differentiation and categorization of languages as separate entities is a 'European invention' resulting from literacy and standardization processes.

psychological, social, and material consequences for many people. Researchers should consider opting for alternatives to such a restrictive, categorical system in critical research on education and multilingualism. The concept of language often does not do justice, or even accurately capture, the multiple discursive practices encountered among speakers (Love, 2017). More flexible and inclusive solutions, such as *translanguaging*, are discussed below. The social reality, however, still relies upon these named entities and categories.

Importantly, despite being mental constructs, language ideologies form the basis of social practices and can result in physical or social discrimination. Following the 'native-speaker ideology' (Chomsky, 1957; 1965) and judging speakers for their 'deviant' accent, for instance, can create barriers between artificially constructed in-groups. This judgement of certain expressions, accents, or even of entire varieties leads to their speakers being (de)valued accordingly, not only on a linguistic level but as social individuals in a wider network; this can foster or impede social justice (Lippi-Green, 1997; Ortega, 2019; Piller, 2016). It follows that belonging to a certain linguistic group can determine how these individuals will be judged and assessed as people and even as a nation (Bylin & Tingsell, 2021). Hymes (1973) explains the connection between language (and ideologies) and social inequality as a natural phenomenon. Being part of a regularly occurring process, certain people will decide to use certain expressions or varieties more than they will others. These forms of speech will rise in popularity and will become a prestigious language almost effortlessly. The expressions or varieties used less commonly will automatically lose their applicability and all of their speakers by the end of the process. The obvious paradox, then, is that people seemingly choose to appropriate certain expressions or varieties, through which an underlying force is created, thereby reaching more and more people. Although voluntary at first, people are forced to follow it by adopting their speech and ways of communication once this movement is underway. This can be seen in changing language hierarchies: Whereas Latin or French found themselves at the top of the language hierarchy for a long time, recent globalization processes have catapulted English to the top. While individuals have their own perceptions of how much prestige and value they attribute to a specific language variety, it is typically a normalized social construct that is perceived similarly by individuals within the same society.

1.4 Lived Experiences of Language

Another important concept used in the study's research questions concerns the *lived experiences of language*; this refers primarily to the subjective dimension of both perception and understanding. According to Boylorn (2008), a lived experience "is a representation and understanding of a researcher or research subject's human experiences, choices, and options and how those factors influence one's perception of knowledge" (p. 490). The aim of researching lived experiences is not so much to produce facts about social reality, but rather to gain a more profound understanding of individuals' experiences and actions (Merleau-Ponty, 2014). Lived experiences of language are understood as experiences gained either through linguistic interaction or the deprivation thereof. Access can be either granted or denied to a certain speech community, depending on one's linguistic repertoire (Busch, 2017c). Therefore, linguistic experiences can be very emotional and are also linked to other personal experiences. Individuals can be forbidden from speaking their L1 and might be forced to use another language instead. They (are forced to) acquire – whether consciously or unconsciously – a certain variety, to adopt a specific accent, and to abandon their linguistic and cultural heritage. Plurilingual individuals particularly are exposed to such emotional experiences revolving around language. These can also certainly be positive, of course, such as when language opens the way to intercultural exchange, private and professional enhancement, and emancipation. Drawing on a phenomenological perspective, the focus here is on the subject itself, how individuals feel, perceive, and position themselves through experiences, actions, and interactions *vis-à-vis* other individuals, the society, and the discourses produced within. Thus, lived experiences of language have a direct impact upon the person, their bodily and emotional dimensions that create feelings of joy, pain, (in)security, embarrassment, and belonging among others. As stated by Kramsch (2009), these personal emotional experiences are decisive in language learning. Positive experiences linked to the feelings of joy, appreciation, and belonging contribute hugely to the success of the learning process, whereas negative experiences attributed to linguistic insecurity, such as embarrassment and shame, hinder development further. The present study investigates students' and teachers' linguistic repertoires and how these shape their lived experiences of language and follows Kramsch's call for more of an emphasis to be placed on, and more research into, language learning experiences and their impact on each individual.

Education, Languages, and Power

2.1 Introduction

This chapter's focus is to situate this study in the wider field of critical multilingual education research by drawing from educational and applied linguistics literature. Its aim is to elaborate the underlying framework of power mechanisms, as well as explicit and implicit language education policies, in schools in order to analyze and interpret study subjects' perspectives on and experiences with language hierarchies and ideologies thereafter. First, the relationship between power and education in a broader sense will be discussed, which will serve as the study's theoretical foundation (2.2). Second, the aspect of language will be integrated into the discussion of power relations in order to demonstrate how language can both connect culturally diverse groups and improve mutual understanding, but how it can also create barriers and engender social exclusion (2.3). The role of English in particular, as *mediator* or *troublemaker*, is examined in section 2.4, following a relatively new research paradigm of *(unequal) Englishes*. These power dynamics are further elucidated through the concept of *critical multiculturalism* (2.5). Plurilingual identities are analyzed with regard to individuals' linguistic repertoires and the concepts of *heteroglossia* and *translanguaging* in section 2.6. Finally, ways in which multilingual education can be practiced through different pedagogic approaches, such as *translanguaging* or *content and integrated language learning (CLIL)*, are presented.

2.2 Education and Power

> The starting-point of critical elaboration is the consciousness of what one really is, and is 'knowing thyself' as a product of the historical process to date which has deposited in you an infinity of traces, without leaving an inventory. (Gramsci, 1971, p. 324)

The two fundamental principles of democracy and equality constitute the modern education system's overt basis (Green, Preston, & Janmaat, 2006; Noddings, 2013). As critical research in educational science has shown, however, schools often actually reproduce the social order characterized by unequal stratifications rather than promoting these values among their students. Schools actively impose patterns of power relations that resemble "a common-sense world" shaped by the values and interests of the socially and culturally dominant classes; these values and interests remain unquestioned and are accepted as such by the dominated groups (Bourdieu, 1986, p. 468; Nash, 1990; for a critical response see Pennycook, 2010). This study attempts to contribute to a larger movement that interrogates social, public structures with the intention of unraveling and questioning their underlying power mechanisms. It advocates for a critical thinking approach that aims to disrupt the self-sustaining circle of elitism, on the basis of privilege, and works toward the flattening of existing hierarchies due to (the lack of) different types of capital or resources. This section draws primarily from the work of Bourdieu, Gramsci, Delpit, and from other critical thinkers for its analysis.

According to Bourdieu, the world can be depicted through the concepts of *habitus*, *field*, and *capital*. First, habitus is "a set of *dispositions* which incline agents to act and react in certain ways. The dispositions generate practices, perceptions and attitudes which are 'regular' without being consciously co-ordinated or governed by any 'rule'" (Bourdieu, 1991, p. 12 [emphasis in original]). Individuals are influenced by previously acquired dispositions on which they base daily decisions, their behavior, and their beliefs. A certain behavior or belief does not, however, result from the habitus itself, but instead needs to be considered as bifurcating the relation between the habitus and the field. The *field*, sometimes called *market*, "may be seen as a structured space of positions in which the positions and their interrelations are determined by the distribution of different kinds of resources or 'capital'" (Bourdieu, 1991, p. 14). Importantly, actions within the fields are oriented at maximizing the individual's capital of any sort (e.g., cultural) which can then be exchanged for a different kind of capital (e.g., economic) (Bourdieu, 1972). These fields are 'governed' by:

'symbolic power', an 'invisible' power which is 'misrecognized' as such and thereby 'recognized' as legitimate...the exercise of power through symbolic exchange always rests on a foundation of shared belief...they [actors in the field] fail to see that the hierarchy is, after all, an arbitrary social construction which serves the interests of some groups more than others. (Bourdieu, 1991, p. 23)

This implies that the cultural capital possessed by dominant and non-dominant groups is unevenly distributed and is acknowledged as such by the working mechanisms of social institutions. This structure reinforces the privileged status that the dominant groups already have and increases the standard against which non-dominant groups are measured. Fraser (2003) defines status as "an order of intersubjective subordination derived from institutionalized patterns of cultural value that constitute some members of society as less than full partners in interaction" (p. 49). The public school represents a large social institution that is run by the government and in which this process of unequal reproduction of social order and status is officially legitimized and presented as the social norm. Put differently, schools teach and transmit the covert knowledge, that is, the way in which the institutions work and how hierarchies and orders are (unjustly) created and reproduced within the educational setting, to its students who absorb this as 'official knowledge' (Apple, 1993).

Apple (2012) later complicates this claim and points out that in order for this 'official knowledge' to be absorbed, and for the reproduction of social orders to be acknowledged, all students would need to be "passive internalizers of pregiven social messages" (p. 13) In fact, students neither simply absorb and internalize what is presented to them in class nor do they content themselves with the authoritative structures with which they are presented. They often judge and interpret the input based on their previous knowledge and belief system and either (partially) accept or reject the information.

Another point unaccounted for by mere reproduction is that "it undertheorizes and hence neglects the fact that capitalist social relations are inherently *contradictory* in some very important ways" (Apple, 2012, p. 89 [emphasis in original]). Schools, therefore, "sort, select, and certify a hierarchically organized student body...and they maintain an inaccurate meritocratic ideology and, therefore, legitimate the ideological forms necessary for the recreation of inequality" (Apple, 2012, p. 89; Flyvbjerg, 1998; Street, 2001). Furthermore, 'official knowledge' can only be transmitted if teachers act convincingly and actively support the curriculum that they implement (Apple, 2012; 2019). In so doing, they adopt the ideology and carry out guidelines created by policy makers and by other authorities. While schools recreate the unequal social structures and reproduce only the knowledge that they decide to include in the curriculum, schools also create new knowledge and produce new groups of students who do not accept the long-established routines, but who instead develop a critical attitude.

Understanding these processes of the state apparatus involves gaining control over the cultural capital that is distributed unevenly throughout society. It is the acceptance of daily practices, conducted in social institutions and commonsense meaning-making processes, that constitutes hegemony. Gramsci (1971) developed a theory of *(cultural) hegemony* based on subaltern[1] groups' acquiescence to hidden power that was exercised by the dominant class. The establishment of consent is achieved by the former coercing the latter into accepting their world view and ideology as both dominant and legitimate. They do so by manipulating the society's belief and value system through social and political systems of daily life. Similar to Bourdieu's 'common-sense world,' this worldview constitutes the dominant group's interests, but is neither questioned nor rejected by subaltern groups, no matter whether it serves them or not (Erickson, 1996; Fuller, 2015). Subaltern groups can be deceived because they lack a critical reflection of the world and of themselves: "When one's conception of the world is not critical and coherent but disjointed and episodic, one belongs simultaneously to a multiplicity of mass human groups" (Gramsci, 1971, p. 324). Thus, subaltern groups are incapable of discerning that they are involved in, approve of, and actively support hegemonic processes that serve the dominant group's interests exclusively because they acknowledge them as the established norm. For Gramsci, individuals need to be aware of the underlying mechanisms of coercion in order to overcome the hegemonic processes taking place, and that go by without comment, in every sphere of daily life. They need to develop an understanding and consciousness in order to defend their own interests and to create social equity combining the interests and needs of every group within the society to an equal extent. Gramsci (1971) continues:

> To criticise one's own conception of the world means therefore to make it a coherent unity and to raise it to the level reached by the most advanced thought in the world. It therefore also means criticism of all previous philosophy, in so far as this has left stratified deposits in popular philosophy. The starting-point of critical elaboration is the consciousness of what one really is, and is 'knowing thyself' as a product of the historical process to date which has deposited in you an infinity of traces, without leaving an inventory. (p. 324)

Thus, we need to be aware of and 'know' ourselves in order to critically reflect and better understand the circumstances in which our identity is socially embedded.

---

[1]   Gramsci uses the term 'subaltern' to describe a group of people who lack autonomy and access to the hegemonial parts of society and who are characterized by structural and economic marginalization.

Such an inventory needs to be created in order to determine diachronic power relations and their impact on daily social practices.

Freire (2005, p. 5) elaborates further on the concept of this much-needed awareness, which he calls *conscientização* or *critical consciousness/attitude*. It requires one to actually "intervene with reality" (Freire, 2005, p. 5), to participate in and transform it, instead of being merely a passive bystander. People without this critical attitude will be overpowered by dominant, sometimes more critically aware groups in society instead of changing the world and integrating their own interests and viewpoints. Being able to critically evaluate one's situation, individuals discover their potential and realize the impact of the underlying mechanisms: "Society now reveals itself as something unfinished, not as something inexorably given; it has become a challenge rather than hopeless limitation" (Freire, 2005, p. 10). This is the counterpart to the "culture of silence" practiced unknowingly by subaltern groups. According to Freire, the public education system's task is to help develop the necessary criticality to question and to assess underlying reproductive mechanisms. The main objective is to liberate oneself from oppression and to become a critical subject that is both responsible for and conscious of one's own potentials, rights, and duties.

This study argues that these hegemonic processes exist within Swiss society and that they obfuscate its citizens' perspectives and understanding of their own viewpoints and of the societal value and belief system. These underlying, invisible ideologies can be illustrated in the nation-wide debate on language learning in Swiss schools. Zurich's decision to reverse the traditional order of language learning, focused on national languages and to introduce English first instead, can be seen as a hegemonic mechanism. Paradoxically, although a few French-speaking journalists and educators felt betrayed or disappointed and contributed to the mediatized debates, the vast majority (including the Italian and Romansh linguistic regions) complied with this decision rather defenselessly. Arguably, one might assume that most individuals support Zurich's decision and the arguments provided to change the language order, due to the lack of heavier reactions or any contesting of the decision by referenda or other political actions. Individuals left out of this policy decision could be said to also want the same reform, either for themselves personally or for their children. In fact, this decision also led to the adoption of the new language order in the cantons in central and eastern Switzerland. Yet, the responsible educational authorities in the French- and Italian-speaking cantons have seemingly, until today, been very much influenced by tradition- and ideology-driven policies and have remained hegemonized in their decision-making processes due to their dependency on German-speaking Switzerland.

These individuals become trapped in these power mechanisms which divide societies into groups of elites and subaltern by adopting the hegemon's viewpoint, not speaking out for themselves, and thus practicing a "culture of silence" (Freire, 2005). As pointed out by Gramsci, these viewpoints or the reasoning thereof by the subaltern groups is incoherent and illogical. Their rationales and motivations to act in a certain way, while following different personal convictions or perspectives, can sometimes seem contradictory. That is, by being strongly influenced by the dominant viewpoint and decision making, they might not even be consciously aware of the fact that they would in fact also like to be able to choose, even though they might argue otherwise.

Since these processes impact language education policies implemented in the education system in this case, these are felt by and consequential for many young individuals who are excluded from the decision-making processes. Therefore, this study aims at unveiling such obscure hegemonic processes in order to make them more transparent and inclusive to individuals that are directly affected thereby. This can be achieved by engaging in and developing critical thinking and awareness strategies that can detect biased, power-laden discourses and manipulations which benefit only a small group of people and which also exacerbate inequity within the society. A closer analysis of how language, education, and power are inextricably intertwined can help to support the integration and amplification of every individual's voice in these power dynamics and can serve to flatten the existing hierarchies. The following section will deal with and clarify the interconnectedness of *language*, education, and power.

2.3 Language, Education, and Power

> Every time that the question of language surfaces, in one way or another, it means that a series of other problems are coming to the fore: the formation and enlargement of the governing class, the need to establish more intimate and secure relationships between the governing groups and the national-popular mass, in other words to recognize the cultural hegemony. (Gramsci, pp. 183–184)

Gramsci's concept of *linguistic hegemony*, Bourdieu's concept of *symbolic power*, and Delpit's concept of *culture of power* all represent different facets of the relationship between education and power from different cultural, regional, ethnical, and academic viewpoints. Gramsci (1891–1937) as an Italian Marxist philosopher, journalist, and linguist advocates for a counter-hegemonic approach in order to challenge social structures based on capitalist power. The primary Gramsci source used in this study – the Prison Notebooks – are the result of his imprisonment by Mussolini's regime and which are considered a unique contribution to 20th century political theory. Bourdieu (1930–2002), a French sociologist and one of the most influential and important representatives of France's intellectual public life in the 20th century, investigates social power dynamics as a critical response to idealism in Western philosophy. Throughout his analyses of social structures, he developed different theories such as *theory of habitus, field theory* or *theory of capital and class distinction* and the forms of capital, linked to language, represent a particularly interesting aspect for this study. Finally, Delpit is an American educator, author, and researcher in the field of race, minority groups, literacy, and language in education. She is known for her commitment to creating equitable educational practices for all students and for challenging the *status quo* by raising awareness of *the culture of power*. All three thinkers highlight language's importance as being inextricably linked to both education and power. Each of the three concepts is elaborated in the sections that follow.

2.3.1 Gramsci's Linguistic Hegemony

Gramsci's concept of *hegemony*, understood as the formation of consent whereby subaltern groups are coerced into adopting the dominant group's world views, manifests itself in an ideology with a focus on institutions and, in seemingly inconspicuous, daily practices. A society's value and belief systems relate to a larger set of ideologies that are spread and supported by institutions. As these institutions become increasingly involved in daily practices and activities, the ideologies tend to become transmitted through them rather implicitly and unconsciously. The primary medium of such transmission is language (Phillipson, 1992). Language is a very important daily practice and plays a major role in school settings, either as the medium of instruction or as the subject as such. Language itself is inseparable from the speech community's culture and history (or civilization in Gramsci's terms) (Tsui & Tollefson, 2004). It is therefore "a continuous process of metaphor...with respect to the meanings and the ideological content which the words used had in preceding periods of civilization" (Gramsci, 1971, p. 450). That is, language exists as a continuous, diachronic process of meaning-making in which historical features of hegemony, power, and prestige become incorporated (see also Blommaert, 1999). Language is not a static entity but develops and changes, particularly when it comes into contact with other languages (and therefore with other cultures and histories). It takes on new forms of meaning and replaces older cultural residues within the language:

> Language is transformed with the transformation of the whole civilization, through the acquisition of culture by new classes and through the hegemony

exercised by one national language over others, etc., and what it does is precisely to absorb in metaphorical form the words of previous civilizations and cultures…The new 'metaphorical' meaning spreads with the spread of the new culture, which furthermore also coins brand-new words or absorbs them from other languages as loan-words giving them a precise meaning and therefore depriving them of the extensive halo they possessed in the original language. (Gramsci, 1971, pp. 451–452)

Gramsci uses the example of a national language taking over other already existing languages through hegemonic processes that are accepted as legitimate by the subaltern groups. What becomes clear from the quoted passage is that speakers belonging to subaltern groups of the society are led to believe that the newly introduced forms are more prestigious than, and are superior to, their speech variety. As a consequence, subaltern groups adapt their language and adopt new 'metaphorical' meanings. It must be taken into consideration, though, that Gramsci was referring to the standardization of the Italian language in 20th century Italy.[2] In the Swiss context, all four of the national languages have each undergone these standardization processes, albeit to different degrees. While the Swiss Italian and French varieties have largely abandoned their regional dialects, in an effort to assimilate to the neighboring standard varieties, Romansh and Swiss German have resisted standardization to a greater extent. In the case of Romansh, different local varieties continue to be used in accordance with a (more recent) standardized written language for the purposes of both administration and instruction. Swiss German enjoys a much higher status and popularity amongst its speakers and is used as a means of communication, regardless of socioeconomic status. However, certain contexts (such as educational settings) require speakers to switch to SSG. The different regional Swiss German varieties have never been standardized and do not exist as an official written code, whereas SSG is a standardized and codified language and counts as the official language.

English as a non-national language brings an additional dimension to Switzerland's multilingual landscape. In fact, it seems to hegemonize structures of how national languages are both spoken and taught. It does so not only by taking over other languages' positions, but also by infiltrating these languages' vocabulary and cultural values. Importantly, Gramsci argues that languages are not prescribed by a certain authority (e.g., state or government) as official media, but that they are instead introduced through *hegemony* and *seemingly* on the basis of a freely made choice. In a second step, languages then become codified and obtain institutional support. As presented in this manuscript's introductory chapter, the same can be said of English in Switzerland. English had become a matter of societal interest which led to

---

2   For a more detailed description of the 'trasformismo' movement, see Ives, 2004a, pp. 103–105.

the revaluation of its status in Swiss schools and, finally, even to its introduction as a mandatory FL. A certain standard for everyone in the same speech community is set through the codification of language in grammar books and dictionaries. Certain institutions, such as government or schools, are responsible to first serve as a yardstick in applying the 'correct' standard variety and second to create language policies and to ensure that their implementation by teachers is executed, for instance. More importantly, Gramsci also provides an explanation for why dominant groups succeed in hegemonizing language policy and its use within a society. Two types of grammar constitute his theory of *linguistic hegemony* (compared to *historical hegemony*[3]): *spontaneous grammar* and *normative grammar*.[4] For Gramsci, "hegemony is the relationship between spontaneous grammars and the prevailing normative grammar" (Ives, 1997, p.99). Each of the two sub-sections analyze these two schools in turn.

2.3.1.1 Spontaneous Grammar

Spontaneous grammar describes the kind of grammar chosen voluntarily, without being influenced by any external forces or any set of rules – characteristics that would usually be connected to the concept of *descriptive grammar*. These grammatical structures can be understood as "patterns we follow while speaking that are unconscious and *seem* natural: 'There is the grammar 'immanent' in language itself, by which one speaks 'according to grammar' without knowing it'" (Ives, 2004a, pp. 90–91 [emphasis in original]). Although spontaneous, a certain adherence to an underlying structure is inevitable because of language's historical development, which is now understood as common sense. This is where language's diachronic or historical dimension becomes important. The following sentences can serve as examples of this distinction:

1. How long have you been waiting for?
2. For how long have you been waiting?

These two sentences illustrate spontaneous grammar in its diachronic dimension. Whereas certain descriptive grammarians would argue that sentence one is grammatically incorrect, and that only sentence two respects established grammatical rules, sentence one is used (more) frequently by native speakers of English. When

---

3 'Historical hegemony', sometimes simply called 'hegemony', is defined as a state of predominance or control in terms of politics, economics or of a state or country's military over others. The type of hegemony that Gramsci is coining, which is applied in this study, is a 'cultural' or 'linguistic hegemony' meaning the dominant class's manipulation of the society's belief and value systems and, therefore, hegemonizing the way of thinking and belief structure of the dominated class.
4 'Spontaneous grammar' is sometimes interchangeably called 'immanent grammar'. For the sake of simplicity, I will only use the former.

asked whether their usage is correct, many speakers tend to agree that sentence two is 'more' correct and standard-like, which demonstrates that they still adhere to diachronic language forms, even though they are becoming increasingly archaic (Ghomeshi, 2010). The first example sentence corresponds to the descriptive or spontaneous use of grammar, whereas the second example sentence falls into the category of descriptive or normative use of grammar. Speakers are influenced by those prescriptive grammar rules that are passed on historically, often through the educational system, while the way of applying grammar is always in flux and adapting to new forms of speech style. These linguistic innovations can be triggered or manifest a society's historical and cultural progress (Gramsci, 1985).

We all unconsciously follow certain patterns that bear characteristics of the development of language and the historically established standard: "But this 'spontaneous' expression of grammatical conformity is necessarily disconnected, discontinuous and limited to local social strata or local centers…the subaltern classes try to speak like the dominant classes and the intellectuals, etc." (Gramsci, 1985, pp. 180–181). Thus, (subaltern) individuals unconsciously internalize and adhere to a certain prevalent standard because their own 'spontaneous' language resources are perceived as being rather 'limited.' Furthermore, they are often unable to see the close intertwining between historical development and synchronic language norms. These synchronic language norms correspond to how language has come to be used contemporarily, even while the diachronic dimension is not readily discernable and the etymological process is mostly opaque. That means that they are disadvantaged in using their own idiolect, given that subaltern individuals do not receive the same opportunities to develop their critical awareness or language skills as dominant groups. They (try to) adopt the contemporary standard without recognizing that these linguistic forms are the result of previous, historically established dominant groups dictating the way in which individuals are supposed to speak. This obscures the hegemonization and coercion processes that lead the subaltern groups to adopt a certain standard, seemingly voluntarily. In addition to this linguistic standard, they are also accepting what is incorporated by it: the status of 'dominant classes' or 'the intellectuals.'

This study responds to the need for more profound understandings of these implicit and explicit mechanisms of standardization and language contact situations, especially in multilingual Switzerland. Greater awareness is needed to acknowledge the artificiality of socially constructed standards, that is, understanding that these standards which dictate correct language use have been established by a small group of elites and that individual speech naturally differs therefrom. Linked to this is the phenomenon of linguistic insecurity which can be a consequence of trying to adhere (unsuccessfully) to such standards. Linguistic insecurity is a complex feeling of self-consciousness, shame, lack of confidence, or anxiety based on one's individual use of language and the perception of linguistic standards and expectations. Speakers who feel that their own speech is 'inappropriate' or that it 'deviates' from the prescribed standards can become (linguistically) insecure. This can have felt consequences on the individual's psychological and physical health (Labov, 2006; Lippi-Green, 1997; Meyerhoff, 2006; Niedzielski, 2010). For instance, Demmerling and Landwehr (2007) illustrate that being ashamed of one's linguistic skills, because they are considered 'deviant' or 'deficient' or because they are not attributed the same social and economic value as other prestigious languages, can result in linguistic insecurity. If the feeling of shame persists or reoccurs continually, individuals can develop severe shyness or even an inferiority complex. They further found that speakers of minority languages with low social prestige often stop using their language in public and in official contexts, suppress it entirely, or even develop speech impediments due to humiliation and fear.

Finally, Gramsci argues that every person is equipped with their own individualized grammar that serves as the basis for everyone's idiolect (Gramsci, 1985) in contrast to Chomsky's (1965; 1986) later attempts to analyze language as a 'universal grammar.' In his theory, Chomsky postulates that certain structural rules are innate to humans (under certain conditions, such as regular sensory activity and language exposure) which develop further into specialized language-specific grammars with more linguistic input and stimuli (Chomsky, 1965; 1986). He argued that when humans follow a regular language acquisition process, the language that they develop will have certain characteristics and properties that are universal (e.g., nouns and verbs or content and function words[5]). Nevertheless, Chomsky has received substantial criticism for his theory since it is said to ignore neo-Darwinian evolutionary principles or to oversimplify linguistic variation in languages (Jackendoff & Pinker, 2005).

2.3.1.2 Normative Grammar

In addition to *spontaneous grammar*, Gramsci developed the concept of *normative grammar* which focuses on the formation and the implementation of grammatical norms and standards. Normative speech behavior is achieved when speakers adhere to the prescribed rules and where they employ them accordingly in their speech. They acknowledge them as legitimate and use them to adjust their individual communicative patterns to fit certain norms and in order for others to understand. This is achieved through a process that he describes as follows:

> [The normative grammar] is made up of the reciprocal monitoring, reciprocal teaching, reciprocal 'censorship' expressed in such questions as 'What did you

---

5 Content words carry semantic content/meaning, e.g., nouns, verbs, or adjectives. Function words, conversely, are primarily employed to signal grammatical relationships between content words, e.g., prepositions, pronouns, or conjunctions.

mean to say?', 'What do you mean?', 'Make yourself clearer', etc., and in mimicry and teasing. This whole complex of actions and reactions come together to create a grammatical conformism, to establish 'norms' or judgements of correctness and incorrectness. (Gramsci, 1985, p. 180)

The central element here are those social processes that take place in daily interactions that shape and define grammatical norms. Gramsci uses a *descriptive* approach deducing patterns from actual speech (bottom up), in contrast to typical *prescriptive* grammarians and linguists who are in favor of imposing rules and standardizing speech behavior from the top down. These 'judgements of correctness and incorrectness' also demonstrate the power relations transmitted through language. Deviations from the norm are judged as incorrect by people or institutions which represent the linguistic standard. Importantly, while Gramsci distinguishes between two types of grammar, he does not separate them as two isolated systems. They are better understood as a cycle since spontaneous grammars are influenced by certain opaque, diachronic norms and continue to be measured against socially constructed linguistic norms.

Figure 4: Cycle of spontaneous and normative grammars

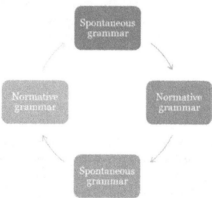

As shown in Figure 4 historically spontaneous grammar started out as the individuals' use of language and way of speaking. The language variety of a certain dominant group (royal family, famous writers, inventors, or privileged regions as in North versus South) was often given a nation-wide official status that depended on the individual's status and power, as well as the speech community's sociopolitical environment. The non-dominant groups were forced to modify their own spontaneous grammar and to adopt elements of the imposed normative grammar in order to qualify as legitimate members of a given speech community. Over time, as can be seen in the boxes increasingly losing intensity in color in Figure 4 above, these sociopolitical embeddings of the standard language are becoming more opaque and more invisible. These two types of grammars are interdependent and develop out of each other.

Importantly, Gramsci's writings are not against a standardized language *per se*. He argues that having limited linguistic resources (only speaking the dialect of a restricted geographic region for example) is equal to having a limited or 'provincial' understanding of the world (Gramsci, 1971) and, therefore, also limited access to economic resources supervised by mainstream capitalism (Cazden et al., 1996). Yet, this does not mean that dialect speakers should give up their linguistic and regional heritage altogether. Gramsci convincingly promotes multilingualism by advocating that these language resources bear different meanings and resources for each speaker. He clearly recognizes the social, cultural, and economic advantages that a common vehicular language brings, whereas dialects may support identity construction and provide a sense of belonging (Gramsci, 1971). Individual spontaneous grammars need to be taken into consideration in order to achieve an equal standard without imposing rules onto the entire society or by electing one particular (prestigious) variety as the national language. According to Gramsci (1971), a national standard language should integrate every idiolect within the society in order to ensure that everyone's voice is heard and represented. Instead of accepting an imposed language, people should respond with a 'linguistic revolution' demanding that their way of speaking be included in the formation of a common language (Gramsci, 1971). Interestingly, Gramsci goes on to argue that this cannot happen successfully without the state's participation as well as by its social institutions. The state should, therefore, be involved in language policy and planning in codifying and officializing people's decisions. This does not imply, however, that individuals should rely on the state in order to become active. Rather, they should speak up for themselves and contribute to the policy and decision-making processes.

Whereas this approach certainly advocates for social justice, by leveraging non-dominant social groups and by promoting linguistic and cultural diversity, it does not necessarily account for the people's interests or for realistic opportunities. The assumption is made that individuals actively want to be unified linguistically and have access to social, cultural, and economic advantages within these approaches, as illustrated in Gramsci's theory of *cultural hegemony*, for instance. One striking counterexample by which to demonstrate that individuals' personal interests, feelings, and desires do not always follow the logic of achieving greater access to socioeconomic opportunities is that of Grisons, Switzerland.

In an effort to promote its minority language Romansh at an official level, the trilingual canton of Grisons opted for the graphization[6] of the three biggest Romansh idioms by *creating* Rumantsch Grischun (RG). This language constitutes common features of the three biggest idioms while simultaneously excluding two smaller ones.[7] Its implementation at government and school level has proven rather difficult, however. This is partly due to the very controversial reactions and attitudes toward the imposed and artificially constructed standard language. For instance, teachers refused to employ newly developed teaching materials in RG or even to use it as a standard language in class, despite sociopolitical and legal pressure. Furthermore, although 83% voted against the use of RG in the public media, it has been made the language for regional news and radio nonetheless (Coray, 2009; Berthele, 2015; Berthele & Lindt-Bangerter, 2011). Whereas the underlying objective was to support linguistic minorities and to give them a chance to compete with the surrounding dominant national languages (as suggested by Gramsci), the initiative was not supported by the individuals who were supposed to benefit from it.

In sum, Gramsci's work provides a very well-suited framework for this study's interests which includes an analysis of students' and teachers' perspectives on language against the concepts of *normative* and *spontaneous grammars*. Furthermore, as contained in the first, fourth, and fifth research questions, it will first deal with the romantic idea of expressing one's voice and identity through a certain variety. This aspect of singularness, as Gramsci argues, often deviates from the standard language. In Switzerland, Romansh, Swiss German, and their different local varieties (as well as other HLs) can be positioned within this category. Second, it will compare the romantic idea of language with the instrumental one aiming at social, cultural, and economic advantages which are often attached to hegemonic power mechanisms and dominant groups. English, as an international *lingua franca*, SSG, and RG all incorporate these advantages and attributes especially well. As Ives (2009) argues, in the case of ELF: "from a Gramscian perspective, the spread of English is a problem to the extent that its role within particular hegemonic blocs prevents subaltern social group consciousness from developing and creating critical and counter-hegemonic responses" (p. 663). Keeping this in mind and also applying it to the question of the relationship among English, national languages, and other HLs in multilingual Switzerland, the study employs Gramsci's analysis of hegemony in the field of education.

---

6   Graphization refers to the development of scripts and orthographic conventions in language planning, (Hornberger, 2006).

7   These five Romansh idioms are Sursilvan, Sutsilvan, Surmiran, Putér, and Vallader. They developed due to the inaccessibility and isolation of villages and valleys in the past. Each idiom exists in a non-standardized spoken and written form.

Gramsci convincingly argues for a multilingual, inclusive, and equal approach toward integrating every social group's use of language so that they might defend their own voice. He helps us to visualize the underlying power dynamics in language, not only when used as a medium of communication but already in its constitution, by not separating the two types of *spontaneous* and *normative grammar*, and by showing language's important historical development. As Ives (2004b, p. 176) puts it poignantly: "In Gramsci's terminology, all language takes place within normative contexts, however spontaneous they may appear."

Yet, the concept of two types of grammar and the idea of basing the *normative grammar* on many individual *spontaneous* ones does not account for the speakers' language ideologies, needs, or perspectives. These might lead them to favor an unstandardized variety, knowingly renouncing personal or economic benefits. A standardization of one's own variety – as has been quickly outlined in the RG-example provided before – can also misrepresent the interests and voices of certain social groups even if the intentions are to attribute more power thereto and to make them more equitable. Finally, although the study fully supports Gramsci's advocacy of critical, social change, it also follows Friedman's (2009) suggestion to combine Gramsci's approach to *cultural hegemony* with Bourdieu's (1991) theory of *symbolic capital*, which "offers us a unique insight into the obstacles faced by agents of progressive social change and, in so doing, sheds light on the limitations of Gramsci's approach" (Friedman, 2009, p. 355).

2.3.2 Bourdieu's Symbolic Power

Another important concept of the study's underlying framework is Bourdieu's theory of language as *symbolic power*. Very much in line with Gramsci and other critical language theorists (Makoni & Pennycook, 2007; Pennycook, 2001; 2010; Delpit, 2006; Blackledge, 2010; Blackledge & Creese, 2010), Bourdieu argues that language standards are artificial constructs created by linguists within a linguistic field who deem certain varieties to be more valuable and seek to legitimize their status through criteria created by themselves. The linguistic field is defined as "a system of specifically linguistic relations of power based on the unequal distribution of linguistic capital (or, to put it another way, of the chances of assimilating the objectified linguistic resources)" (Bourdieu, 1991, p. 57).

As a consequence, the society is split into two groups: One is the dominant group that provides the norms for *the* national or standard language and simultaneously accrues linguistic capital in the process; the other is the dominated group being disadvantaged because they do not match the official norms which, therefore, diminishes their chances of compensating and competing. Once the dominant variety establishes itself as being superior, the dominant group constantly and almost effortlessly gains more linguistic capital and is able to manipulate the system to its advantage. This cycle can be seen as the reproduction of symbolic domination. It leads to a distinct social position for the dominant group, one which becomes visible in every social interaction. For them, language is a very powerful tool to dominate processes in every social sphere, whereas the dominated group continuously struggles between expressing their own (ethnic or regional) identity and speaking 'appropriately' and 'correctly.' Moreover, language is also employed "to impose the legitimate definition of the division of the social world and, thereby, to *make and unmake groups*" (Bourdieu, 1991, p. 221 [emphasis in original]). Groups or spaces are distinguished by criteria such as ethnicity, religion, and culture where access is either granted or denied depending upon the correspondence between one's own speech variety and the prevailing standard. As Bourdieu (1991) observes:

> ...this struggle is not only personal but also economic:
> Linguistic exchange...is also an economic exchange which is established within a particular symbolic relation of power between a producer, endowed with a certain linguistic capital, and a consumer (or a market), and which is capable of procuring a certain material or symbolic profit. In other words, utterances are not only (save in exceptional circumstances) signs to be understood and deciphered; they are also signs of wealth, intended to be evaluated and appreciated, and signs of authority, intended to be believed and obeyed. (p. 66 [emphasis in original])

A linguistic exchange is thus never neutral. What is also important to highlight here is that utterances,[8] which serve primarily to communicate and make meaning, are likely to contain and convey different underlying characteristics or messages such as *wealth* and *authority*. In order to read and understand these signs, the 'consumer' must acknowledge them as such. The problem here is the consumer's seemingly voluntary submission to the norms set by dominant speakers. If these rules were not accepted and recognized as superior, then linguistic exchange would not equate to an economic exchange. Additionally, the submission does not only apply to the linguistic norms, but is also valid for the social and economic position that the speaker occupies. The speaker's social and economic position and language are inextricably intertwined. The relationship is twofold: the higher the position, the greater access the person has to the official speech; the more proficient the person is in using the official language, the higher the position. Individuals who do not have sufficient exposure to the official language, and who therefore do not possess the linguistic capital required, are excluded or 'censored' from these positions. According to Bourdieu (1991):

---

8   In linguistics, utterances refer to different units of speech.

> Among the most effective and best concealed censorships are all those which consist in excluding certain agents from communication by excluding them from the groups which speak or the places which allow one to speak with authority. In order to explain what may or may not be said in a group, one has to take into account not only the symbolic relations of power which become established within it and which deprive certain individuals (e.g., women) of the possibility of speaking or which oblige them to conquer that right through force, but also the laws of group formation themselves (e.g., the logic of conscious or unconscious exclusion) which function like a prior censorship. (p. 138)

An individual's survival can depend on a person's ability and permission to speak in extreme cases. Censorship can revoke this permission and can suppress an individual's voice. This can either be due to external sociopolitical pressure imposed onto individuals or can be the result of linguistic insecurity, where people consider themselves unworthy of speaking (a certain variety, in a certain place, to certain people, etc.) (Butler, 1997).

The principles of censorship, linguistic exchange, and the reproduction of symbolic domination can be applied in the present study in various ways. There seem to be inequalities in the approaches to language learning where the accumulation of linguistic capital is overtly ascribed to certain social groups, whereas 'certain agents' (e.g., teachers) are effectively excluded from decision-making processes. Not including their expertise and understanding can create tensions, misunderstanding, and inequity. Teachers might refuse to carry out imposed policy decisions so that (possibly well-intentioned) social transformation cannot be achieved. Conversely, including their perspectives, beliefs, and informed opinions about language teaching into policies might reveal that, in fact, these policies do not serve to actually ameliorate teaching and learning experiences. They could primarily pursue a political agenda while ignoring the actual needs and interests of the actors involved in education. Hence, it is important to find out the ways in which certain languages' prestige and status contribute to the reproduction of symbolic domination (Abendroth-Timmer & Fäcke, 2011; Bourdieu, 1999; Gogolin, 2007). With this information, policy makers and educators can then attempt to render access more equitable and can either shift or redirect the distribution of linguistic capital (Rudby, 2015).

Although Bourdieu's concept of *habitus* and the *symbolic power* that he attributes to language fit the study's underlying theoretical framework well, it lacks crucial elements and is inapt to advance critical, social change. As Friedman (2009) summarized it poignantly: "The consequences of Bourdieu's emphasis on the forces of social reproduction over those of social change have been widely remarked upon, often by way of contrast with Gramsci" (p. 362). For instance, Bourdieu's concept does not properly account for other personal factors or social justice approaches that influence language learning, use, or promotion such as emotional or affective factors or minority language advocacy. As Bartlett (2007) observes: "Theories of language and power that draw on Bourdieu identify the politics of communicative practices, but they have ignored the intense and important influence that emotions have on the interplay between language, individual experiences and social structures" (p. 560). Problematically, Bourdieu bases his analysis almost exclusively on an institutional, market-based approach that exposes language hierarchies ranging from highly valued, prestigious varieties to economically irrelevant ones. In so doing, he does not take the fact that language is inextricably linked to one's identity and that a certain linguistic behavior can be irrational into consideration and, therefore, inhibits efforts aimed at maximizing one's linguistic capital. Put otherwise, instead of sending their children to additional classes in the official, regional language, some migrant parents might decide to prioritize HL learning in order to transmit their heritage culture and values. They do so even though their children's future opportunities might be financially more advantageous if they were to study the language(s) taught at school more to a more significant degree.

Furthermore, this more empirical/humane perspective, which language typically also incorporates, is generally rather lacking in Bourdieu's concept. Language is largely seen as a 'good' that creates opportunities or exclusion, but rarely as something unique and precious to an individual person. Concepts such as *linguistic pride* or *insecurity* need to be taken at least as seriously as *symbolic power* and considered on an individual basis. Finally, languages are always applied and never remain on a theoretical dimension only (Keller, 1994). What Bourdieu is missing in his concept is a level of intra- and intersubjective exchange or communication that provides an authentic setting in which languages are negotiated based on real-life experiences. Furthermore, a clear distinction between dominant and non-dominant groups is hardly realistic in complex societies. Individuals can be members of multiple groups and *act* or *perform* to a certain extent as though they pertained to a certain group based on poststructuralist performativity (Butler, 1999). As Butler argues, group membership and one's identity are embedded in a process of constant social construction through performative habitual speech acts[9] and nonverbal communication (Austin, 1962), which *per se* (re)produce power and authority through discourse.

In his study on English usage at workplaces in Switzerland, Lüdi (2016) argues that the shift from national languages to English is not based on empirical results or recommendations to modify language policies but on ideologies. This issue is especially interesting in workplaces with multinational employees. His results show that English is increasingly climbing in importance as a corporate language, but that it does not replace already existing (national) languages. It is employed as a

---

9   Typical examples of performative speech acts include inaugurations or legal sentences (Austin, 1962).

highly individualized *lingua franca* and demonstrates traces of other L1s. Generally, international employees make use of their full linguistic repertoire and do not adhere to a monolingual language policy when at work. As a consequence, employees benefit from a linguistic and cultural exchange and can contribute within their own linguistic limits (Lüdi, 2016; see also Lüdi, 2010). Grin, Vaillancourt, and Sfreddo (2009) investigated the economic added value of Swiss professionals' language competences for the first time ever in political economy research.[10] The LEAP ("Langues étrangères dans l'activité professionnelle" [Foreign languages in professional activity]) project's main result is that multilingualism in Switzerland creates a competitive advantage of 10% of the GDP or 50 billion Swiss francs yearly (Grin et al., 2009). Bi- or multilingual employees are hugely profitable and are twice as indispensable for Swiss companies as monolingual co-workers. This is not only true for companies oriented toward exportation or tourism, but particularly in Swiss corporate service and informatics domains. The added value of multilingualism is more than 22% in the corporate service and informatics sectors alone. At the same time, it is individually financially lucrative for employees to speak more than one language. As Grin et al. (2009) point out, Swiss German professionals who also speak French earn 10% more than their colleagues with similar training and experience, except for the language skills. For employees from the French-speaking part of Switzerland who can speak German this advantage increases to 14%. Another important point raised by the authors concerns the diversification of language skills: It is more advantageous to focus on internationally economically important languages, such as Mandarin or Hindi, than concentrating time and financial resources on (the more widely spoken) English, for instance (for more details see Grin, Sfreddo & Vaillancourt, 2010; Duchêne & Del Percio, 2014).

2.3.3 Delpit's Culture of Power

In addition to Gramsci's (1971) concept of *cultural hegemony* and Bourdieu's (1991) concept of *symbolic power*, this study also draws from Delpit's (2006) concept of *culture of power*. Her theory is well-suited and accounts for a valuable, more innovative, and contemporary part of the scholarly literature on the study's topic and examines the relationship among language, culture, and power. Whereas Bourdieu argues that determining the appropriate linguistic means to communicate is an unconscious act, Delpit capitalizes upon the training and raising of awareness about these unconscious linguistic choices. Linguistic and cultural practices can be internalized and learned in order to apply them appropriately and to take part in the culture or

---

10 Earlier studies had focused on this issue in Switzerland, but had not provided such conclusive and wide-ranging data (Grin & Korth, 2005).

society through training and awareness. Delpit's (2006) *culture of power*, which comprises the following five main components, addresses power issues in educational settings:

1. Issues of power are enacted in classrooms;
2. There are codes or rules for participating in power; that is, there is a *culture of power*;
3. The rules of the culture of power are a reflection of the rules of the culture of those who have power;
4. If you are not already a participant in the culture of power, being told explicitly the rules of that culture makes acquiring power easier;
5. Those with power are frequently least aware of – or least willing to acknowledge – its existence. Those with less power are often most aware of its existence (p. 24).

These five theses are explained below and are contextualized in the present study's setting. First, issues of power in classrooms are typically enacted by several actors and according to factors: teacher-student relationships; the power of both publishers and curriculum designers transmitted through intentionally chosen content in textbooks and curricula; the state determining (compulsory) schooling; and the society imposing a certain standard. The school's responsibility as an institution is also to prepare students for the job market and pre-selecting possible entries, depending on academic achievements. Second, Delpit's (2006) concept of the *culture of power* is linked to linguistic codes and rules directly, which symbolize membership in a certain group of power. Using a specific linguistic code can, therefore, be equated to participating in and belonging to the culture of power. Third, since these codes and rules are tied to institutions such as schools, the achievement accredited by these institutions depends upon the acquisition of the codes and culture of those who determine them. Thus, students socialized in the culture of power are automatically higher achievers than those who are first exposed to it at school. Fourth, Delpit contends that knowledge of any culture, of how to participate in a certain culture, and of how to become a member is typically transmitted implicitly among members. This implicitness can be the source of cross-cultural miscommunication and a lack of understanding since the cues detected by members may not be visible or even accessible to members of any other culture. She argues that making these cues for how a given culture works should be made explicit in order to simplify cross-cultural communication and the adaption to other cultures. In the contexts of school, students who are less well-equipped with the right linguistic and cultural codes should receive proper and detailed training about how to better understand the requirements and to gain access to the culture of power. Fifth, the imbalance of power is most acutely felt and visible for those with less power, while the more powerful individuals are often ignorant of their superior position. Since the culture of power's *status quo* reinforces a given power dynamic's 'normalcy', it also often remains unquestioned by those who are in the position to change the dynamics. At school, policy makers might be unaware of the power they impose on school leaders, which they in turn impose on teachers, which they in turn impose on students. To sum up, in order to interrupt this cycle, awareness needs to be raised of implicit power dynamics and corresponding linguistic and cultural patterns for everyone to participate in the culture of power legitimately and competently.

These appropriate linguistic codes are expressed through the correct form of the language (i.e., the sentence structure and grammar) which allows for a rather simple distinction to be drawn between 'standardness' and 'non-standardness' (Delpit, 2006). Although standard speech is essential in order to access the culture of power and to achieve social status, "language *use* – the socially and cognitively based linguistic determinations speakers make about style, register, vocabulary, and so forth" (Delpit, 2006, p. 49) is particularly important in linguistically diverse school environments. Focusing on language use rather than form is crucial when cognitive development, as well as raising awareness and recognition of the linguistic diversity among students, are the objectives. Furthermore, Delpit (2006) argues that learning these new codes or entire languages "comes with exposure, comfort level, motivation, familiarity, and practice in real communicative contexts" (p. 49). Drilling students to adopt a new language with which they cannot identify or with which they are not familiar or not comfortable will reduce their ability to (re)produce these linguistic codes. It can have a negative impact on both their cognitive and affective development and can cause issues with group identity, which is important to their wellbeing (Delpit, 2006).

Thus, for immigrant students and learners of FLs, who may or may not be proficient in the school language(s), it is not so much the learning of the form, but rather the language's use that has more profound effects on them. For instance, not being allowed to speak their L1, suppressing it in official contexts, and being penalized for possibly 'wrong' pronunciations or 'deviant' sentence structures in the local language can all be interpreted as a personal failure or can be negatively linked to their family and community of origin. That being understood, Delpit, like Gramsci (1971), also emphasizes the equal need for a formally correct language learning of the standard language since students would be socially and economically disadvantaged if they lacked these skills entirely. She suggests that language classes pursue an integrated approach that combines students' other L1s, which are crucial to their identity, *and* the standard languages that are important for socioeconomic success. She invites teachers to explicitly acknowledge students' language repertoires, expose them to standard language input, and to provide authentic, but sheltered, opportunities for them to engage in exchanges with peers or other language activities, such as drama or role-play.

Promoting linguistic diversity is not only beneficial to those who have different L1s, though. Delpit (2006, p. 54) convincingly argues that "it is possible and desirable to make the actual study of language diversity a part of the curriculum for all students." It is important to point out that the promotion of linguistic diversity in class must not be forced onto students. Their choice of how to express themselves, their identity, and their culture must be respected. The linguistic tools provided by the teachers ought to be seen as a pragmatic enlargement of their language repertoires in an attempt to provide equal opportunities for all students, despite their different L1s and the social prestige associated therewith. According to Delpit (2006), the classroom should be seen as a safe space in which students receive appropriate exposure and training as well as "the opportunity to practice that form *in contexts that are nonthreatening, have a real purpose, and are intrinsically enjoyable.*" (p. 54 [emphasis in original]). Teaching should therefore not only focus on the correct form, but should also train students to choose the appropriate way of speaking according to the context. The broader their linguistic repertoires from which they can draw, the easier it will be for students to adapt to varying social requirements without having to suppress their linguistic and cultural identities altogether.

For students who already are proficient in the standard language, being sensitized to different ways of speaking and corresponding social contexts can enhance understandings of linguistic and cultural diversity and issues and difficulties with which only certain groups of individuals are confronted in society. This awareness might further contribute to their understanding that certain individuals *have to* adapt and to adhere to socially constructed requirements whereas others do not. Delpit's underlying intention, when calling for the promotion of linguistic and cultural diversity in classrooms, is a change of mentality. Educational settings can no longer simply *tolerate* diversity and try to integrate and assimilate students into one homogenous group, but should rather embrace and legitimize their 'otherness.' According to Delpit (2006, p. 67), "all teachers must revel in the diversity of their students and that of the world outside the classroom community." Existing personal and language hierarchies among actors in the classroom can be flattened by opening themselves up to linguistic and cultural diversity. For instance, this can be achieved when students present their L1s and cultures in class or when the curriculum leaves room to include poems, stories, songs, or television shows from another linguistic and cultural background. The culture of power can be fully shared and equitable only when all languages and cultures receive recognition. It must also be kept in mind that the classroom represents a safe space in which these hierarchies can be showcased and flattened, which does not necessarily always mirror the reality outside. Occupying the interface of theory and praxis, it is the teacher's job to prepare their students for this reality where much attention is paid to correct, standard language and where certain cultural backgrounds are privileged over others. As Delpit (2006) puts it:

> While linguists have long proclaimed that no language is intrinsically 'better' than another, in a stratified society as ours, language choices are not neutral. The language associated with the power structure – 'Standard English' – is the language of economic success, and all students have the right to schooling that gives them access to that language. (p. 68)

Importantly, an integrative approach to language diversity opens the way to the social recognition of less prestigious languages and of their disadvantaged speakers. Disadvantages can be turned into advantages by raising awareness and understanding of such language hierarchies, and the direct consequences they incur for certain groups of individuals. When pluralism becomes the new norm, then linguistically and culturally diverse students will be able to benefit from their repertoires, "gain access to the global culture" (Delpit, 2006, p. 69), and transform the long-established culture of power. Linked to this is a mindset associated with (geographical, i.e., national) borders and a fixed *status quo*. What is much more needed in contemporary schools is a dynamic mentality that incorporates different cultures and languages, which transforms students into "citizens of the global community" (Delpit, 2006, p. 69).

2.4 (Unequal) Englishes

> To achieve equality within a given language, it would never be enough to change the way people speak. One would have to change what the way people speak is taken to mean. In this regard, one can hardly avoid the thought that a latent function of schools has been to define a certain proportion of people as inferior, even to convince them that they are so, and to do this on the seemingly neutral ground of language. (Hymes, 1980, p. 110 [emphasis in original])

This section addresses the unequal and increasingly diverse nature of English (and its many local/regional varieties). It discusses existing definitions, including English as a *lingua franca* and the economic variables associated with the different varieties.

2.4.1 (Unequal) Englishes – Concepts and Definitions

(Unequal) Englishes is a rather new research paradigm which, by using the language English in the plural, incorporates the increasing diversity lived through language and its speakers. It establishes that language should not be viewed as one homogeneous, autonomous entity, much like a static system that is identical for all speakers and which places the 'ideal native speaker' (Chomsky, 1965) as a standard model in the center. Instead, this pluralist approach promotes the idea of language being dynamic, interpersonal, and culturally (co-)constructed in contexts by speakers (Blackledge & Creese, 2010; Daryai-Hansen et al., 2015; Lüdi & Py, 2009; Pennycook, 2010). A mentality of deficiency and linguistic insecurity are created by aiming at native-speaker proficiency, which is still a pursued goal in public schooling, albeit very often an unreachable one. This goal has been challenged by the (unequal) Englishes paradigm, especially with regard to plurilingual individuals. Canagarajah (2007) also promotes this idea and argues that speakers make use of their whole linguistic repertoire and social environment, especially in *lingua franca* communication.

With the spread of English and its uncontested place as the most commonly taught FL worldwide, English has been conceptualized in several manners to account for its increase in popularity and usage: *English as an international language* (McKay, 2003), *global English* (Crystal, 2003; Graddol, 2006), *world Englishes* (Canagarajah, 2007; Kachru 1990), *English as a lingua franca* (Seidlhofer, 2005; Jenkins, 2007) or even *hypercentral language* in De Swaan's (2001) global language system (for an overview see Crystal, 2003; Görlach, 1998; Graddol, 2006; McArthur, 1998; 2004; Jenkins, 2015; Schneider, 2007; 2011; Widdowson, 1997; for a critical response see Mufwene, 2010). Despite their specific differences, the common underlying argument is the same: English is learned by non-native[11] speakers for international

---

11 The terms *native* and *non-native* are used here only due to a lack of better terminology. The concept has received substantial criticism for creating an artificial dichotomy between different groups of people, focusing more on ethnocultural differences than on linguistic features. Arguably, if every native speaker of English were tested on their language skills, they would possibly not meet all the required criteria needed for non-native speakers of English to pass such an assessment. In fact, a study conducted by McNamara (2011) found that air traffic communication is in fact most often hindered by pilots whose L1 is English; this is caused by their disregard of the communication protocol based on simple English and phraseology. Such terminology is also often used as a means to discriminate against people who do not qualify as 'native-speakers', whereas language is only employed to cover other non-desired qualities or characteristics of a person in job- or visa-seeking contexts. The concept has also been criticized for basing the norms and standards to be followed on one small group of people that are equated with a given language's native speakers. In reality, language functions more like a continuum of different competence levels for L1 speakers and learners. However, it is also true that the differentiation between native and non-native is a concept on which many peo-

and sometimes intranational communication. More recent definitions also include native speakers of English when speaking to non-native speakers (Jenkins, 2015). In so doing, new varieties of English that are characterized by their adoption of local linguistic features are emerging. That is, English spoken in China by Chinese nationals, for instance, typically differs from so-called 'standard' varieties such as British English (BE) or American English (AE) in grammatical features and vocabulary.

When referring to English in educational settings, English is often referred to as *English as a second language* (ESL) in so-called 'Outer Circle' countries (see below).[12] In countries in which English is neither a national nor a former colonial language, the so-called 'Expanding Circle' countries, the term *English as a foreign language* (EFL) is still most currently used (Kachru 1992; Yano, 2009; Rajadurai, 2005; Bruthiaux, 2003; Mollin, 2006; Park & Wee, 2009). One important characteristic of ESL and EFL is that they (still) aim to develop a linguistic competence in 'standard' English in order to use it in the English native speakers' countries of origin, e.g., in the UK or USA, Canada, Australia or New Zealand. Thus, EFL classes typically have monolingual and monocultural transmission of knowledge as their objective. This approach and the conceptualization of static English varieties and groups has been called into question because of the growing diversity and dynamism that English is incorporating and representing. It has also been interpreted as a sign of postcolonial resistance (Lok, 2012). Lok (2012) drawing on the work of Said (1978; 1994) emphasizes "the dangers that are posed by the alliance of language, knowledge and culture in essentializing differences, an oppressive alliance that is both a product and accomplice of the imperialistic ambitions of governments...and the necessity to foster...cultures of resistance" (p. 420). ELF as an umbrella term for authentic, real-world English communicative practices has been suggested by many researchers (Jenkins, 2009; Mauranen & Ranta, 2009; Seidlhofer, 2011) following the paradigm shift of deconstructing languages as fixed entities and focusing on individual speakers' translingual practices instead (Canagarajah, 2013; Makoni & Pennycook, 2007).

---

ple rely and use in daily practices in the educational and professional sectors to assess their language skills (Anchimbe, 2006).

12 Kachru developed a theory of three concentric circles of language to specify how English is used in different country contexts. He distinguishes between the 'Inner,' 'Outer,' and 'Expanding Circle.' The 'Inner Circle' is the site from which English originates and in which it is spoken as L1, e.g., the UK, USA, and Australia. The 'Outer Circle' represents former English colonies or other important historical ties linked to the English language. Countries that fall into this category are, for instance, India, Nigeria, Kenya, or the Philippines. The third circle, the 'Expanding Circle,' incorporates countries without any historical ties to English-speaking countries. English here is a foreign language and is commonly used as a means of intercultural communication between, say, China and Germany or between Switzerland and the USA.

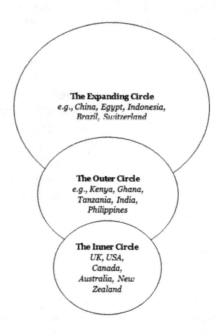

Figure 5: Three Concentric Circles of English, adapted from Kachru (1985)

2.4.2 English as a Lingua Franca

In contrast to ESL or EFL, ELF attempts to provide a solid linguistic base for intercultural (inter- and intranational) communication, rejecting any hierarchical order of different English varieties. Seidlhofer (2011, p. 7) defines ELF as *"any use of English among speakers of different first languages for whom English is the communicative medium of choice, and often the only option"* [emphasis in original]. She further points out that "EFL learners become ELF *users*" (Seidlhofer, 2011, p. 187 [emphasis added]) because of their rapid applicability and adaptability within – but not exclusively – their own country contexts. Learning ELF implies using ELF, since its language acquisition process is not centered on faultless language skills, but rather on applying the language and communicating through it. The interesting idea behind this concept is that ELF is supposed to be detached from any native-speaker norms and, therefore, can provide a 'neutral' terrain in which linguistic and national borders are deconstructed. Speakers engage in a common meaning-making process based on finding a consensus and mutual support, especially because they both face comparable difficulties expressing themselves in a language which is not their L1 (Seidlhofer, 2004). Another of ELF's innovative characteristics, mentioned by Meierkord (2004), is its formation on the basis of interaction between speakers of different L1s who do not apply specific ELF norms. Therefore, as she continues to argue, ELF may never be a standardized or codified variety of English, but will always be spontaneously produced with a different composition depending upon the speakers' L1s and on their specific linguistic features. ELF may be a variety of English that not only reduces language barriers and creates global interconnectedness, but also teaches its speakers cultural sensitivity and communicative strategies.

Importantly, language and power mechanisms are inextricably intertwined, however, as Marácz (2018), referring to Bourdieu (1991) and Ives (2015b), emphasizes. These power mechanisms do not simply disappear when the communication takes place in a *lingua franca*-setting among speakers of different L1s. Marácz (2018) considers the equality among languages an 'illusion' since a liberal approach to languages, in which languages are primarily individual resources and have no fixed boundaries or norms, will not resolve linguistic injustice. This is particularly true for institutional language use and learning that not only incorporate and transmit norms, but which also measure students' achievement by their adoption of such norms (Skutnabb-Kangas, 2009). Marácz (2018) continues to argue that minority languages in particular, which would typically be dominated by English in ELF situations, rely upon the concept of language hierarchies. If they were to be flattened or declared non-existent, then language policies, which aim at establishing equitable linguistic diversity and supporting minority languages' revitalization and their speakers, would be 'superfluous.' Finally, flattening power dynamics by opting for language use regardless of sociolinguistic norms does not remove the underlying hegemonic processes that attribute power and status to given groups of speakers. Rather, by adopting an 'anything goes'-attitude, minority and HL speakers in particular are disadvantaged because they lack the necessary English language skills that are practically demanded by sociopolitical norms (Marácz, 2018) even as English is hegemonizing and endangering their very own HLs and cultures (Phillipson, 2018).

Furthermore, as convincingly stated in Seidlhofer's (2011) own definition, attention needs to be drawn to the fact that when English is used in intercultural communication, speakers most often do not have a choice. Being the only option reflects unequal power dynamics that are represented by varying language skills and, therefore, linguistic capital. ELF (like any other language) is thus never neutral; this is especially the case in linguistically unequal interactions between a non-native and a native speaker of English (Wierzbicka, 2014), but also between two non-native speakers of English (Delpit, 2006).

Moreover, it is worth pointing out Grin's (2018) argument that ELF may not be the kind of English variety that learners wish to acquire, given the Swiss educational context in which this study is embedded. Learners, as well as language course providers and schools, often seek native-speaker instructors as their 'model speaker' (Clark & Paran, 2007; Mahboob & Golden, 2013; Moussu & Llurda, 2008). This, of course, has to do with the prestige that is still attributed to 'standard' varieties and to their speakers. Unquestionably, this needs to be considered when promoting ELF on a pedagogical basis.

Another important – yet somewhat simplistic – feature of ELF's definition is its predominant focus on communication. This study argues that language cannot be reduced to this function only.[13] It also serves as a regional, national, ethnic, and/or cultural identity marker and creates a sense of belonging (Kramsch, 2009; Edwards, 2009). It further carries information about a person's education, socioeconomic status, and position within society. In addition to this, language mirrors linguistic struggles over standardization, historical development, and political decisions (Ives, 2009). Another characteristic that is in need of critical reflection is the historical and etymological meaning of the term *ELF* itself. As Phillipson (2007) points out, *lingua franca* originally refers to the language of the Franks, whose goal it was to eliminate Islam. He draws the link to English 'in disguise' pretending to bring democracy and economic success, when in reality it endangers minority languages and creates linguistic barriers. Although this is not necessarily in line with ELF researchers who first introduced the term in the field to describe a far-reaching vehicular language among speakers of different L1s (House, 2003; Seidlhofer, 2005; Jenkins, 2007; Mauranen & Ranta, 2009), from a critical perspective, this term should still be used precisely because of its (abiding) negative connotation. Applying and problematizing the term ELF can raise awareness of its 'covert mission' or can at least 'uncover' it and point out the impact that English has on language communities, particularly smaller, endangered communities where it is not an official language (historically). Other terms, such as *English as an additional language* (EAL), *English for speakers of other languages* (ESOL) or *languages beyond English* (LBE), have been coined to account for speakers for whom English is not necessarily the second but any language acquired after the first (Wright, 2010; Cunningham, 2019).

English in Switzerland can be said to hold a hybrid status, one positioned on a continuum between ELF and EFL. While it is officially *taught* as an FL using BE or AE in class, its *use* among speakers of different languages within the country and translations of official documents on a federal level correspond more to its *lingua franca* function. Since EFL and its underlying teaching objectives emphasize the dichotomy of 'foreignness' versus 'nativeness,' this approach seems incompatible with the linguistic diversity of today's classrooms and students' familiarity with English. Rather, the paradigm of *Global Englishes*, which combines EFL and ELF and also "incorporate[s] many peripheral issues associated with the global use of English such as globalization, linguistic imperialism, education, language policy, and planning" (Galloway & Rose, 2015, p. 224) seems more suitable. Instead of promoting English

---

13 A more detailed definition of 'language' and the way it is used in this work can be found in section 1.3.

as a target language to acquire, in a manner similar to its native speakers, language teaching can enforce the idea of an 'additional resource' (Saraceni, 2009) that can be appropriated by both teachers and students as part of their proper idiolect.

2.4.3 The Economic Nature of (Unequal) Englishes

Having access and exposure to and being proficient in the 'right' variety of English can enhance one's linguistic capital and therefore one's socioeconomic status, as has been shown. English is nowadays often seen as *the* incorporation of linguistic capital and the ability to speak it fluently (or in a 'native-like' manner) is often equated with a bright future and both symbolic and material success (Phillipson, 2007). However, empirical findings suggest otherwise. English does not provide the same social, cultural, and economic advantages to everyone evenly (Ricento, 2015a). This is partly due to the inequitable access, availability, and quality of English instruction in different parts of the world. Meanwhile, it has also been shown that, English no longer counts as a distinct skill to ameliorate one's career opportunities – a process which Grin (2015, p. 129) has called "the *banalization* of English" [emphasis in original] since the English language industry has created a huge number of proficient language users. As a consequence, English (most typically a 'prestigious' variety such as AE or BE) in combination with other 'valuable' (either economically important ones or rare ones) languages *and* other relevant qualifications are needed (Ricento, 2015b). English's increasing predominance leads to ever more people wanting to learn and benefit from it, which guarantees the language's value as a prestigious FL to be learned. By the time non-elitist groups are also given the opportunity to learn English, it has already lost some of its value, which can only be compensated by other economically relevant qualities and skills (Ricento, 2015a). This process, Ricento (2015b) argues:

> is conditioned by and correlates with processes of economic globalization and expansion of the digitalized knowledge economy, which greatly, and disproportionately, benefit some workers in some sectors of the formal economy in certain geographical regions, but mostly benefits the corporations that employ those workers. This preference has a secondary effect on the utility of local/non-dominant languages in local and regional economic development that, in the long run, will influence the status and viability of nondominant languages in those societies. (p. 41)

Although almost all countries are impacted by the effects of a highly economically and digitally connected world, officially multilingual countries, which already deal with differing proportions of speakers and different language groups, experience a greater difficulty. First, this is due to the complexity of capturing the linguistic differences and rights in special policies. Second, officially multilingual countries need to guarantee mutual understanding among language groups and simultaneously keep up with globalization movements and international linguistic influences. Looking at Switzerland and how English, as a language incorporating the digitalized knowledge economy and neo-capitalistic mechanisms of globalization, interacts with local or even national languages will be examined in the present study.

The expansion of neo-capitalistic, economic, and digital globalization focusing on instrumental values such as efficiency, output, and standardization, as represented through the global spread of English (Ricento, 2015a; 2015b), will most likely end up coming into conflict with ethnic or national identities, heritage, cultures, and languages. For instance, English might interfere with qualities L1s have materialized through cultural capital, an identity marker, and a connection to their regional or traditional heritage. Furthermore, for some individuals, personal voices, and experiences, tied to their position within the society, can only be properly expressed in their L1. In fact, they are often unable to translate or to verbalize them in another or universal language such as ELF. Williams (2015) argues that the individual's identity as belonging to an ethnic or national group becomes "a collective subject that is, simultaneously, a political subject" (p. 100). Language is an important element in identity construction and is a binding element for ethnic or national groups that share this piece of identity with other members of the same community (Edwards, 2009).

In Switzerland, language is considered to be a very strong marker of both national and regional identity with not only four national languages, but many more regional and local varieties which create a connection between speakers and their communities or regions (Haas, 2010). English, not being a national language in the setting of this study but used as an AL in almost all educational institutions or as a *lingua franca* intra-nationally, further complicates its status among national and other HLs. This does not mean that English cannot function as an innovative identity marker within the Swiss linguistic landscape, but it does imply that the Swiss linguistic landscape cannot be maintained in the way it is currently being maintained. The change being brought about by digitalization, economic globalization, and migration is rapidly transforming tradition-based territories and taking over functions and meanings that had been attributed to a smaller local market previously (Ives, 2015a; Bale, 2015; Brutt-Griffler, 2002). English is part of similar phenomena that rearrange the economic order by deterritorializing national 'products,' i.e., local dialects, minority languages, and other linguacultural artifacts[14] (Williams, 2015).

These (neo)liberal movements consequently 'destabilize' and 'reproduce' formerly established 'national linguistic norms' (Bale, 2015) as well as the nation-state. An interesting point is raised by Kubota (2015) who observes that in non-

---

14   Linguacultural artifacts are objects or traditions that are shared by a certain culture or speech community related to their language behavior. For instance, collaborative narrative practices can be seen as a linguacultural artifact (Odegaard & Pramling, 2013).

English-speaking countries "the perceived omnipresence and usefulness of English in the world is paradoxically contrasted with the local expectation for immigrants to acquire the locally dominant language" (p. 22). In fact, although the Swiss local population is often eager to learn English and to be closely involved in internationalization processes, the Swiss language policy still imposes national languages upon the immigrant population. They expect certain linguistic competences to be held by immigrants, whereas a significant part of the local population prioritizes English over other national languages themselves for seemingly ideological reasons. Linguistic integration in this case seems to be a marker of the community's cultural identity that is exclusive to those who have sufficient knowledge of the local language. People without this specific linguistic competence, even if they have English language skills, are censored from this kind of identification process and are excluded from the community. A 'natural' reaction to this is to protect one's ethnic or national identity and one's linguistic rights. One solution for which societies opt, in order to reduce overt inequality and maximize equal, official status involves the formal creation of language rights. However, this does not account for all of the varying interests among speakers and is again an imposition on their individual rights and language use. As Bale (2015, p. 74) sums it up: "Ultimately...language rights are unable to resolve discrimination because there are too many discrepant stakeholders exploiting language rights to satisfy too many competing interests." Moreover, "linguistic regulation not only *reflects* racialized neoliberalism but in fact can *drive* it" (Bale, 2015, p. 91 [emphasis in original]). Having the state develop and impose language rights can exacerbate and legitimize discrimination among groups. Paradoxically, the state is needed or considered responsible for managing and controlling access to, and the quality of language instruction in, most societies. With regard to ELF, Williams (2015) argues rather unconvincingly that ELF does not endanger national languages because it is not to be understood as an identity marker, but as a deterritorialized, communicative tool.

The approach proposed by Wee (2011), which can be defined as liberal multiculturalism, focuses on individual rights in a deliberative democratic framework (see also Pogge, 2003), relevant to Switzerland as a deliberative democracy. Its underlying principle is that "individuals may and should have the ability to question, challenge, and renegotiate the norms of their own or other's culture" (Wee, 2011, p. 198). What is needed is mutual respect, appreciation, and the integration of different voices in the public discourse. This is important to account for the dynamic nature of linguistic and cultural diversity. Kubota (2015) and other critical applied linguists have expanded the concept of *liberal multiculturalism* by adopting a critical perspective. Critical multiculturalism, its conceptualization, and its connection to the study's underlying theoretical framework and setting are presented in the section that follows.

2.5 Critical Multiculturalism

> All animals are equal, but some animals are more equal than others.
> (George Orwell in Animal Farm)

Linguistic standards need critical (re)examination in addition to raising awareness of one's own rights, the integration of different voices, and the questioning of the *status quo*. Kubota (2015) argues that critical multiculturalism is based on "critical recognition of and enactment against power, inequalities, and discrimination that affect not only individual members of society but also groups of people divided by various social categories" (p. 28). According to May (2009):

> A critical multicultural approach can thus foreground sociological understandings of identity – the multiple, complex strands and influences that make up who we *are* – alongside a critical analysis of the structural inequalities that still impact differentially on so many minority groups – in other words, what such groups *face* or *experience*. (p. 42 [emphasis in original])

According to Tupas and Rudby (2015), the ideologies about English's high prestige and standard speech relate back to colonization transforming the former colonial legacy into an unquestioned and legitimate symbol of global interconnectedness and economic success (see also Holliday, 2008; Pennycook, 1994; 2001; Phillipson, 1992). One major task non-English-speaking countries face is the democratization of English, that is, its liberation from former inherent power mechanisms involving personal appropriation of the language for an individual's own benefit (Canagarajah, 1999; 2013; May, 2012; Pennycook, 2010).

This circumstance, as Kubota (2015) argues, is intensified by 'neoliberal academic activities,' which on the one hand acknowledge a pluralist view of English (e.g., research conducted in the field of ELF and World Englishes), but that also undergird the unequal nature and hierarchization in the field on the other. Such activities include English-only conferences and journals that require non-native academics to present and publish in English in order to be competitive. Another interesting point that Kubota (2015) makes concerns liberal multiculturalism's current, dominant approach. The paradox that she describes lies in the fact that both 'sameness' and 'otherness' are accepted and respected equally. Whereas this approach might seem honorable on the surface, it hides the actual struggle of unequal power dynamics. The socially constructed categories of class or ethnicity, for instance, are blindly acknowledged out of good will and are not examined critically. Therefore, liberal multiculturalism should be seen from a critical theory perspective that is combined with elements of critical race theory (Delgado & Stefancic, 2017; Bonilla-Silva, 2015). More precisely, as Kubota (2015) observes, "racism is conceptualized as not only individual intolerance but also structural inequalities and racially biased social and academic knowledge...critical race theory also examines intersectionality among race, gender, class, sexuality, and other social categories that shape our lived experiences" (p. 29).

Individuals can develop the reflective competences needed to appropriately assess the society and culture in which they live by engaging in critical thinking. The meta-level perspective is useful to critically assess the circumstances in which we live and our positionality within the prevailing sociopolitical and economic mechanisms. Adding critical race theory to the framework of multiculturalism provides yet another dimension that considers aspects of race, power, and law. It promotes a race- and color-*conscious* approach to social transformation and diversity-engagement, instead of colorblindness and acceptance (Magno, Becker, & Imboden, 2022).

This study adopts critical multiculturalism as its underlying theoretical foundation. It advocates for the 'mutual accommodation' (Nieto & Bode, 2018) of dominant and non-dominant social groups alike, instead of the unilateral acculturation of the latter to the former, to increase equity and emancipation. The study attempts to uncover and to sensitize people to structural inequalities and power mechanisms that split society into groups of privileged versus marginalized. The same critical awareness is needed regarding the teaching and using of English. Instead of doing away with norms, as is often the case in ELF or translanguaging approaches, a critical multicultural approach would argue that these norms should be addressed in educational settings in order for learners to understand and deconstruct them. As Kubota (2015) points out further, the reality of language teaching often requires a set of rules, which is why it is better to problematize them than to either ignore or uncritically acquiesce to them. In order to do that, teachers and students need to be aware of today's social norms' embeddedness in historical, sociopolitical, economic, and ideological processes. The common understanding, according to Kubota (2015), which needs to be created for speakers of any given language, and particularly within educational institutions, is that standard language is a socially constructed norm with no 'native-speakers.' All speakers of any official variety inherently speak their idiolect, which is some deviated form of the national standard. The national standard is usually determined by a small group of elitist individuals who do not necessarily prescribe *de jure* language norms, but are imitated by the majority of people who attempt to adjust their speech to the socioeconomic or politically dominant class (Milroy, 2001). (English) language teaching could adopt this view and present it not as somebody's language, which in the case of English is often done with reference to the 'Inner-Circle-English,' but as an additional linguistic resource that is open to everyone (Saraceni, 2009). Standard language is a political construct that enables institutions to separate and select people (Milroy & Milroy, 1999). A shift toward a pluri-dialectal and plurilingual society should be initiated by acknowledging that every individual has distinct linguistic features (Candelier, Daryai-Hansen & Schröder-Sura, 2012). Language teaching can set an example of an influential attitude change by applying integrated approaches where artificial and discriminatory categories are deconstructed (Ladegaard, 2000; Hilgendorf, 2007; Davis, 2003). Holliday (2008) argues for de-centering English language instruction in the following:

> There is a need for decentralized research which records the realities of home settings, and for de-Centred curriculum content in which students are exposed to the ways in which English relates to their communities. This content might include interaction between English and local languages, the politics of English, translations and literature authored in English by non-native speakers, the representation of native English cultures as 'one among many', texts written by English-speaking Western people from diverse ethnic backgrounds which discourage simplistic images of speakerhood, the writings of critical linguists in English and other languages, the de-Centering of textbooks with local teachers [sic] own realities, moving away from Western universities and publishers. (pp. 125–126)

Strikingly, more than ten years have passed since Holliday's suggestions about how to de-center English language instruction. However, a study conducted in the meantime in which non-native English language teachers favor 'Inner Circle' varieties and Western textbooks over transcultural or local approaches in English (Rai & Deng, 2014) indicates that the mentality has not (completely) shifted yet. Other studies still report discrimination against non-native ESL/EFL teachers, due to their linguistic and ethnic background (Mahboob & Golden, 2013; Sung, 2011; Braine, 2010). It becomes clear then that more research promoting attitudinal change is needed. It is essential to raise critical awareness among students, teachers, and policy makers to finally overcome any hegemonic processes through English (or any other language) that are still ongoing, due to its perceived necessity and utility for socioeconomic success. People need to be able to counteract the global capitalist movement created by the monopolization of English in economically important sectors of everyday life (Rudby, 2015). The importance that English is attributed around the world, as visible in language policy and planning (LPP) for instance, "through promoting the extensive use of English in education, [has] contributed to the creation and maintenance of a new global economic and political imperialism" (Rudby, 2015, pp. 53–54).

Importantly, a clear distinction needs to be drawn between the type of English required to access these global political and economic markets and the one typically acquired through regular teaching in schools. The language proficiency usually achieved after compulsory education is rather applicable to low-income employment (if needed at all) or to consumerism, whereas particularly fluent and authentic language use is (still) rather reserved for "the cosmopolitan community of well-educated scholars and technocrats and by the transnational, highly mobile elite of executives and top-level professionals" (Carlucci, 2017, p. 133; see also Ricento, 2015b). This is highly problematic since the internationally relevant and respected variety of

English is becoming a 'good' that is only accessible to those who can afford prestigious (private) schools, additional tuition, and linguistic exchanges in 'Inner-Circle-countries.' By investing time and money in the proficiency of English, "they are legitimizing their privileged social position through meritocratic rhetoric" (Carlucci, 2017, p. 134).

As outlined above in Gramsci's theory of *linguistic hegemony*, every individual's voice should be heard in daily sociolinguistic exchanges and norms established by the dominant group in question. The same goes for the English language industry that offers exclusive, authentic language classes to socially high-positioned individuals and certifies their participation to enhance their career possibilities further (Kubota, 2015). Although this process of privileging is seemingly accepted, and becoming a part of it is considered unrealistic by subaltern groups, its consequences are clearly visible and felt especially in terms of economic capital and the job market. Possessing less linguistic and economic capital can decrease one's career opportunities drastically and can lead to dissatisfaction and protectionism (Carlucci, 2017). Carlucci (2017) argues that this can turn into nationalism and measures to exclude foreigners from the job market and, therefore, make it less competitive in the long run.

What is essential is, first, a critical attitude to question and unveil these institutional mechanisms of reproducing and legitimizing the privileged status of a few selected languages and their speakers, and second, linguistic confidence and relativity. That is, languages need to be recognized as equal and should no longer be juxtaposed against artificially constructed standards or varieties incorporated by socioeconomically high-positioned speakers. It is the present study's aim to elucidate these institutional mechanisms, which are depicted through long-established power discrepancies, individual perspectives (and stereotypes), inequitable language policies, and the challenge of heterogeneous, multilingual classrooms. It further promotes a critical attitude to detect and reverse such mechanisms and offers an equitable approach to multilingualism. Language teaching needs to rethink its mission and (re)include social justice in its agenda in order to flatten the language hierarchies, based on socioeconomically important and prestigious languages. This is where innovative language education policies can shape and improve individuals' future opportunities and ultimately their lives.

2.6 Plurilingual Identities, Heteroglossic Linguistic Repertoires, and Multilingual Educational Approaches

> Bilingual education has the potential of being a **transformative** school practice, able to educate all children in ways that stimulate and expand their intellect and imagination, as they gain ways of expression and access different ways of being in the world. (García, 2009, p. 11 [emphasis in original])

This section expands upon the concept of *language* in 21st century, super-diverse multilingual societies. In contrast to traditional English language instruction, based on 'standard' varieties such as BE or AE, teaching in the Global Englishes paradigm tries to level language hierarchies and provide a medium of communication for everyone regardless of their sociocultural background and linguistic competences. That is, without any native-speaker rules to be followed, but many diverse linguistic repertoires of speakers of other languages to integrate, the main goal is successful, intercultural communication. In line with critical multiculturalism, however, ignoring existing (that is, socially visible and felt) hierarchies does not diminish the fact that English (like any other language) is not a neutral language to be applied freely without any inherent characteristics of power and inequality or learned without any rules to which to stick in educational settings. These uneven power distributions among dominant and non-dominant languages have been challenged by Bakhtin's (1981) concept of *heteroglossia* as well as García's (2009) concept of *translanguaging*, among others. Due to their importance and impact on the 'multilingual turn' (see below), these two notions will be discussed in the following sub-sections and the study's stance toward the concept of *language* will be explained further.

The section also includes a discussion of linguistic identity because these two concepts focus strongly on the internal, subjective dimension of language experiences, and perspectives. The concept of *linguistic repertoire*, based on Bakhtin's (1981) understanding of heteroglossia, is defined in line with how language is experienced and how individuals engage with language. The aspect of how languages as named entities are constructed and used within a society are analyzed in addition to the subjective dimension of language. Finally, especially innovative integrative methods, such as the didactics of plurilingualism and Content and Language Integrated Learning (CLIL), are promoted by this study and these multilingual approaches are discussed *vis-à-vis* school settings. Importantly, the promotion of multilingualism must not be done blindly or uncritically hailing it as the ultimate goal to be achieved.

Rather, a reasonable approach that includes a vision of how languages are used in real life and what values and hidden messages they can transmit, is indispensable.

2.6.1 The Multilingual Turn

The study's primary focus on the concepts of *plurilingual identity* and *multilingual education* need to be understood within the 'multilingual turn' (Conteh & Meier, 2014; May, 2014), which occurred in Europe around the year 2000. Importantly, as Meier (2017) points out, this development is not limited to the European context; instead, it encompasses the global education sector and can be attributed to the wider field of critical pedagogy. The 'multilingual turn' as a critical development in education advocates the rethinking of long-established concepts of *language, learners,* and *language learning*. Generally, the 'multilingual turn' postulates that languages are always embedded in status and power mechanisms. Learners are seen as "diverse multilingual and social practitioners" and language learning accordingly "as a multilingual social practice based on theoretical pluralism, consistently guided by critical perspectives" (Meier, 2017, p. 131). Since the study is situated in Central Europe, it will focus on the European development and policies. Reified in the CEFR, the intention to form plurilingual European citizens for better cultural understanding and social cohesion among the different member states spread across the European countries and is continually adopted in other non-European countries as well.

The Council of Europe (CoE) (2001) published the CEFR to standardize language competences of FL learners across Europe as one of the major results of the project 'Language Learning for European Citizenship'. The underlying reason was to protect and foster European diversity of (minoritized) languages and cultures as well as to enable and facilitate mutual understanding and respect while simultaneously relying on a common (European) value and belief system. These objectives are meant to reduce discrimination, stereotypes, and protectionism. By promoting the learning of at least two languages in addition to one's L1 in all European countries, while paying special attention to individual speakers' communicative needs, the goal is to create an open, welcoming linguascape for unrestricted mobility, cooperation, and exchanges in education, science, and culture as well as trade and industry. Mutual comprehension and respect (are meant to) reduce xenophobic movements or nationalist political orientations, which endanger democracy, free border traffic, and the European community in general. To sum up, common underlying values and beliefs as well as mutual respect for diversity are necessary, according to Coste and Simon (2009, p. 169), for a "sustainable development of the species.'"

The CoE distinguishes between pluri- and multilingualism by adopting a more speaker-oriented, that is subjective, approach to language learning.[15] The latter, according to the CoE, corresponds to the linguistic situation on a societal or institutional level. Typically, Switzerland is (commonly cited as) a stellar example of a multilingual country. On a societal level, multiple languages benefit from a *de jure* equal official status and are used for public and administrative purposes. Swiss residents, however, are not necessarily *plurilingual* despite the country they live in being *multilingual*. Multilingualism can typically be influenced and encouraged by language education policies that determine which FLs are learned, at what level, by whom, and so on.

Plurilingualism, conversely, refers to one's personal lived experiences of language including the language(s) one speaks at home, within the society, etc., and the implications thereof on a subjective level. Languages are not (primarily) counted as separate entities, but as linguistic experiences that transform into communicative skills that are stored within the individual's linguistic repertoire. These skills are interrelated, interactive, and dynamic. This understanding of interconnectedness and dynamism is also true for *pluriculturalism* in which the concept of *plurilingualism* is embedded. The more varied the linguistic repertoire, the more speakers have access to different cultures and peoples. A greater variety also facilitates and enriches the cohabitation of diverse cultures within contemporary, multicultural societies. These cultural experiences and skills act as dynamically as languages. They are not stored as entities but are compared and connected to previous knowledge and tradition so that the more intercultural exposure individuals have, the more pluriculturally competent their identities can become. Likewise, the more language exposure one has, the more plurilingually competent one's linguistic repertoire (see below) can become.

However, there is no fixed or static objective to eventually 'complete' one's linguistic repertoire. Therefore, the level of 'ultimate attainment' attached to 'native-speaker ideals', as a legitimate concept in curricula or learners' biographies, can be questioned (Lambelet & Berthele, 2015). That is, as a curriculum objective, it is neither very likely nor desirable to obtain a 'native-speaker' competence of an AL to which students are only exposed in class. The concept of *plurilingualism* refutes such descriptions because knowledge about language, even in one's L1, can only ever be partial. There are huge differences in language competences across the entirety of a speech community. To be sure, the language proficiency among speakers of the same L1 varies greatly so that a 'native-speaker' comparison with learners is rather meaningless. The CEFR's aim is therefore to develop, assess, and certify skills based on *can-*

---

15   This distinction is particular to the European-centered literature. Research conducted in the field of comparative education on language issues published in North American scholarly literature typically does not make this distinction (Benson, 2013).

do statements[16] that emphasize the learners' progress in a positive way (what I *can* already *do* in the new language) in contrast to a deficiency orientation that points out the discrepancy between a learner's and a native speaker's competence. The overall linguistic objective of each level[17] and area of competence within the CEFR is to fulfill one's communicative needs without imposing a necessary proficiency in all areas of all linguistic experiences:

> a plurilingual and pluricultural competence presents a transitory profile and a changing configuration. Depending on the career path, family history, travel experience, reading and hobbies of the individual in question, significant changes take place in his/her linguistic and cultural biography, altering the forms of imbalance in his/her plurilingualism, and rendering more complex his/her experience of the plurality of cultures. This does not by any means imply instability, uncertainty or lack of balance on the part of the person in question, but rather contributes, in the majority of cases, to improved awareness of identity. (CoE, 2001, p. 133)

Thus, the objective of the LPPs established by the CoE is to form 'social actors' with a plurilingual and pluricultural competence; this is comparable to an additive, dynamic collection of experiences and skills that interact with each other and provide the flexibility to understand and act competently in increasingly more complex, intercultural situations (Coste & Simon, 2009). These different situations have a varying impact on each individual's language repertoire as well as identity construction. Beacco (2005, p. 20) compares the concept of *identity* to that of *crossroads*, where several influencing factors meet, interact, and are flexible enough to continue in different directions. It can be influenced by language policies and/or education where either, to remain with the metaphor, roads can be closed off, repaired, or built upon. Similarly, the linguistic repertoire is highly dependent on environmental factors as the individual absorbs different varieties under varying circumstances. The following section elaborates on these two notions in greater detail.

---

16   Example of a *can-do* statement: As an intermediate user of a certain language, I *can* understand the main points of clear standard input on familiar matters (school, work, etc.).
17   The six different levels to pass in the CEFR include the following:
   A1: Breakthrough
   A2: Waystage
   B1: Threshold
   B2: Vantage
   C1: Effective Operational Proficiency
   C2: Mastery
   These levels contain descriptive criteria in the areas of oral and written comprehension as well as oral and written production that need to be fulfilled (usually assessed in certified exams) in order to achieve a certain level of linguistic competence.

2.6.2 Linguistic Identities and Repertoires

In a globalized, 'super-diverse' world (Vertovec, 2007), familiar patterns that have been internalized during one's early socialization and learning processes (Vygotskij, 1978) are increasingly becoming more insufficient to managing today's social heterogeneous complexities. Not only are more innovative communicative strategies constantly required, to which only individuals with the right and sufficient linguistic capital have access (Bourdieu, above), but the linguistic variety and its corresponding cultural qualities also impact every speaker's own (national, regional, social) identity. Language, according to Edwards (2009), is one of the primary markers of identity.

Thus, one's L1(s) and the status it provides more generally, specifically the prestige or connotations it has within the society, play a major role in defining and shaping identity. For instance, speaking Portuguese at home, but not being allowed or able to use it in other public or official contexts, has an impact on one's linguistic and social identity (Little, 2012; Krumm & Plutzar, 2008). Speakers of multiple languages can develop linguistic insecurity in communication with monolingual speakers if they perceive their own language skills to be 'inferior' or regarding specific registers typically used for official purposes. That is, non-native speakers are hugely disadvantaged whenever they are exposed to official communication contexts involving authorities, politics, or law, where the expectation prevails to express oneself particularly eloquently (and to be 'native-like'), and to adopt a certain context-specific register. They are less certain about how to express themselves adequately so that they might refuse to enter these spaces altogether or when they do, they might not be taken as seriously or made justify themselves more so than native speakers. Additionally, a sense of belonging and cultural heritage often established through language can be lacking or weakened if one's L1 is devalued, suppressed, or even forbidden.

2.6.2.1 Linguistic Identities
A language of identity, as Beacco (2005) defines it "is a linguistic variety chosen and/or accepted in order to signal or designate membership of a community" (p. 11). It is typically one's L1, which is often simplistically assumed to be identical with the national language. The process of learning one's first or any additional language in one's surroundings does not necessarily happen voluntarily. A language can be imposed on the individual and still be crucial for identity construction (Derrida, 1996).

Yet, languages are not only important media of communication and modes of expression, but they also carry implicit meaning. They are transmitters of cultural memories, norms, and a value and belief system. Identities seem, therefore, to be socially constructed (Bucholtz & Hall, 2005b; 2008; Foucault, 1972; Fuller, 2015;

Heller, 2007). Cultural identities are not seen as innate or stable, but always "as shared self- or hetero-categorisations that social actors develop, activate or modify in the...historical or social circumstance, according to the specific interest that prompts them to act as a group" (Beacco, 2005, p. 7). For speakers of more than one language, this requires a constant positioning on an identity continuum of assimilation and accommodation (Hu, 2003b). The impact that this has on identity formation is particularly important for minority language speakers or speakers of languages that are generally considered less prestigious or devalued in any form. The missing social respect and appreciation can have a negative effect on one's self-confidence (Cummins, 2000; Hu, 2003a; 2003b; Kramsch, 2009) and cause linguistic insecurity (Lippi-Green, 1997). Abendroth-Timmer and Hennig (2014, p. 28), drawing on Krewer and Eckensberger's (1991) concept of *identity*, define categories that determine the individual's linguistic, cultural, and social identity:

- Self-concept: What languages does the individual speak in which contexts and in which situations? How does the individual define him- or herself as a linguistic or cultural person? How does the individual describe and define his or her (plurilingual) communication practices? In which social contexts does the individual live? What is his/her (socioeconomic/linguistic etc.) status in society?
- Self-esteem: What value and prestige does the individual assign to his or her languages and the respective (socio-)cultural contexts and in what way is this estimation influenced by migration contexts or intercultural contact experiences? How is the individual viewed by people having more/less access to power in society?
- Self-confidence: How does the individual perceive and evaluate his or her competences with regard to his or her different languages? How far can the individual contribute to changes in society?

Therefore, linguistic awareness as well as the concept of "a diversified experience of otherness" (CoE, 2001, p. 34) are of major importance for one's own identity construction. Reflecting on questions regarding one's self-concept, self-esteem, and self-confidence and sharing lived experiences can help establish a more equitable understanding of languages. Their embeddedness in one's personal language and culture biography, which especially nowadays is often intercultural and plurilingual, requires a dynamic, fluid, and flexible concept of *identity*. The incorporation of different languages and cultures to varying degrees replaces the notion of the static monolingual and monocultural identity. "Forms of imbalance in [a person's] plurilingualism" (CoE, 2001, p. 133) represent the complex social diversity, as well as the prevailing chaos, rather than restrictive order (Maxcy, 1995). Importantly, a conscious appreciation of one's own linguistic repertoire is needed to overcome linguistic insecurity or the notion of "imbalance" and become more self-confident.

Language education can promote this shift toward plurilingual and pluricultural identities by integrating and supporting various linguistic and cultural resources, which students already bring with them (CoE, 2001). What is relevant for multilingual education is a better understanding of the linguistic repertoire and how it can be integrated into language teaching.

2.6.2.2 Linguistic Repertoires

The concept of *linguistic repertoire* was originally coined by Gumperz (1964) and focused primarily on interactions among speakers in a certain speech community (see also Grosjean, 1985). Conducting research in one town in India and one in Norway, he analyzed everyday-communication and the correlation between the words chosen by the speakers and the meanings that they intended to convey in their message. This is what Gumperz considered to be the linguistic repertoire: Making use of the language, dialect, style, registers, and speaking routines that individuals acquire during the process of socialization with certain grammatical and sociopolitical constraints. Put differently, in his view, speakers are free to choose among all of the linguistic elements stored in their repertoires except for the limitations established through grammatical and social norms. Grammatical norms here represent an accepted societal standard for speaking. For example, speakers who say '*I ain't going*' instead of '*I'm not going*' do not (want to or know how to) adhere to the established grammatical rules of speech. The context in which the utterance is made determines the appropriateness of what is being said. This depends on register, (specific) vocabulary, political and grammatical correctness, and formality and is assessed by the speakers' surroundings. The underlying idea of the linguistic repertoire promoted by Gumperz (1964) is that it is an open, versatile, and changing resource of which speakers make use to position themselves within an interactional space. The grammatical and social constraints notwithstanding, they voluntarily employ elements of their repertoire to individualize their way of speaking.

What is missing from this concept, in my view, are the bodily and sociopolitical consequences which result out of inappropriate speech behavior. For example, speakers who use *ain't* instead of *am not* (as described above) can either benefit from this behavior, that is, they can be accepted as members of a certain speech community (in-group), or they can be penalized by being excluded from several privileges reserved to standard speakers only (out-group) (see Bourdieu, section 2.3.2.) Another element that is necessary to account for are the speakers' individual characteristics. However extensive or substantial an individual's linguistic repertoire is, speakers will almost always also be assessed and (de)valued depending on their race, gender, and class. That is, their ways of speaking will most likely have to match expectations that exist about the speech style of a person with a given race, gender, and class.

Drawing on the *interactional linguistic repertoire* (Gumperz, 1964) as well as on the concept of *heteroglossia* as described by Bakhtin, Busch's (2017b; 2017c) conceptualization of the linguistic repertoire is a more contemporary and convincing one, which will be adopted in this study. Busch (2006; 2010; 2014; 2017b; 2017c; 2018) adds a poststructuralist dimension that establishes that individuals form themselves and are formed through language and within discourse. The linguistic repertoire is, thus, an expression of the self and comes into being when individuals engage in meaning-making processes with each other (Busch, 2017a). I would argue that not only do inter-subjective processes help individuals to form and position themselves, but that also intra-subjective processes do likewise because plurilingual individuals in particular often adopt and express more than one voice and identity (Becker, 2021). The poststructuralist orientation is better suited for a globalized, dynamic, and pluralist *community of practice* (Wenger, 1998), in which daily language practices are shaped by migration and transnational communication.

According to Busch (2017c; see also Busch, 2012; 2014), the linguistic repertoire is *not* to be understood as "a set of competences, a kind of toolbox, from which we select the 'right' language, the 'right code' for each context or situation. The range of choices available to a speaking subject is not limited only by grammatical rules and knowledge of social conventions" (p. 356). Rather, the linguistic repertoire incorporates, as defined by Busch (2017c):

> particular languages or ways of speaking [which] can have such strong emotional or linguistic-ideological connotations that they are unavailable or only partly available at particular moments. Our repertoire is not determined solely by the linguistic resources we *have*, but sometimes by those we do *not* have; these can become noticeable in a given situation as a gap, a threat or a desire. The linguistic repertoire can be understood as a heteroglossic realm of constraints and potentialities: different forms of language use come to the fore, then return to the background, they observe each other, keep their distance from each other, intervene or interweave into something new, but in one form or another they are always there. (p. 356 [emphasis in original])

The linguistic repertoire is embedded in a biographical approach that concentrates on the subjects' lived experiences of their language use and relation to given sociopolitical circumstances from an internal perspective, rather than looking at languages or varieties as independent systems of first or second languages. It combines language's biographical and historical-political dimensions with a focus on the internal features of language and speakers emphasizing subjectivity, feelings, thoughts, and desires. It avoids categorization of languages or dialects and leaves it up to the speakers to define their linguistic repertoires (Derrida, 1996). This approach also implies that no one is monolingual or mono-dialectal because we have all learned (voluntarily or not) to adapt our speech to external conditions (e.g., interlocutors, sociocultural settings) (Bakhtin, 1981; Wiater, 2010).

Importantly, it is not so much about how proficient one individual is in a specific language, such as French for instance, but rather how a certain variety, dialect, or code represents a voice within the individual and either can or cannot be expressed depending on ideological or sociopolitical constraints. Speech communities can vary enormously, and speakers can find themselves taking part in several linguascapes simultaneously employing different elements out of their linguistic repertoires, especially in a more globalized and interconnected world shaped by digital communication. Nevertheless, as Busch mentions in her definition of the linguistic repertoire (see above), the choice of which linguistic element to employ is not free. Each *social space*[18] (Lefebvre, 1991) in which communication takes place "has its own language regime – its own set of rules, orders of discourse, and language ideologies – in which linguistic resources are assessed differently" (Busch, 2017c, p. 343; see also Kroskrity, 2000). The notion of space is also taken up by Blommaert (2008) who defines the concept of the *polyglot repertoire*. According to him (2008), the polyglot repertoire "is not tied to any form of 'national' space, and neither to a national, stable regime of language. It is tied to an individual's life and it follows the peculiar biographical trajectory of the speaker" (p. 16).

The rules predominating the regime of language are always both context- and culture-dependent, which consequently requires a more fluid and flexible linguistic repertoire (Pennycook & Otsuji, 2014). Busch (2017c) claims that the repertoire is "formed and deployed in intersubjective processes located on the border between the self and the other" (p. 346) and is not itself part of the individual. That is, it is not a static or given entity, but is developed and shaped externally in social interactions. This implies a "shift of perspective: from discourses that form the subject to the subject itself that is enabled, through its very formation, to perceive, feel, experience, act, and interact, thus, to position itself vis-à-vis others and with regard to discourses" (Busch, 2017c, p. 349; see also Martinez, 2015; Spies & Tuider, 2017). Linguistic repertoires that incorporate both individual language biographies and identities are, therefore, inextricably interconnected and are always in flux. The more plurilingual and pluricultural encounters individuals experience, by either moving to different places, working abroad, or simply being part of a multicultural society, the more their identities are shaped by those. Consequently, each linguistic repertoire and the different languages, experiences, and the competences that it combines are unique (Coste, Moore & Zarate, 2009; Jenkins, 2015).

---

18   According to Lefebvre (1991), space within human society and its underlying interactions among individuals is necessarily social. A social space allocates actual and figurative places to social relations and functions as such as a product of social life.

According to Otheguy, García, and Reid (2015), these unique repertoires ought to be seen as *idiolects*, as one's personal language which should be used freely without adhering to any socially- or politically constructed boundaries or categories. This is in line with the postmodern way of thinking in which individuals continuously (need to) reposition themselves, integrate new elements into, and reconstruct their identity. This is an important aspect worth highlighting, especially when it comes to debates of language learning in which many actors and institutions have tended to regard language as something purely instrumental (Kramsch, 2009). Language is strongly connected to one's identity and can be linked to positive and negative emotional experiences, which can then either facilitate or hinder acquisition processes and identity formation. The study's focus on teachers' and students' personal language biographies and experiences in a (restrictive) multilingual context is an attempt to fill the gap in research on this topic and to stress its importance in an increasingly interconnected world. That is, the more people travel and move across the globe, the more their linguistic repertoires expand and become fluid. Their trajectories are not only captured in their passports, but significantly shape both their linguistic biographies and identities. This deserves some reflection before passing national language laws discriminating against and limiting people when the social reality calls for the recognition of a more dynamic and mobile polyglot repertoire. Therefore, a more holistic approach is very valuable when it comes to prescribing rules that concern one of people's most precious identity marker – language.

2.6.3 Heteroglossia

Individual biographical trajectories and their link to the linguistic repertoire and language's lived experiences are nicely and adequately captured in the concept of *heteroglossia*. Heteroglossia consists of the two Greek words: *hetero* which means 'different' or 'other' and *glóssa* meaning 'tongue,' 'language', or 'speech.' It is the translated version of the Russian term *raznorečie*, coined by the literary analyst and language philosopher Mikhail Bakhtin in his essay "Discourse in the Novel" in 1934/35.[19] It refers to different speech types within a language, i.e., its 'internal stratification' of dialectal, professional, or generational differences (Bakhtin, 1981). However, less emphasis is put on actual linguistic differences in form. The primary focus is on speaker-oriented sociolinguistic variation. By coining the term *raznorečie*, Bakhtin's intention was to raise awareness of and promote the legitimacy of intralingual variation within the Russian language, due to individuals' socioeconomic position or their rural and ethnic origin. This variation was judged negatively because these

---

19 Bakhtin's oeuvre remained unavailable under Soviet regimes until it was first published as a compilation of four essays in 1975. The notion of heteroglossia first received scholarly recognition after the publication of the English translation by Emerson and Holquist in 1981.

'speech types' deviated from the official standard norm. According to Ivanov (2001, p. 95), the concept of *heteroglossia* describes "the simultaneous use of different kinds of speech or other signs," i.e., what has been described as intralingual (social) variation; "the tensions between them, and their conflicting relationship within one text" (Ivanov, 2001, p. 95).

Of particular interest to this study is the link between the simultaneous use of different languages, i.e., multilingualism, and the sociopolitical implications that derive from tensions and conflicts. Similar to Gramsci's *linguistic hegemony*, a major source for conflict is the tension between standardization and the individualization or localization of (national) languages. As Bakhtin (1981) put it:

> The centripetal forces of the life of language, embodied in a 'unitary language', operate in the midst of heteroglossia [while] the centrifugal forces of language carry on their uninterrupted work; alongside verbal-ideological centralization and unification, the uninterrupted processes of decentralization and disunification go forward. (pp. 271–272)

These two forces constantly act on language and language users. It is important to note, though, that these forces act within a heteroglossic space, which is the default state according to Bakhtin. Therefore, multilingualism represents the (societal) norm for Bakhtin, yet it is always influenced by unifying forces that impose a certain (national) standard variety. Providing space for social diversity and multi-voicedness, he prefers the modern novel over other genres since it can include, and therefore depict, multiple perspectives of genuine social life better than others. He argues for the integration of multiple voices to create an authentic space in which every idiolect regardless of the social recognition it receives can be included and heard. Yet, he is concerned that the obstinate homogenization and officialization of language, based on 'verbal-ideological thought' (within the novel but very much so also in real life), endangers the linguistic variety that individuals bring to a society.

Moreover, the ideological embeddedness of language and the speakers' positioning within this ideology-laden space renders languages' neutrality impossible. Every word only exists in and derives its specific meaning from a certain context that is shaped by extralinguistic, sociopolitical, and historical forces. Again, in a similar vein to Gramsci (1971), Bakhtin (1981) argues that:

> unitary language constitutes the theoretical expression of the historical processes of linguistic unification and centralization, an expression of the centripetal forces of language. A unitary language is not something given [*dan*] but is always in essence posited [*zadan*] – and at every moment of its linguistic life it is opposed to the realities of heteroglossia. But at the same time it makes its real presence felt as a force for overcoming this heteroglossia, imposing specific limits to it, guaranteeing a certain maximum of mutual understanding and

crystalizing into a real, although still relative, unity – the unity of the reigning conversational (everyday) and literary language, 'correct language.' (p. 270)

Here again, Bakhtin points out that heteroglossia displays the reality, whereas any attempt to unify or standardize individuals' idiolects is a mere imposition; doing otherwise neglects the variety of unique characteristics. In addition to the imposition of a language norm usually representing a certain prestigious variety, a certain way of thinking, that is, a specific world view, is transmitted as well (e.g., which terms are appropriate, what ideas are allowed to be exchanged, etc.; see also Gramsci, 1971).

Heteroglossia is a very well-suited foundation to develop the concepts of *plurilingual identity*, *linguistic repertoire*, and *multilingual education* further. It serves as an instrument to analyze language in its web of diachronic sociopolitical relationships and struggles. While not focusing on the linguistic form but emphasizing the ideological and sociopolitical forces that drive language use and policies, heteroglossia can be seen as describing the linguistic situation of multilingual Switzerland quite well. The diglossic situation of SSG in particular and the plethora of existing Swiss German variants are captured well in the concept of *heteroglossia*, given that each of the dialects represents their very own regional voice, thereby contributing to the diversity and tradition of the German-speaking part of Switzerland. On a social macro-level, constant centrifugal and centripetal forces are shaping political debates on national cohesion as well as language learning and curricula in *de jure* monolingual schools facing a multilingual reality (Bakhtin, 1981).

2.6.4 Translanguaging

In this section, the concept of *translanguaging* is presented as a possible alternative to regular, isolated language learning approaches in schools. It provides the opportunity to engage in inclusive, student-oriented, and multicultural and multilingual learning. Translanguaging is a suitable approach to capture and promote multilingual and multicultural practices in a pluralist society that aims at an equitable representation and usage of every individual's linguistic repertoire. Originating from two Welsh educationalists, Cen Williams and Dafydd Whittall, translanguaging was coined in the 1980s to describe a Welsh-specific language learning strategy employing two languages – one for input and one for output – to foster acquisition and cognitive processes (Lewis, Jones & Baker, 2012). It has since been used in wider educational (research) settings with a focus on bi- *and* multilingualism despite its original intent to foster *bi*lingualism.

2.6.4.1 Definitions and Conceptualization

More recently, translanguaging has been typically associated with *multi*lingualism, although García (2009), for instance, employs bilingualism as an umbrella term. Among the numerous definitions available, the present study adopts the following: Translanguaging means *"using one's idiolect, that is, one's linguistic repertoire, without regard for socially or politically defined language labels or boundaries"* (Otheguy, García & Reid, 2015, p. 297 [emphasis in original]). Although the emphasis has commonly been placed on bi- or plurilingual speakers, it needs to be highlighted that 'monolingual speakers' also possess a broader linguistic repertoire than what would typically be referred to as one named language and can also be said to use translanguaging techniques. That is, there are different registers, styles, sociolects, and dialects, which the speaker adopts according to the appropriateness of the communicative context within the 'monolingual repertoire'. However, 'monolingual speakers' can also face certain limitations, due to grammatical or sociopolitical constraints, since L1 competences can vary enormously and not everyone has learned standard speech, for instance. Nevertheless, the restrictions are more severe for bi- and multilinguals. Following monolingual language policies, they must always suppress a large part of their linguistic repertoire to act according to the expected social norm. Translanguaging, as defined above, provides a space free of language hierarchies where speakers can use their linguistic repertoire without being assessed or discriminated against.

Translanguaging, according to García and Li (2014), "works by generating trans-systems of semiosis, and creating trans-spaces where new language practices, meaning-making multimodal practices, subjectivities and social structures are dynamically generated in response to the complex interactions of the 21st century" (p. 43). Swiss schools can rediscover language teaching without long-established cultural and linguistic stereotypes and outdated concepts, which target native speaker accuracy and consider monolingualism as the norm by applying the approach of translanguaging, instead of imposing socially and/or politically constructed categories of named entities such as *French* or *German*, for example (Gogolin, 2008). Importantly, the use of translanguaging in educational practices must not be understood as an 'anything-goes' attitude or deviances from the target language to be learned. Translanguaging is neither an incoherent or imperfect 'learner variety', nor is it meant to be a temporary support to facilitate the FL acquisition, but is instead an approach to strengthen every learner's idiolect in a value-laden classroom setting. (García & Li, 2014; Cenoz & Gorter, 2015).

2.6.4.2 Translanguaging as Empowerment

By defining it as the desired state of the (language learning) classroom, translanguaging can increase power and amplify voices of (plurilingual) students. Students gain feelings of security, confidence, and willingness to speak up for themselves after having been allowed and able to express themselves without any covert or overt language policies, which would typically silence them. This is needed to stop the circle of acquiescing to the unequal power relations found in education and other authorities. This equitable and inclusive approach creates a space of empowerment in which students can freely construct their (linguistic/cultural) identity, ameliorate their language skills in more than just the target language, and can develop a more profound understanding of multicultural diversity. García and Li (2014) summarize this succinctly as follows:

> Translanguaging offers a way to do this by transgressing educational structures and practices, offering not just a navigational space that crosses discursive boundaries, but a space in which competing language practices, as well as knowledge and doing, emerging from both home and school are *brought together*...translanguaging *transgresses* and *destabilizes* language hierarchies, and at the same time *expands* and *extends* practices that are typically valued in school and in the everyday world of communities and homes. (p. 68 [emphasis in original])

The integration of language practices from the school and home contexts in the language classroom are the key to doing away with language hierarchies. Students need to see their HLs as valued in an official context. Those who also speak the official school language as their home language can learn more about other languages and cultures. That said, schools need to raise awareness of the sociolinguistic reality, in addition to the promotion of equitable language learning and the destabilization of language hierarchies within the classroom setting. Students must learn about how their linguistic repertoire can be applied appropriately within a society that is based on monolingual standards and favors prestigious languages. They need to be conscious about their choices, opportunities, and how they can best 'market' their repertoire. A translanguaging approach would be illusory without this step of painting a realistic picture of the social reality. This is especially relevant for multilingual contexts in which seemingly more prestigious languages, such as English, dominate other important national and heritage languages. Translanguaging can even function as a mediator in the heated battle of languages that ought to be learned in Swiss schools. As García and Li (2014) observe:

> A theory of translanguaging offers educators a non-competitive perspective between 'languages' of instruction....by doing away with the distinction between an L1 and an L2, a translanguaging theory offers educators the possibility of understanding that bilingual practices do not compete with each other because there is but one system from which students select appropriate features. (p. 73)

2.6.4.3 Toward Equitable Language Teaching

Translanguaging is very well suited to addressing the problem of inequitable opportunities of language learning in schools. It attempts to create social cohesion by involving speakers in a common meaning-making process and by inviting them to make use of their language repertoires without adhering to socially constructed standards against which they would be juxtaposed (Gal, 2012; Kubota, 2015). Translanguaging changes social conceptions and structures by legitimizing the value of what were previously called deficient or non-standard linguistic competences (Quirk, 1990). "In so doing, orders of discourses shift and the voices of Others come to the forefront, relating then translanguaging to criticality, critical pedagogy, social justice and the linguistic human rights agenda" (García & Li, 2014, p. 3).

Translanguaging is an innovative, transformative approach that tries to capture and include the contemporary multilingual reality in schools which continue to impose monolingual standards, thereby impeding plurilingual identity formation and language learning. It intends to eliminate hierarchies, discrimination, and prejudice based on languages and advocates the recognition and appreciation of all languages. As has been pointed out by García and others to a certain extent, the reality, especially in an institutional classroom context, often differs hugely. I would go further and claim that translanguaging is not a pedagogical strategy that can be applied by teachers, for which trainings or workshops can be organized or exercises in textbooks developed easily without a more profound paradigm change. In fact, translanguaging can probably better be described as a *mentality* that is more easily adopted by people whose linguistic repertoire consists of more than one language and who frequently engage in multilingual communication. Even within plurilingual individuals, they might not always be aware of or want to use the different linguistic competences they have to hand. These might be triggered by their surroundings, linked, or restricted to certain interlocutors and/or contexts or cause feelings of shame, conflict, or insecurity (Becker, 2021). Speaking different languages can also be restricted by sociopolitical factors that punish individuals either explicitly or legally, or implicitly – by exclusion or discrimination. I support Otheguy, García, and Reid (2015) in their call for empowerment especially for speakers of minority languages and for their integration into an equitable, multilingual classroom. However, I believe that translanguaging cannot (yet) happen regardless of these sociopolitical constraints as they state in their definition (see above). On the contrary, I would argue that individuals have internalized social and political attributes that languages possess during their acquisition and socialization processes and have learned how to employ their linguistic repertoire as successfully as possible through their lived experiences of language. It might, therefore, be their personal choice not to use a certain language in a certain context.

2.6.5 Content and Language Integrated Learning

Coyle, Hood, and Marsh (2010) apply the translanguaging framework to another innovative multilingual approach, which is also important for this study. Using content and language integrated learning (CLIL) in a translanguaging framework can reduce the tensions in the sometimes-heated debate about FL instruction. By allowing the use of more than one language in the classroom and thus (institutionally) integrating students' heterogeneous language repertoires, translanguaging is beneficial for more students who would otherwise be excluded or disadvantaged due to their linguistic competences. That is, instead of insisting on the use of FLs in the FL classroom, the switch among several languages can release the pressure and increase students' participation (Berthele, 2010). It has also been established that education can highly improve the status of a language and influence people's language beliefs (Skutnabb-Kangas, 2000). To better understand how CLIL can be useful in this study, its concept will be explained in the following sub-section.

2.6.5.1 Definitions and Conceptualization

CLIL, as defined by Coyle et al. (2010, p. 1), "is a dual-focused educational approach in which an **additional language** is used for the learning and teaching of both content *and* language" [emphasis in original]. The additional language (AL) can be any second or foreign language in which the teachers are either trained or have sufficient linguistic resources. What is particular about this approach and what differentiates it from already-existing approaches, such as bilingual or immersive education, is its primary emphasis on content and the fact that the medium of instruction is most often a 'foreign' language, i.e., a language without any official status or function in the country in which the school is situated[20] (Nikula, Dalton-Puffer, & Llinares, 2013). CLIL is less focused on language learning and more on specific topics such as technology or environment which are dealt with in class in an AL. This does not imply that (foreign) language learning is neglected altogether. It simply occurs more naturally through content-driven input and a more active engagement with corresponding vocabulary and grammatical structures. Often, CLIL is realized in co- or team-teaching with a subject and a language teacher to guarantee that both areas are covered. The language teacher typically facilitates interaction and does not necessarily teach language-related topics, such as grammar, in isolation. AL exposure can vary, depending on the model used. In extensive programs, more than half of the curriculum can be taught through CLIL (Coyle et al., 2010). Other programs may limit CLIL to a certain time frame or might choose only a few subjects to be taught in an AL.

---

20 For example, English is taught as a foreign language in Swiss schools, whereas Italian is typically referred to as a second language for all non-Italian-speaking Swiss students.

This shows that CLIL cannot (yet) completely replace separate language classes, unless the school's curriculum is entirely based on CLIL and where its methodology has long been established (as is mostly the case in Luxembourg, for instance).

2.6.5.2 Student-Centered and Future-Oriented Language Teaching

CLIL incorporates the necessity to shift from static, inflexible, curriculum- and teacher-oriented teaching methods toward a more integrated, participatory, and contemporary approach representing the needs, experiences, and interests of the students and the challenges of 21st century education. As Ricento (2015) points out, since CLIL instruction is mostly conducted in English, it also serves the interests and the spread of the 'knowledge economy'. Intensive use of and reliance on technology and the internet have also impacted teaching practices. The constant and immediate availability of information ready to be consulted from anywhere in the world changes what and how we teach. The mentality has changed from "'learn now for use later' [to] 'learn as you use, use as you learn'" (Coyle et al., 2010, p. 10; see also Coste & Simon, 2009). Another characteristic of modern education is the move toward integration and inclusion. CLIL combines these aspects in preparing students not only in relevant societal issues but, on top of this, in a vehicular language which students can use in international – and in the case of Switzerland – even in national exchanges. The integration of content and language is, thus, an efficient way to incorporate real-life experiences into teaching. The table below taken from Coyle et al. (2010, p. 17) summarizes CLIL's advantages.

Table 1: Common reasons for introducing CLIL

Context	Preparing for globalization, e.g., developing the whole school curriculum through the medium of other languages.
	Accessing international certification, e.g., outside a national examination system such as International Baccalaureate.
	Enhancing school profiles, e.g., offering CLIL gives strong messages about plurilingual education.
Content	Multiple perspectives for study, e.g., modules in history where authentic texts are used in different languages.
	Preparing for future studies, e.g., modules which focus on ICT which incorporate international texts.
	Skills for working life, e.g., courses which deal with academic study skills equipping learners for further study.
	Accessing subject-specific knowledge in another language.

Language	Improving overall target-language competence, e.g., through extended quality exposure to the CLIL language.
	Developing oral communication skills, e.g., through offering a wider range of authentic communication routes.
	Deepening awareness of both L1 and CLIL language, e.g., those schools which offer 50% of the curriculum in other languages in order to develop a deeper knowledge and linguistic base for their learners.
	Developing self-confidence as a language learner and communicator, e.g., practical and authentic language scenarios, such as vocational settings.
	Introducing the learning and using of another language, e.g., lessons which are activity-oriented are combined with language-learning goals, such as in play-oriented 'language showers' for younger learners.
Learning	Increasing learner motivation, e.g., CLIL vocational courses which explicitly target confidence-building through the use of the CLIL language where learners feel they have failed in traditional language-learning classes.
	Diversifying methods and approaches to classroom practice, e.g., courses integrating learners who are hearing impaired, where the sign language is the CLIL language.
	Developing individual learning strategies, e.g., upper-secondary courses in science which attract learners who are confident in the CLIL language, but much less confident in science, who might not otherwise have opted for further study in the L1.
Culture	Building intercultural knowledge, understanding, and tolerance, e.g., module of psychology on causes of ethnic prejudice.
	Developing intercultural communication skills, e.g., student collaboration on joint projects across nations.
	Learning about specific neighboring countries/regions and/or minority groups, e.g., 'school hopping', which engages students and teachers in border regions in sharing resources and curricular objectives.
	Introducing a wider cultural context, e.g., comparative studies involving video links or internet communications.

Taken from Coyen et al., (2010, p. 17)

Table 1 vividly shows how multiple and diverse the advantages of CLIL instruction are. Not only can students' language skills, linguistic awareness, and self-confidence be improved, but they can also benefit in terms of preparation for future studies or work life and can obtain precious intercultural knowledge in an authentic way. On a general basis, the CLIL method is embedded in a globalized context and considers this as the default circumstances in which the students will be studying and working in the future.

2.6.5.3 CLIL and Empirical Studies

CLIL teaching approaches have seen a rise in research in the last few years. Serra (2007) conducted a longitudinal study in Switzerland to assess CLIL and oral production in the second language (L2) in three classes of German-speaking primary schools. Fifty percent of the mathematics curriculum was taught in Italian or Romansh as an L2. Serra's (2007) findings show that language alternation between L1 and L2 proved most successful and has produced positive results for CLIL's implementation. It was important to make meaning and to make oneself understood to also guarantee the adequate instruction of content. The results achieved in mathematics were comparable to monolingual classes. Proficiency in students' L1 and L2 was high. This bilingual model is now open to more students, particularly immigrant children with different L1s. This "confirms the non-elitist avenue this bilingual programme has taken" (Serra, 2007, p. 601). It needs to be pointed out again, though, that this bilingual program only focuses on two languages (German and Italian or Romansh) and neither automatically incorporates multilingual teaching nor includes other L1s spoken in the classroom. A more recent study by Pfenninger (2016), which received scientific awards and public criticism by former EDK president Christoph Eymann (Pichard, 2018), interrogates the relationship among early English learning, CLIL, and motivation in 200 grade 12 students (between 17 and 20 years old). Half of them followed a CLIL curriculum and EFL classes and the other half was only exposed to regular EFL classes. She found that students who start later in CLIL classes can catch up to students who started earlier in CLIL classes, which is probably due to the oral-based, communicative approach and its primary focus on vocabulary knowledge and fluency. This finding is hugely important for the debates in Swiss primary schools and the prevailing question of when to start teaching ALs. Notably, it contradicts arguments used to introduce English *before* another national language in primary schools. On the contrary, the study also shows that morphosyntactic[21] accuracy does not improve in CLIL classes. Motivation to learn an FL, however, is increased in CLIL classes (Pfenninger, 2016). Pfenninger highlights CLIL's positive influence on secondary school students' motivation to learn FLs and calls for a better implementation in Switzerland's established curriculum. An interesting aspect to bear in mind was raised by Heinzmann's (2010) study, which analyzes the impact English-before-French-learning has on students' motivation to learn French in school. Her results show that the teaching of early English in primary schools has neither a positive nor a negative impact on the motivation of subsequent French learning. It is, however, influenced by "the learners' language attitudes, their self-concept, gender and the language background of learners" (Heinzmann, 2010,

---

21 In linguistics, morphosyntax refers to the area of grammar that analyzes how forms or inflections of verbs, nouns, etc. (morphology) interact within a given sentence structure (syntax).

p. 7). This is especially relevant for the present study as particular attention is paid to students' and teachers' perspectives on language learning.

In sum, introducing CLIL as a pedagogical strategy to combine language and content learning has many advantages. These include, for instance, international certificates, diversification of teaching methods and content, an increase in motivation, and multilingual learning experiences or preparation for tertiary education. However, CLIL is most often *bilingual*, as was pointed out in Serra's (2007) study exemplarily. CLIL also typically incorporates prestigious media of instruction, such as English or French. Often, other L1s, especially HLs, are not included in the CLIL setting. This is partly due to the lack of teaching material in these languages and teachers' lacking linguistic skills and training in (the inclusion of) HLs.

I argue that CLIL can serve a specific function in the study's setting of multilingual Switzerland, however. Two of the central arguments in the language debate of FL teaching concern the *order* in which the languages are introduced and the *number*. Certain actors in the debate argue that too many languages at an early age are overwhelming and impede language learning. The other crucial factor is which AL (a national one *or* English) is introduced first. I argue that CLIL in either a national language or English can help to alleviate the tensions among the different linguistic regions concerning language learning at school. It can do so by combining language and content learning and can, therefore, reduce the number of (language) lessons, something which can be used to teach both languages. Furthermore, CLIL taught in either a national language or in English can compensate for the fact that one was introduced before the other. The CLIL language can certainly change depending on the teachers' and students' needs and objectives. This is more feasible since teaching materials in these languages exist and at least German and French are mandatory languages to be learned in all of Switzerland. Italian and Romansh learning materials exist, but these subjects are often taught as voluntary options only – if at all. The more volatile factor is the teachers' linguistic competences to teach in either English or in other national languages. This requires personal and logistical efforts by the schools' actors to ensure the provision of these multilingual offers, something which can be supported and subsidized by cantonal and federal organizations.

Methodology

The present study is situated in the methodological paradigm of phenomenology and in its primary focus on individuals' 'lifeworlds,' that is, on everyday social practices and individuals' perspectives that shape their lives and that concern investigating how human experience is perceived (Denzin & Lincoln, 2017). It corresponds to the underlying project's conception of social phenomena as dynamic, evolving, and changing especially in the super-diverse social context encountered at the beginning of the 21st century.

The study follows an interpretivist approach, since multilingualism is constructed by speakers *and observers* as the social reality as a societal phenomenon (Rubin & Rubin, 2005). By observers I mean to include researchers like myself as well. The broader ontological stance adopted here is post-structural or critical realism (Heidegger, 1962). As defined by Heller (2008b) this position "assumes that reality may be socially constructed, but it is constructed on the basis of symbolic and material structural constraints that are empirically observable" (p. 250). Therefore, individuals construct and co-construct the meaning, beliefs, and knowledge of their world with others, but these social practices always depend on "practical conditions" and "cultural frames of meaning" (Heller, 2008b, p. 250). This is important to bear in mind throughout the study since my personal, ontological, and epistemological beliefs influence the selection of the phenomena to be studied, how they will be investigated, and how they are portrayed in the analysis (see also 3.5). I further agree with Heller (2008b) that "researchers are active participants in the construction of knowledge" and that "we therefore have to think about research as a meaningful social activity which can have social, economic, and political consequences" (Heller, 2008b, p. 250). Considering the influence that a researcher has on the study's accuracy, it is important to choose a methodology with which one is comfortable and agrees. Phenomenology incorporates many elements with which I strongly identify and in which I am personally interested. I support van Manen's (2017) understanding of research and the ongoing process of knowledge construction and learning: "Indeed, phenomenological research is often itself a form of deep learning, leading to a transformation of consciousness, heightened perceptiveness, increased thoughtfulness and tact, and so on" (p. 163)

The different instruments employed, such as the questionnaire and interviews with students and teachers in three different cantons and language regions respectively, allows the work to reach a greater variety of individuals' voices and to capture a more multi-faceted representation of the social phenomenon under examination. The following section first presents relevant research in the field conducted previously before elaborating the study's own research questions, research design, protection of human subjects, researcher bias, data collection and analysis, information on the pilot study, data collection/analysis issues, translation, and finally the study's limitations.

3.1 Relevant Research in Phenomenology/Multilingualism

The National Research Program on "Language Diversity and Language Skills in Switzerland" (NRP 56), carried out by the Swiss National Foundation until 2009, advanced the research field immensely to which the current study aims to contribute. Stotz (2009) examined the ways in which AL learning enriches children's and teenagers' identity formation, how it shapes their educational experiences, and what type of multilingualism should be supported and developed by schools. The study's focus is on the language reform introducing 'early English' programs in two primary schools (ten classes) in the cantons of Appenzell Innerrhoden and Zurich. These two cantons were the first ones to start teaching English in grade three and two respectively, thereby including two FLs in the curriculum of primary education. In a first step, discourse about the decision-making process to reform language teaching was analyzed. Semi-structured interviews with the Ministers of Education and several project leaders responsible for the decision were conducted. The data were used to reconstruct the language reform's history. In a second step, demographic as well as language biographic information about students and teachers was collected. Teaching practices were also observed. Teachers as well as students were interviewed to examine their language experiences in- and outside of school. They were also asked to elaborate on their opinions about languages in general and about the language reform in specific. The discourse analysis and the interviews with the Ministers of Education as well as project leaders revealed four principal arguments in favor of English and a simultaneous delegitimization of national languages. Due to their relevance for the current study, they will be presented in detail in what follows:

- Equal opportunities: Public schools must act and provide equal opportunities for learning English for those who cannot afford private classes to balance out the advantage privileged students have, due to their additional, private (and often costly) English tuition.

- Globalization and economization: Schools in the 21st century need to prepare their students for the information and communication society and economy's demands.
- Early language education: Tensions and uncertainties were detected concerning the learning of two FLs in primary school. On the one hand, empirical results are cited and somewhat overgeneralized, but it is believed that children are overwhelmed with two FLs on the other. This argument is often used to discredit national languages since an earlier introduction of French is never discussed.
- English presence: English is said to play a major role in daily Swiss-German language practices; it is also the language of the youth culture and technology, which is why children and teenagers are commonly exposed to it.

The study's findings show a big support for the language reform, which changed the language order from French to English first in both cantons, Appenzell Innerrhoden and Zurich, by teachers and students. It further suggests that the four arguments, cited previously in favor of the language reform, were only used to legitimize the preference of English over French. Furthermore, the study points out that the adaptation of the content as well as the methodological-didactic approach associated with the reform has been neglected. Teaching material and topics treated in class do not relate to the students' interests ("youth culture" as argued above). Stotz (2009) pointed out that students prefer a clear line between school and their spare time. This means that English instruction, which is typically associated with higher motivation, more interesting topics, and a closer connection between students' lifeworlds and school, is neither necessarily perceived nor wanted as such by the students. The argument that teaching English would be equivalent with the integration of the youth culture is far-fetched. The suggestion was made by a student to incorporate socially relevant and intercultural topics into language teaching instead.

Bossart (2011), who collaborated in the study conducted by Stotz (2009) and draws upon the same data in her dissertation, investigated how plurilingual students position themselves within an officially multilingual state. Her findings suggest that students feel at ease in different lifeworlds, based on language and culture. Students from both rural and urban backgrounds embrace pluri- and multilingualism openly and are curious about the changing multilingual reality. A more inclusive approach to language learning was suggested.

Pietikäinen et al. (2008) investigate the lived experience of language for a plurilingual Sami boy, using drawings, interviews, and a sentence completion task. They conclude that the multilingualism, to which he is exposed, is both a precious resource and a barrier. In addition to this, different languages position him differently: Using Finnish makes him part of the majority, speaking Sami puts him in the role of a minority language speaker. The boy consciously chooses English as a global language, and in so doing, he positions himself within globalization and internationalization processes.

McClain's (2010) study on parental agency in decision-making processes on their child's school curriculum in a Mexican American family draws on van Manen's (1990) phenomenological framework embedded in an ethnographic research design. Through interviews and observations, McClain was able to reconstruct the reflective process of the parents' and child's educational lifeworld in order to better understand (the meaning of) the situation to several actors. Given the insights that she gains through her methodological procedure, she suggests that parents be more actively involved and their voices, especially those of immigrant and low-income families, respected in educational decision making. Hickey's (2012) study investigated the lived experiences of learning English by drawing on the phenomenological approach of Gadamer (2004), Heidegger (1962), and van Manen (1990), to emphasize the learners' own voices and feelings during their learning experiences. Interestingly, she argues that her phenomenological study led herself to re-examine her own linguistic practices and experiences so that she ended up "un-learning to learn" (Hickey, 2012, p. 145). This study is a fascinating example of how phenomenology is also a learning process for the researcher who can experience a transformation to better understand the participants' voices. Kirova and Emme (2006) employed van Manen's (1990) phenomenological methods, emphasizing the children's lived experiences, in an attempt to examine the lifeworld and the consciousness of the position occupied within the lifeworld of immigrant children in school. They contend that the visual representation of the children's experiences and trajectories through *fotonovelas* enriched their phenomenological analysis and allowed for a more profound reflection for participants and readers. They found that the migrant children's interpretation of visual, instead of text-based narratives, allowed for a better reconstruction of their lived experiences in particular, which might have been distorted without phenomenology.

3.2 Research Questions

Using a phenomenological research design, I seek to deepen the understanding of experiences, perspectives, and practices in educational settings, by asking the following research questions:

1. How are students' and teachers' linguistic repertoires constituted and how are they employed so as to position individuals and groups within (restrictive) linguascapes?
2. What are students' and teachers' lived experiences of language?

3. What are students' and teachers' perspectives on Switzerland's multilingualism and its multilingual education?
4. How do students and teachers (de)construct and legitimize (existing) language hierarchies?
5. How do they (de)construct and legitimize (existing) sub-hierarchies within certain languages?

3.3 Research Design

The study's underlying research design is phenomenology. The origins of phenomenology were described almost 80 years ago (Speigelberg, 1960) as a movement toward an individual-centered research methodology to include exploration, meaning, and feelings and to move away from numerical-logical-based studies of control, assessment, and improvement. Phenomenology derives from the Greek verb *phainesthai* (to show itself/to appear) and was first used by Immanuel Kant in 1764 (Heidegger, 1962). It investigates societally and individually important phenomena based on a biographical account of individuals' perceiving, feeling, positioning, and existing. As Heidegger (1962, p. 27) explains, "the meaning of the expression 'phenomenon' is *established as what shows itself in itself*, what is manifest. The *phainomena*, phenomena,' are thus the totality of what lies in the light of day or can be brought to light" [emphasis in original]. According to the literature in the field, phenomenology that draws upon biographical life trajectories of speakers in a multilingual space is a well-established methodology (Treichel, 2004). As a researcher using phenomenology, the aim is to focus on a phenomenon, to help us to understand it in as many of its facets as possible, and to raise awareness of the positive and negative effects it can have on a micro-, meso-, and macro-level. By uncovering daily routines, practices, and habits, which have been internalized and are carried out mainly unconsciously, I follow van Manen (2017, p. 163) when aiming at "new levels of self-awareness, possible changes in life-style, and shifting priorities." Language is a socially and individually important phenomenon because we all use language to express ourselves, to form a representation of ourselves in the world and in relation to other individuals (Jakobson, 1960). Merleau-Ponty (2014), a well-known phenomenologist, supports this position and argues that language is a capacity that comes from the body to express the body and to relate it to the world and other interacting bodies.

Central to phenomenology as a research design is the concept of lifeworld, which was coined by one of the founders of phenomenology,[1] Edmund Husserl (1913; 1970),

---

[1] Zahavi (2008) criticizes the term because almost all phenomenologists after Husserl distanced themselves from him in their argumentation and developed their own methodologi-

and is a translation of the German word *Lebenswelt*.[2] *Lebenswelt* or lifeworld refers to the world of lived experiences. Of particular interest are those phenomena that are taken for granted or that are part of a person's common sense. Their existence is not recognized (anymore) by the people who experience and live them every day, while these phenomena continue to impact their lifeworld unconsciously. According to van Manen (2017), one of the most important contemporary practicing phenomenologists adopting a human science perspective, the lifeworld or the experience lived in one's personal world, "is both the source and the object of phenomenological research" (p. 53). He emphasizes that, unlike in Cartesian dualism, it is concerned with the world as it is lived and experienced by people, not simply with phenomena existing separately from human interaction. Heidegger (1962), drawing on and expanding upon Husserl's work on phenomenology, adapted the term *Lebenswelt* to include not only lived experiences but also modes or ways of being or existing in the world.

According to Christensen, Johnson, and Turner (2014), phenomenology's main goal is to understand given social phenomena or concepts through the eyes of participants who experience these phenomena, that is, their perspectives, and how these shape their everyday lives. It is important for the researcher to understand the connection between the phenomenon to be investigated and the individual's positioning toward it within a certain social space. Meaning, therefore, must be constructed out of the relationship between the two (Merriam, 2015). It is the researcher's task to collect rich, personal data from people who experience a certain phenomenon or concept in their lifeworld, to describe it appropriately, and to compare the data among all of the participants in order to better understand the phenomenon's complexity and what exactly was experienced in what way (Moustakas, 1994). In this study, the phenomenon analyzed is (restrictive) multilingualism from a subjective/individual and educational perspective. Data was collected from social actors (students and teachers) as verbalized perspectives on their lifeworlds and educational practices. Given the focus adopted in phenomenological research on individuals, their experiences, and lifeworlds, it suits the study's underlying research questions and theoretical framework best. As pointed out by Creswell and Poth (2018), a central phenomenon needs to be identified which is relevant both to a group of people within society and to the researcher. It is also crucial for a phenomenological study to examine a social phenomenon of which a more profound and detailed understanding would contribute to a better everyday life in society and higher social justice for all social groups. The study focuses on the lived experiences of language, that is, real-life linguistic practices and the perspectives

---

cal framework. Phenomenology is therefore said to have "no common method and research program" (p. 661).

2   For additional information on the concept of *Lebenswelt* see Husserl (1970).

that participants have on their personal plurilingualism and on Switzerland's societal multilingualism. Furthermore, a phenomenological study aims to contribute to the amelioration of these experiences through the thorough investigation of these lived experiences, perspectives, and practices. In this study, this can be achieved by recommendations on language policies and practices and by raising critical awareness and recognition of one's own multi-faceted language biography.

Heidegger approaches consciousness as a collection of lived experiences in an effort to uncover the positive and negative impacts that certain phenomena have on people's daily lives and to enhance meaning making in and of the world. These experiences have been collected in the process of socialization and represent the individual's life trajectory or their "'texts' of life" (Creswell & Poth, 2018, p. 77). These lived experiences need to be understood and interpreted since only the capability of interpreting one's surroundings appropriately, and thus to apprehend cultural meanings and expressions, is considered unique to humans (Heidegger, 1962; Kvale & Brinkman, 2009). Heidegger further argues that every individual is embedded in sociocultural and historical contexts that shape their understanding and positionality in the world. It therefore follows that reality is not something that exists separately in the world, but is always constructed individually based on (historically) differently shaped backgrounds.

The study's focus on individual perspectives, their bodily and emotionally felt consequences for their language biography, and on the impact on their lifeworlds can be positioned in the existential or hermeneutic phenomenology. More specifically, this study draws more on the Heideggerian phenomenological framework since lived experiences of language are investigated through reliance on the understanding and interpretation of the individuals impacted. In line with Gramsci's (1971) concept of *cultural hegemony*, it is important to recognize the hegemonic processes that influence our positioning in and meaning making of the world. This implies that the study does not follow Husserlian phenomenological philosophy, in which individuals are simply considered pre-existing beings that have a (clear) understanding of their biographical trajectory separate from the world. Instead, it integrates a poststructuralist element that views individuals as subjects who position themselves and are positioned within a given historical-political, power- and-ideology-laden space full of both norms and categorizations (Althusser, 1971; Butler, 1997). Their biographical trajectory and perspectives are, thus, clouded by the position they occupy and are attributed within this space. As Gramsci (1971) noted: "The starting-point of critical elaboration is the consciousness of what one really is, and is 'knowing thyself' as a product of the historical process to date which has deposited in you an infinity of traces, without leaving an inventory" (p. 324). Another important element taken from the poststructuralist approach to methodology is its focus on disruption, exclusion, and suppression that can be experienced throughout one's life trajectory based on language (Derrida, 1996). Instead of viewing the phenomenological and poststructuralist approaches as opposing each other, their strengths should be considered together and should be adapted to each study context accordingly.

Van Manen (2017, p. 30–31), in his seminal work on phenomenology as a research methodology, describes a six-step methodological procedure, which is applied in this study:

1. Turning to a phenomenon that seriously interests us and commits us to the world;
2. Investigating experience as we live it, rather than as we conceptualize it;
3. Reflecting on the essential themes that characterize the phenomenon;
4. Describing the phenomenon through the art of writing and rewriting;
5. Maintaining a strong and oriented pedagogical relation to the phenomenon;
6. Balancing the research context by considering parts and whole.

The phenomenon at the center of this study are language hierarchies within Switzerland's diverse linguascape and its multilingual education. The phenomenon is of serious interest and relevance to many individuals, educators, and policy makers (Demont-Heinrich, 2005). This investigation is very much based on lived experiences rather than mere conceptualizations or descriptions because it asks individuals how they perceive, experience, negotiate, and (de-)construct language hierarchies within a multilingual country on an everyday basis.

Van Manen's (2017) six-step methodological procedure can be applied to the present study in the following way: first (1) the phenomenon of language hierarchies in a multilingual society was chosen as a research focus. The study wants to find out how these language hierarchies are experienced, (de)constructed, and negotiated by individuals to provide a better understanding and to raise awareness of potentially (unnoticed) inequitable social practices. Second (2), the phenomenon was appropriately and systematically analyzed through scholarly and newspaper articles and in terms of language (education) policies. Third (3), essential themes were detected. These include, for instance, *de jure* language policies such as the LangA that provides equal status to four national languages, *de facto* language policies with Swiss German as the majority language dominating over other national and HLs and the rise of English as a preferred FL to be learned. These themes were first described in their historical and geographical context and are connected to existing empirical research. Fourth (4), the study's contribution to a better understanding of the phenomenon consists of written data (interview transcripts and questionnaires). The detected patterns, codes, and themes were written and rewritten to achieve a fuller picture of the phenomenon under investigation. Fifth (5), the analysis was conducted while bearing the pedagogical implications it would have on multilingual teaching and on individuals' lifeworlds affected by the phenomenon in mind. Finally (6), the study also takes into consideration that it is embedded in a value-laden research environment in which many actors, including myself, pursue different interests and in which various competing voices need to be integrated to arrive at a more profound and inclusive understanding and learning experience.

3.4 Protection of Human Subjects

In a study drawing on phenomenology, where the focus is on individuals' personal lifeworlds, perspectives, feelings, and their everyday practices, it is hugely important to protect the participants involved. Therefore, participants were recruited on a voluntary basis. They were given the possibility to withdraw from the data collection process at any time. All data were treated confidentially, only by me, and were anonymized. During data collection, I made sure that the participants were as comfortable as possible when talking about their lived experiences of language by providing space for them to talk. I repeatedly informed them that they had the option not to answer any questions that they thought were too intrusive or personal, to rephrase something they said, modify answers they gave in the questionnaire, ask additional questions, or make comments on my interview guide. Since the interviews were all conducted in the participants' preferred language (with the limited choice of Swiss German/German, French, Italian, and English), it was assumed that they could speak freely, aiming at a fair treatment and opportunity of expression for everyone. The audiotapes were deleted after the transcripts were created.

3.5 Researcher Bias

Everyone needs to be aware of their own biases, especially in a qualitative study in which the interaction between researchers and participants is key and where researchers step into the lifeworlds of the study's participants to better understand a certain social phenomenon. For instance, I believe that languages are not neutral. Social constructs such as mono- or multilingualism are not neutral and neither is the act of studying these phenomena (Heller, 2008b). By adopting a phenomenological perspective, I strive to find out which languages are meaningful to them and why, how linguistic (in)security impacts their daily lives by interrogating, and I seek to challenge their perspectives on language hierarchies. Through conversations with them, I wish to give them the space that they deserve and to amplify their voices. In my accounts, I do not want to and cannot simply tell their story as my own. I will share my understanding of, and try to tell, their stories as their own relying on their own words and experiences. This reconstruction is naturally subjective. It is not a depiction of reality as it is, but my (informed) interpretation thereof. As a researcher,

I am aware that I am responsible for thorough and systematic fieldwork as well as for the accurate presentation of participants' accounts. I have taken multiple precautions to document my own biases against and reactions to, all forms of collected data and to record aspects of intersubjectivity through MaxQDA's 'logbook.'

I have expectations of and beliefs about multilingualism and multilingual education because I have an academic background in education and linguistics, being myself a speaker of multiple languages and living as I do in a multilingual environment. I believe that hegemonic processes affect the education system and often hinder its actors from speaking up for themselves to improve their learning practices and experiences. I believe that language hierarchies exist in society and facilitate the accumulation of linguistic capital for the speakers of prestigious languages and that this represents politically and economically dominant social groups. Speakers of heritage and national minority languages, conversely, are disadvantaged due to the low status and value that their L1 is attributed within the linguistic market. I expect these processes to be mirrored in the negotiation of language hierarchies in the classroom with the education system's reproduction and legitimization of the monolingual and monocultural habitus (Gogolin, 2008). Therefore, always being aware of my own stance and inevitable influences when engaging with the participants and analyzing the data is indispensable.

That said, being aware does not mean remaining neutral or objective. I believe that being a researcher who shares aspects of the phenomenon of interest with the participants, and who cares about amplifying their voices and creating more equitable multilingual and educational practices, cannot be completely neutral or objective. I am well aware that I have a great influence on the way in which the study is conducted and how the data are analyzed. Hence, I see myself rather as a participating researcher than as a neutral observer. Denzin (1997) argues that researchers who are (participant) observers in the field can never be objective. This is an important divergence from positivist, quantitative research where criteria such as validity, reliability, and objectivity are deemed necessary. Phenomenological research, on the contrary, calls for more flexible procedures and techniques that depend on the situation, issue, or space to be examined, the participants involved as well as the underlying institutional mechanisms and structures to a significant degree. The researcher's ideology, emotions, experiences, and worldviews are always present and need to be made transparent. In this study, the aim is not to paint a picture of objective reality, but to provide a subjective account based on the participants' voices in a manner influenced by my own positionality.

I rigorously documented my data collection and analysis in order to make my procedures as transparent and comprehensible as possible. Additionally, employing and sticking to a semi-structured interview guide guaranteed a standardized procedure independent of the interviewee and setting. The documentation included meticulous field notes, a digital research journal, audiotapes of the interviews, and their verbatim transcripts. The research journal served as a vehicle in which to immediately write down my own impressions, feelings, ideas, understanding, and preliminary analyses of my experience. This enabled me to compare the spoken and written data with my personal accounts. Furthermore, I gave participants the opportunity to ask questions before, during, and after the interview and provided my contact information so that they could reach me after data collection was finished. Finally, I offered to provide a copy of my results as well as a summary to the participants personally and even to their institutions if they were interested. I collected personal email addresses from those who were interested in case they would no longer be associated with the participating schools by the time the work was finished.

3.6 Data Collection

The data were collected through in-depth interviews with students and teachers while students also filled in a questionnaire to examine lived experiences of language, practices, and perspectives within the qualitative research paradigm. More precisely, the questionnaire was initially sent out to gather information about the students' linguistic and cultural backgrounds, their individual language biography, use, and preferences. Based on these results, the sample for the student interviews was selected.

3.6.1 Research Setting

The study took place in three different research settings, given the study's intention to represent as many Swiss language regions as possible and to consider the particularities of each region. I chose the cantons of Grisons (GR) for Romansh, Zurich (ZH) for German, and Fribourg (FR) for French. The canton of Grisons, Switzerland's only official trilingual canton, was the natural selection for Romansh as an official language since it is geographically limited to this region. It has a rich history of multilingualism and has constantly faced challenges in language rights, activism, and policies. The canton of Zurich, an official monolingual canton, was chosen since the canton's former Minister of Education, Ernst Buschor, initiated the first-ever introduction of English before a national language that ought to have been learned at school. In addition to this, Zurich is an economically strong canton and home to many international companies. The canton of Fribourg was chosen due to its long history as an official bilingual canton separating Switzerland's German- and French-speaking populations through a 'language border.'

3.6.2 Site Selection

In line with the research design, the research sites were chosen intentionally and carefully (Creswell & Poth, 2018). Following Marcus (1995) and Hannerz (2003), this study adopts a multi-sited research approach. Focusing on multiple sites, instead of one in-depth case study, the analysis of social processes, movements, and trajectories, which cross different 'educational policyscapes' can provide more valuable knowledge (Carney, 2009; 2011; Gogolin, 2002; Zimmermann, 2017). Looking at the ideological, symbolic, and material representation of languages, it is key, as pointed out by Appadurai (1996), to not only apprehend static sites, but also to capture the fluidity and circulation of either the languages' representations or their speakers. The criterion to be met was the exposure to and the lived experiences of multilingualism in a primarily monolingual school restricted by language education policies.

Students and teachers from this school type were chosen, given the limited research on Swiss upper secondary schools. The schools within these cantons were carefully chosen to make sure that Romansh, French, and German were the official school languages at the corresponding institutions. The school in Zurich was selected based on the only positive response that I received from the requests that I had sent out. The school chosen for French is, in fact, an intercantonal school to which students from the French-only canton of Vaud and students from bilingual Fribourg go, so French is the more dominant language here. This was considered important, given the intention to represent the French-speaking perspectives. In the case of Romansh, there is only one public upper secondary school for the whole canton of Grisons. This implies that students from the entire canton complete their upper secondary education in this school. To complicate matters further, these can be students who are speakers of any of the five different Romansh idioms. The challenge for the school with Romansh as a medium of instruction, therefore, is to either standardize the different idioms into Rumantsch Grischun or to provide separate classes taught by teachers who can switch between them. The image below illustrates this particularity.

Figure 6: Languages and idioms spoken in the canton of Grisons

[Vallader, Putèr, Surmiran, Sutsilvan, Sursilvan, German, Italian; top to bottom]

Importantly, despite the multiple requests to gain access to an upper secondary school in the Italian-speaking canton of Ticino, I did not receive a response from the cantonal authorities. Hence, the fourth Swiss language region is not part of the site selection. Nevertheless, by including and comparing three upper secondary schools in the French-, German-, and Romansh-speaking regions of Switzerland in this study, the aim is to represent the speakers of the three national languages within the educational field and to demonstrate how each of the chosen site copes with different linguistic and cultural realities.

3.6.3 Questionnaires

This section presents the questionnaire, one of the instruments used for data collection, the sample, and the procedure.

3.6.3.1 The Instrument

The questionnaire was primarily employed to collect demographic information on the students' language use, competences, preferences, and perspectives for descriptive statistics. It is a suitable tool to better understand and to describe the study's sample, which can be helpful when providing recommendations for language policies and curricula. Understanding and getting to know the participants and their lifeworlds is an essential element, given the phenomenological nature of the study. The questions on language biography and use are mainly based on the European Language Portfolio for adolescents and young adults, a tool often employed in schools for language testing, biographies, or other exercises in the (foreign) language classroom. Being approved as an official complementary language teaching material in Swiss schools, the portfolio provided a useful reference and framework for the questionnaire regarding the formulation of, and the familiarity with, the topics to be included. In this study, a digital questionnaire with 31 questions (5 demographic and 26 content questions) created through Google Forms was used (see Appendix A). It is divided into six sections and contains information about the person, the participant's linguistic and cultural background, language biography, family languages, school languages, personal language use, and language preferences. The information about the linguistic and cultural background gave more insight into the diverse nature of each linguistic repertoire based on the person's upbringing. To what extent this linguistic repertoire expanded in school, was examined in the next section. Students were asked which languages they learned in school, how much they liked them, and what their grades in the current school year's report were. In addition to this, the questionnaire examined the students' use of languages other than their L1(s). They were asked to determine their competency in FLs based on a scale ranging from 1 (I can introduce myself, understand and use familiar everyday expressions, e.g., where do you live?) to 6 (I can use language for virtually everything in unfamiliar situations). The explanations of the scale were based on the CEFR's language levels from A1-C2. They were further asked to specify where, how, and with whom they learned and used these languages. The last section investigated the students' language preferences starting with two rankings of languages which the students used or would like to use. The first ranking consisted of personal languages, e.g., languages used with family and friends, for leisure, associated with heritage and identity. In the second ranking, languages were to be classified according to their value and utility on a professional level, e.g., studying abroad or working in international companies. Students were also asked to rank how satisfied they were with language teaching at school, whether the learning of English should be prioritized, whether other L1s should be more actively integrated, and whether the cultures and languages represented in class should be more debated on a 5-point Likert-scale. Open-ended questions invited the students to elaborate on whether they would prefer learning English over either French or

German (this question was specified depending on the language region). If the students' L1 was not officially used in school, then they were asked to explain whether they thought it should be more actively included, how so or if not, why not. Finally, they were asked if they wished to drop a language that they were learning in order to introduce or intensify others and explain why. I considered it important to reach as many students as possible through questionnaires to sensitize them to the issue since students' perspectives are often neglected in policy-making decisions, and since they do not often have the chance to openly express their interests themselves.

3.6.3.2 Sample

I was granted permission to send the questionnaire to two classes of students within one school in each of the three cantons. Due to financial reasons and lack of time, the questionnaires were only provided in the school's official language. Since the participating students were all enrolled in upper secondary school, I assumed that they would be able to fill in the questionnaire easily in the local medium of instruction. A total of 94 students filled in the questionnaire: 38 in GR, 36 in ZH, and 20 in FR.

Table 2: Questionnaire sample

Item	ZH	FR	GR
N	36	20	38
Gender	52.8% female 47.2% male	68.4% female 26.3% male 5.3% prefer not to say	54.8% female 45.2% male
Place of birth	91.7% Switzerland 1 Vietnam 1 Germany 1 England	85% Switzerland 1 USA 1 Germany 1 France	100% Switzerland
Year of birth	2000 – 2002	1999 – 2004	2000 – 2004

Nationality/ies (By passport)	77.8% Swiss 4 Swiss/German 1 Swiss/Macedonian 1 Swiss/Turkish 1 Swiss/Pakistani 1 Swiss/Italian	50% Swiss 2 Swiss/Italian 1 French/British 1 Swiss/Portuguese 1 Swiss/US 1 Swiss/French 1 Swiss/German 1 Spanish	78.9% Swiss 2 Swiss/German 1 Swiss/Canadian
Age when arrived in Switzerland (if born in a different country)	11 days – 4 years	2 – 8 years	N/A
First language(s)	92% Swiss German and German 8% German *without* Swiss German 22% bilingual German and Bosnian, Vietnamese, Hungarian, Italian, Romansh, Urdu, Turkish, Macedonian, Swahili, Tirolean dialect	70% French 30% bilingual French and Italian English, German, Cantonese, Japanese, Portuguese, Italian	95% bilingual Romans–wiss German/German 1 English and Swiss German 1 Romansh, German, and Dutch
Language proficiency[3] in L1s (Self-evaluation)	86.1% very proficient in their first L1 69.2% very proficient in their second L1	70% very proficient in their first L1 20% very proficient in their second L1	85% very proficient in their first L1 82% very proficient in their second L1

The vast majority of the participants were born in Switzerland. This is mirrored in the students' nationalities who all (except for one in Fribourg) are (also) Swiss nationals by passport. Similarly, all students speak the official regional language – German for Zurich, French for Fribourg, and Romansh/German for Grisons. Their second L1s are more varied, however. Almost all students in Grisons are bilingual,

---

3   Language proficiency here refers to students' reading and writing competences and the options for self-evaluation range from very few words to full texts without any difficulties.

whereas this proportion is 22% in the canton of Zurich and 30% in the canton of Fribourg. That said, students in Grisons almost always have Swiss German/German or Romansh as their L1s, whereas students in the other two cantons speak other HLs such as Urdu, Macedonian, or Cantonese at home. Based on their self-evaluation in language proficiency, it is higher for the first L1 and comes close to the same proficiency for Romansh – Swiss German/German bilinguals. The difference is striking especially in the bilingual canton of Fribourg where only 20% are very proficient in their second L1. Generally, between 70% and 86.1% of students are very proficient in their first L1, which is also the school's official language. This implies that 13.9% to 30% of the upper secondary students perceive their skills as not very proficient, implying difficulties when it comes to reading and writing in school.

3.6.3.3 Procedure

Due to the Covid-19 crisis and school closures, I was unable to be physically present when students filled in the questionnaire. Therefore, the link to the questionnaire was sent to the responsible teachers who forwarded the email or sent directly to the students whenever their email addresses were available. The questionnaire included open-ended questions that would require some (short) sentences of writing. Other formats were multiple choice questions and grids as well as question statements on a five-point Likert-scale. Given that students were aged between 16 and 20, their familiarity with the internet was expected. The teachers were asked to dedicate approximately 15 minutes of their lesson to the completion of the questionnaire in order to guarantee a higher participation than if they were to do it at home. This could be done on the students' smartphones or, in case they did not possess one, they could open the link to the questionnaire on a school computer or at home. If they had questions concerning the questionnaire, they had my contact information and were able to write questions into the comment sections of the questionnaire. Furthermore, they were asked to provide their names for the researcher's use only so that I had the opportunity to contact the students directly to invite them for an interview. Wherever the students' email addresses were not provided, I contacted the teachers again to ask for them.

3.6.4 Interviews

In phenomenology, qualitative interviews are considered an essential and constitutive element of the research design. Since the study focuses on the human, lived experiences of language, their felt consequences, and personal perspectives on important societal issues, actively listening and talking to individuals impacted by these phenomena is crucial (Kvale & Brinkman, 2009; Marshall & Rossman, 2010). I wanted to provide a certain freedom and openness to the participants who could share their experiences in whatever way they felt by conducting interviews that consisted of a biographical and a semi-structured part. As Rubin and Rubin (2005) point out, the interview permits the researcher and the interviewee to have a conversation about personal experiences, to delve into their lives together, and to mutually co- and re-construct important elements. This allows the researcher to better understand a certain phenomenon to which they are not directly exposed themselves, but are keen to investigate to unravel the potential positive or negative impacts on certain individuals or the society as a whole. Qualitative interviews, therefore, help us to uncover individual understandings and interpretations of the world. Additionally, they also reconstruct habitual processes and events, which the participants often undergo unconsciously (Rubin & Rubin, 2005). Importantly, especially in a context in which interview questions deal with participants' everyday practices and lifeworlds, "it is a professional interaction, which goes beyond the spontaneous exchange of views as in everyday conversation, and becomes a careful questioning and listening approach with the purpose of obtaining thoroughly tested knowledge" (Kvale, 2007, p. 7).

Although every interview is unique, two different semi-structured guides for students' and teachers' interviews with questions linked to my research questions were created in order to ensure comparison among the participants and different samples. The questions were derived from the study's theoretical framework and drew on methodological guidelines of how to conduct phenomenological interviews with a focus on pluri- and multilingualism (van Manen, 2017; Rubin & Rubin, 2005; Koven, 2001; Pavlenko, 2007; Bourdieu, 1999). These include, among others, being concrete, asking about specific examples, situations, events, persons involved, locations/spaces, times, being patient, being wary of generalizations, being ready to ask questions to make the discourse more concrete, and providing the opportunity or asking interviewees to use several languages and/or translanguaging techniques to capture their entire linguistic identities.

3.6.4.1 Students' Interviews

The guide for students' interviews was designed based on the scholarly literature and was further guided by the questionnaire's results. The answers solicited through the questionnaire were available during the discussion and were used as a starting point or stimuli to render the discussion livelier. This was considered useful and comforting for the students because they might be shyer or intimidated by the somewhat artificial situation (Barbour, 2007). Knowing that they had already spent time on the questionnaire and were, therefore, somewhat familiar with the topic, they might feel more at ease to talk about their language biography with somebody that they did not know.

The discussion served to arrive at a more subjective representation of the students' language biography and their understanding and perspectives on multilingual education. The questions helped to create scenarios in which the students would describe their lived experiences of language and how they impacted other spheres of their lives. Since this contribution argues that language is inextricably linked to one's identity, this aspect was explored in greater detail during the discussion. Such connections and feelings cannot always be explained on a written basis, in a short answer in the questionnaire, but instead need elaboration in an open space in which their voices are taken seriously and valued. In addition to the identity aspect of language, languages can also take on instrumental functions and therefore incorporate or concern better economic opportunities. This topic was approached in more detail to see which languages students would typically associate with higher personal and professional opportunities. Students in this age group (16–20) and this school type (upper secondary) are more immediately concerned with university, economically higher impact jobs, or other international activities and are, therefore, more likely to be exposed to multiple FLs.

The interview guide (see Appendix A) consisted of 13 questions and covered topics such as students' lived experiences of language, their understanding of language teaching, and their (de)construction and negotiation of language hierarchies on societal, school, and classroom level. Sub-topics examined students' language use in more detail, specifically whether they faced restrictions or censorship or whether they could benefit from their (plurilingual) language repertoire in their daily lives. They were further asked to explain their personal preferences of languages, including their rankings into hierarchies and their favorite language(s). Other questions investigated their perspectives on language and identity, the importance of communicating in multiple languages, CLIL, and language education policies and laws. A total of 14 student interviews were conducted, which lasted 30–45 minutes each: 9 in GR and 5 in ZH. Fribourg students did not respond to my or their teachers' repeated invitation to participate in an interview.

3.6.4.2 Teachers' Interviews

The interview guide for teachers (see Appendix A) draws on the study's theoretical framework of language biography and is meant to provide as much space as possible for the teachers to share and elaborate upon their own language biography, feelings, perspectives, and teaching practices. They were addressed as individual speakers with their own personal lived experiences of language separate from their role as teachers. A total of 20 upper secondary teachers participated in an interview, which lasted between 45 and 90 minutes each: 6 in FR, 5 in GR, and 9 in ZH.

Similar to the students' interviews, the topics covered the teachers' lived experiences of language, their understanding of and perspectives on language teaching, the (de)construction of language hierarchies, and finally the negotiation of these hierarchies in- and outside the classroom. They were asked about their linguistic repertoires, the relationship between language and identity, and language and economic opportunities. The questions further investigated their teaching practices and whether they were positively or negatively influenced by the curriculum. Other sub-topics were the federal language policy and the EDK's language strategy. They were further invited to comment on sociopolitical debates on language learning, explain their perspectives on the integration of students' HLs into (their) classroom, and give examples of how they (would) implement this. Teachers were then asked about the status of English more specifically, its link to personal and professional opportunities for students, and its importance on a societal level. It was assumed that teachers would feel comfortable to conduct the interview given that they were able to start it off by talking about their personal lived experiences of language, their language biography, general perspectives, and feelings.

3.6.5 Data Collection Procedures: Gaining Entry

A request to conduct a study and to collect data in upper secondary schools was sent to the cantonal authorities in Zurich, Grisons, Ticino, Vaud, and Fribourg. The requests and the project description were sent in the official, cantonal language.

First, I wrote a summary of my project, explaining why and how I wanted to collect data in schools. I then sent it to the cantonal authorities (Ministries of Education) along with a permission request to contact individual schools and to ask them to participate in my study. In the case of Ticino, I had to fill in a particular form and questionnaire providing more details concerning my planned data collection. The automatic response that I received after submitting the questionnaire stated that I would be contacted in case it was decided that the study was considered relevant for the Ministry of Education. I quickly received permission from the canton of Zurich to contact six upper secondary schools for which I was provided with a list of contact information. Of the six schools I contacted, three replied. One principal responded and declined, due to my planned data collection, which he considered very time-consuming and because of the high number of requests they received. Another answered similarly, saying that the school did not have the resources to participate in the study. The third answer that I received was positive and we exchanged further information and details about the project. Five months later, I was provided with a list of teachers who were willing to participate in an interview as well as a list of classes to which I could send the questionnaire and select students for interviews. I then contacted each teacher individually to determine a date for classroom observation (see below) and to arrange an interview at their school. All of the teachers who had signed up agreed to an interview. I then asked for permission to contact some of the students who participated in the questionnaire to determine a date for an interview.

I also received a positive response from the cantonal authorities of Fribourg, which granted me access to one upper secondary school. I contacted the school leader, who was willing to support my project and who gave me the possibility to write a letter to teachers to be shared in the school. Teachers could read more about the project and could sign up if they were interested. After three months, I received a response including seven teachers' email addresses who had signed up to participate. I contacted those to explain my project and data collection further and to, finally, ask for an in-person meeting at their school to conduct classroom observation and interviews. However, only two teachers responded and agreed to meet for an interview. Two other teachers responded and said that they were no longer available. Two of my fellow graduate students personally knew teachers working at the same school so I asked them to encourage other colleagues to participate in the study. Finally, four more teachers contacted me and agreed to participate in an interview. Although I had sent the request in French, since I was interested in speaking to French-speaking teachers and students from the canton of Fribourg, only one interview was conducted in French. All other teachers, who responded to the request, were either German-speaking or bilingual.

The canton of Vaud demanded an interview to present and further explain my research project to the person responsible at the Ministry of Education. After the interview, it was determined that it was too time-consuming for teachers and students given that I already had the permission to conduct my study in a French-speaking environment in the neighboring canton of Fribourg.

The cantonal authorities of Grisons informed me that it was the school leader's decision to participate in the study. I, therefore, contacted the school leader of Grisons' upper secondary school who replied that he would have to discuss the request with colleagues. I followed up again by email after a month to find out whether they had already decided. Three months later, I received a positive answer from the person responsible at the school, who suggested an in-person meeting to first present my project to teachers and students and to discuss the detailed procedure of data collection. A few weeks later, I went to Grisons to present my project and my planned data collection to different classes of students and to teachers. We created a schedule collectively to organize classroom observations and in-person student and teacher interviews.

I waited three weeks after sending the request to the Ministry of Education in Ticino before following up with an email. Since I received no response, I called and was told that they had received my request, but that it was still pending. In the meantime, I contacted two upper secondary schools in Ticino to see if there were school leaders interested in participating in my study, on condition that I receive the approval. Both school leaders responded that they could not decide this on their own, but that the Ministry of Education would have to approve any intervention in the school beforehand. I then recontacted the cantonal authorities by phone and asked whether there was an update regarding my request. I was told that if there had not been a written response to my request it was because the study was not of immediate interest to the canton.

3.7 Data Analysis

Data analysis comprised three main steps. First, I prepared and organized the two different data sets which resulted out of the questionnaires and interviews by classing them and transcribing the data verbatim (see Appendix B for the transcription conventions used). Second, I reduced the data into themes and codes using MaxQDA2020, while paying particular attention to how language itself was both medium and the subject of the data analysis. In a final step, I visually and textually represented the data as findings (Madison, 2012; Creswell & Poth, 2018). Analogous to the study's underlying methodological framework of phenomenology, van Manen's (2014; 2017) phenomenological qualitative data analysis technique was employed for the interviews and the open-ended questions of the questionnaire. The questionnaire was analyzed using descriptive statistics. The details of each analysis procedure are listed below.

3.7.1 Transcription

For the transcription, I listened to each interview at least three times. At first, I listened to the full interview before transcribing it. I then began writing a word-by-word transcription while listening to the recorded audio. In a third step, I listened to the interview again to ensure my transcript's accuracy and grammatical and orthographic correctness. This was considered necessary since the interviews were conducted in German, Swiss German, Italian, and French. Given the specific focus on language, and in order to protect participants' privacy, all interviews were recorded and transcribed by me using MaxQDA, a qualitative data analysis software. In this way, I was able to already engage in the research activity and to start reflecting and pre-coding the transcript (McLellan, MacQueen & Neidig, 2003). In addition to the more personal connection I had with the text by transcribing it myself, I also detected my own researcher biases. While transcribing, I noticed that I had constructed memories of information during the interviews which was not stated as such by the participants, but already involved my own interpretation. By comparing my researcher notes, also stored electronically in form of a 'logbook' on MaxQDA, with the transcript, I could easily track and differentiate these two dimensions of the data. That said, it is also crucial to keep in mind that even the transcript is influenced by the researcher's familiarity with and attitude toward the topic and is, thus, not a neutral account of data (Mero-Jaffe, 2011).

Interviews in which participants spoke Swiss German, for which neither a common orthography nor grammar exist, were partly transcribed in German; this caused the data to lose some authenticity and meaning. This was a challenging and uncomfortable task since I did not want to 'correct' or to change my participants' way of speaking. According to Oliver, Serovich, and Mason (2005), it is crucially important to critically assess one's power in participants' representation. I tried to be as reflective, transparent, and accurate as possible while considering how my interpretation of the text automatically influences the transcription and the subsequent analysis, all the while remaining aware of my own biases and assumptions during the transcription process (Fairclough, 2015).

3.7.2 Questionnaires

The questionnaire analysis was twofold. The raw data were taken from Google Forms and were converted into an Excel spreadsheet. They were then organized to conduct descriptive statistics. The analysis included measures of central tendency such as mean, median, standard deviation, and minimum and maximum values. These were then transformed into numbers and text and summarized in tables. All of the data in the tables were rescaled and standardized in order to be compatible on the same scale, since some of the data were retrieved through Likert scales (1–5) whereas other questions required a grade scale (1–6) (Mukherjee, Sinha & Chatterjee, 2018). No further quantitative, statistical methods were employed since the sample was rather small (N=94), and is therefore not representative. The open-ended questions, which each resulted in a few sentences of text, were taken as raw data from Google Forms, were converted into a Word file, and were then analyzed using MaxQDA in concert with the answers solicited through the interviews.

3.7.3 Interviews

The interviews and open-ended questions in the questionnaire were analyzed using phenomenological data analysis and the software MaxQDA2020. Several researchers have developed different analysis techniques in phenomenology. The most popular ones were designed by Moustakas (1994), Giorgi (2009), and van Manen (2014; 2017), with the former two being psychologists and the latter focusing on education and pedagogy. This study adopts van Manen's (2014; 2017) approach to phenomenological data analysis. Van Manen (2017, p.79) argues that analyzing phenomenological data "is more accurately a process of insightful invention, discovery or disclosure." The process of analyzing, he continues, is a human desire to make sense and meaning of the world. Within these experiences, certain themes become apparent that are an example of something. Van Manen (2017, p. 86) posits that in order to understand the lived experiences through the examples that the participants provide, the right question to ask as a researcher is: "What is this example an example of?" Themes help to organize lived experiences; they are "fasteners, foci, or threads around which the phenomenological description is facilitated" (van Manen, 2017, p. 91).

Within van Manen's (2017) phenomenological data analysis procedure, which he calls "hermeneutic phenomenological reflection," he differentiates among "(1) the wholistic or sententious approach; (2) the selective or highlighting approach; (3) the detailed or line-by-line approach" (p. 92–93). This study employed approach (3) to guarantee a detailed analysis of participants' accounts. This first required a thorough reading of the transcript, in order to obtain an overall impression and to look for key passages. I then began pre-coding significant, i.e., relevant for the study's interest, reoccurring, statements by highlighting and underlining them in MaxQDA. I then read the transcript a second time to pay particular attention to the previously highlighted sections and thereby distinguished more narrow codes. I marked them with different colors and re-read the transcript at least one more time to make notes and to document my preliminary impressions and ideas for data analysis. I then printed the transcripts and repeated the entire process of reading, highlighting, and coding the interviews in order to compare parallels and differences between my two analyses. I considered this to have been useful because I had experienced a different processing of information when reading it on my computer screen and on paper. Furthermore, since I did not have a second person reading and coding my transcripts, I wanted to reduce my bias as much as possible. As an underlying guide for reflection, van Manen (2017) proposes the "fundamental lifeworld themes...*lived space* (spatiality), *lived body* (corporeality), *lived time* (temporality), and *lived human relation* (relationality or communality)" (p. 101). These themes were always considered in relation to the overarching phenomenon of lived experiences of language and language hierarchies and applied to the interview transcripts and the open-ended questions in the questionnaire.

3.7.4 Emerging Themes

I noticed reoccurring codes throughout the process of transcribing, reading, highlighting, and coding. I summarized broader codes in an Excel spreadsheet and compared them with the highlighted sections when re-reading the student and teacher interviews. The list included the following codes:

- Selective or restrictive linguistic diversity;
- Linguistic stereotypes;
- Feelings/attitudes toward heritage and national languages spoken in Switzerland;
- Native speaker ideology/authenticity;
- Confidence with (first/second/heritage) language skills;
- Perspectives on education/visions and dreams for the future linked to English;
- Media;
- Traveling/freedom/agency.

When re-reading the interviews based on the more wide-ranging codes and comparing them to the Excel spreadsheet, I noticed that some of them were present in almost all transcripts (e.g., perspectives on education) while 'media,' i.e., the over- and underrepresentation of different language groups in the media was only mentioned by a few participants. I then created another Excel spreadsheet with more narrow codes that were present in most transcripts and which were essential themes and concerns. The following themes emerged after a final reading of both the digital and printed interview transcripts, and after contrasting the list of themes with the written data:

- Plurilingual identities within restrictive linguistic diversity;
- Monolingual habitus in the education system;
- Language hierarchies;
- Native-speaker and standard-speech ideologies;
- Symbolic violence.

3.8 Pilot Study

The pilot study was conducted with 13 students at BA level who were enrolled in my class on multilingual education and with doctoral students and colleagues a few months prior to data collection in order to test the instruments. These students were asked to pilot test the questionnaire and the student interview because of the small age difference of about 1–4 years between the BA and the upper secondary students. The students filled in the online questionnaire and provided valuable feedback in the comment sections as well as during our discussion in class. I changed certain formulations and layout settings that were considered unclear based on their comments and questions. The general feedback was that the questions were interesting and that it was a topic that was not commonly covered in either school or university. Students said they wished that they had dealt with this topic during their school time. The student interviews were tested twice. First, the interviews were conducted in a 90-minute class on multilingual education with both students and I switching between the roles of interviewer and interviewee. Second, they were used as a basis for the students' own data collection with other participants chosen by them for their class presentations. Additionally, the interview guide (created specifically for teachers) was tested with two doctoral students and with one colleague. The feedback led me to reduce the number of questions, to slightly paraphrase certain questions, and to plan more time for potential clarifications and explanations between the questions from my part.

3.9 Data Collection/Analysis Issues

I began planning data collection in schools in September 2019. It was scheduled to start in schools in March 2020, during the same time at which the COVID-19 pandemic was transforming the planet, wreaking death and suffering to many people. The whole of society was under lockdown for a few months, in an effort to decrease the virus' spread, and naturally schools were also closed. This situation made it impossible for me to proceed with my data collection as originally planned. My change of plans is rather insignificant when compared to what many people have gone through, and how COVID-19 has wreaked havoc on the entire world collectively. Nevertheless, I was no longer able to first conduct classroom observations and second carry out in-person interviews with teachers and students combined with a creative language activity due to school closings in all three of the cantons that I had chosen. Not knowing how long the schools would remain closed for, and how long it would take to find time for teachers and students to re-organize interviews afterward, I decided to ask for virtual interviews. I emailed teachers and students inviting them to an interview by phone, Skype, MS Teams, FaceTime, Zoom, or via any other software program with which they would be comfortable and to which they had access. Given the chaotic and sudden changes in everyone's personal and professional lives, I am very grateful to those many participants who had already agreed to an interview and were still willing to talk to me virtually. That said, it was extremely challenging to reschedule new interviews with many personal and professional constraints, to overcome logistical/technological difficulties in an improvised home office setting, and to make the interviewees feel comfortable in this unusual and artificial situation. Many were unfamiliar with videoconference tools and preferred to talk over the phone. This negatively impacted rapport-building, as well as the voice quality for recording, thereby making transcription more difficult.

3.10 Translation

Regarding data treatment, I translated the Swiss German, German, French, and Italian transcripts into English while the original language was included wherever a translation would have distorted the intended meaning or where it ran the risk of misrepresenting the participants' voices. Due to the translation, it is possible that the meaning and participants' voices are not as identically represented as they would be without a translation, however. That said, it was considered necessary in order to make the results accessible to a greater audience, even among Swiss language regions, and to harmonize the multiple languages examined in this study. As a result, the practical nature of using ELF for academic purposes simultaneously demonstrates how power is woven into this study, by necessity, and how such a choice in itself contributes to the reproduction of language hierarchies.

3.11 Limitations of the Study

As indicated above, data collection could not be carried out as planned due to the Covid-19 pandemic. I had planned to triangulate the interview and questionnaire data with classroom observations in schools in order to assess whether participants' verbal accounts and LEPs were in fact being implemented as described. This 'policy-practice dilemma' (Cohen, Moffitt, & Goldin, 2007) requires a stronger focus on the social agents who are carrying out policy decisions and on their daily teaching practices. Furthermore, despite my effort and intention to specifically include and to leverage the minority language-speaking groups, the data do not represent the Italian-speaking groups (except for one interview) and only rely on French-speaking students' questionnaire answers to portray student voices in the *Romandie*. The work could be stronger had I managed to obtain access to these language groups. Similarly, although I tried to select as many plurilingual/HL-speaking students as possible for the interviews based on the questionnaire results, I realized throughout data analysis that the voices of HL-speaking students and teachers or those with a migration background would have warranted an even stronger emphasis in my sample selection. Overall, though, the majority language speakers' perspectives are also meaningful (and necessary) to understand the interdependency of both perspectives.

Findings

This section of the study presents findings retrieved through a data analysis of the questionnaires, along with the interviews conducted with students and teachers, and is divided into themes that have been further divided into subthemes. The results derived from the questionnaire, through descriptive statistics (summarized in a table in Appendix C), are embedded in the following sub-sections, although information on Fribourg students could only be provided for 4.1, 4.2, and 4.3 due to the lacking interview data. Findings are separated by student and teacher and by canton in the case of students' and teachers' interviews. All of the names have been changed to guarantee participants' privacy (see Appendix D for a list with pseudonyms). Participants' accounts are expressed through direct quotes (whenever possible) throughout the findings section. The verbal data, taken from the questionnaires, do not have any line numbers whereas those taken from the interviews indicate the exact transcript line numbers in parentheses.

4.1 Plurilingual Identities within Restrictive Linguistic Diversity

> Despite its focus on linguistic diversity, Switzerland is a restrictive multilingual country which often limits the development of diverse, non-linear language biographies, the opportunities for meaningful lived experiences of language, and full identity expression for plurilinguals.

The findings illustrate that there is a great variety of different languages and cultures present in Switzerland today, yet this diversity does not happen in practice since policies and laws dictate which languages are officially allowed in each canton. Therefore, although all of the participants are speakers of multiple languages, they cannot always freely choose which one to use and not all are equally aware of their linguistic potential. Restrictive language policies, which emphasize (certain) national languages and which exclude individuals' HLs, have bodily-felt consequences and lead to a certain homogenization or assimilation. The participants' own perceptions of themselves were sometimes contradicted by their narrated language biographies; in some cases, this led to a change from identifying as a speaker of one language to a speaker of multiple languages. The data also demonstrated that determining fixed categories, such as L1 or FL, often neither accounts for individuals' non-linear trajectories, due to migration or globalization processes, nor for the emotional or intellectual attachment that speakers have to certain languages which they may consider neither 'first' nor 'foreign.' Finally, the often-lacking opportunities for participants to make meaningful lived experiences with their entire linguistic repertoire increases linguistic insecurity, particularly in those languages most crucial for authentic identity expression and this distorts how individuals assessed their language skills *tout court*.

Students from Zurich and Fribourg specifically are exposed to many different HLs, which they primarily speak at home. However, while their linguistic repertoires might be more diverse, they report generally having lower competences in their HL compared to their second L1, the local language. Students from Grisons, conversely, are typically perfectly bilingual in their two L1s – Romansh and Swiss German/German. English has become an integral part of students' everyday lives and is employed mainly in online activities that occupy much of their time outside of school. French is perceived as a burden by some students in Zurich, who also complain about mandatory language exchanges, even though the average attitude is rather neutral. French is not at all associated with their personal interests and leisure activities. This is not the case for students in Grisons who generally do not learn French in school unless they purposefully select it as either an optional or specialization subject. They show a rather positive attitude toward it and consider it an important subject, given its status as a national language. In fact, many students regret not learning French as a *mandatory* language subject in school. Furthermore, students in Fribourg who learn GFL show a similar pattern in attitude and behavior to students in Zurich concerning French. For instance, one student mentioned that "I've learned German…but I simply don't like it, so I was less motivated." They seem to associate German strictly with school and forced language activities; as one participant reported: "German – only in school if necessary." Italian is generally linked to vacation and, therefore, is perceived less as an obligation. It is not a mandatory subject in any of the three schools (in Grisons, this is true for the Romansh-speaking section). Finally, Romansh only plays a role for students in Grisons who are enrolled in a Romansh-German bilingual program. It is not a school subject in either Zurich or Fribourg.

4.1.1 Students in Grisons

Almost all of the students in Grisons spoke primarily Romansh and Swiss German/German. They would sometimes also use Italian or English, depending on where they lived or which exposure they had due to hobbies, for instance. The majority of them associated English with social media, internet, and Netflix where they had the opportunity to make international or "e-friends," as Jovin called them. It became evident in their answers that the vast majority shared a passion for English, since it enabled them to communicate with people from all over the world online, to watch series not (yet) made available in Romansh or German, and to travel. Italian was associated with vacations in Italy in specific, a common destination for many. Additional languages mentioned by a few students were Norwegian, Dutch, Spanish, and Portuguese. Whereas Norwegian was autonomously learned via a smartphone application, Dutch, Spanish, and Portuguese were languages spoken by either family or friends. Sebastian spoke Dutch at home with his father, Melina was surrounded by Portuguese through her best friend, and yet others had family or friends in Spain or South America with whom they spoke Spanish.

While many of them grew up bilingually, either with one parent speaking Swiss German/German and the other speaking Romansh, others learned Romansh exclusively in school. Jovin explicitly pointed out that being asked to determine his L1 (on surveys or in administrative contexts, for instance) was impossible since he felt unable to make his linguistic repertoire fit into normative categories: "…it is always a bit of a conflict when I have to put German as my first language, it [Romansh] is simply equivalent for me" (Jovin, 18–20). Many participants stated that they were constantly exposed to multiple languages and switched accordingly. These included not only switching among languages but also among identities, habits, and personality traits associated with certain languages. Yet, others demonstrated that they were more convinced of monolingual practices and policies linking it to a more structured and traditional society in line with their values. They believe that Romansh is an authentic indicator of belonging and true Grisons origins, associating immigration and foreign cultural, moral, and political imports with chaos. They also perceived an attack on their language, through mockery or ignorance, as an attack on their personality as it is closely linked to the local dialect.

Multiple participants further reported that they either consciously or unconsciously looked for Romansh speakers when they were in locations in which Romansh was not spoken. For instance, Timo remembered being on vacation with his family in Scotland and overhearing another family speaking Romansh at dinner. He said that he had felt confident talking to them because they shared Romansh as a connection, and this led them to meet again the next day. He is certain that he would not have done so if it had been any other language. Several students had very positive experiences when they used Romansh as a 'secret language' in different places outside Grisons. Hanna said that she had been asked about the language that they were speaking by strangers and when she replied "Romansh," they were fascinated and curious to find out more about it. The interest in Romansh, as she said, positively impacted her self-esteem and made her proud. Furthermore, Jovin explicitly stated that he had no knowledge of French, but would soon be sent to the Romandie to conduct his mandatory military training. He was determined to find speakers of the same language, which would also provide a sense of belonging and group membership, something that he did not expect to find in a French-speaking community. Sebastian shared the same experience; instead of talking to people from other language regions, he would instead limit his interactions to speakers of the same language. The group identity seems to be even stronger in exactly those linguistically and culturally different places, outside of Grisons, and really function as a connecting element.

That said, Romansh identity is also promoted within the Romansh-speaking community, which was highly appreciated by students. There are specific activities that bring Romansh-speaking individuals together within Romansh-speaking territory, connecting them to their linguistic and cultural heritage and that even celebrate the community itself. For example, these included parades and village fairs that function as strong identity markers and an essential part of Romansh speakers' experiences. Yet, the focus on creating this specific in-group, and of being part of the community can also be perceived as forced and unnatural. As Jovin (9–10) admitted: "…then I learned Romansh from my father, almost forcibly I would say." He experienced other restrictions caused by linguistic ideologies, held by some Romansh speakers, which also negatively impacted his mother's self-esteem. Originally from the German-speaking part of Switzerland, Jovin's mother still does not feel legitimate when speaking Romansh after many years of living there, as he reported. Although she understands and is able to speak it, she prefers using Swiss German while justifying herself for not speaking Romansh (although Swiss German is a local language as well). Furthermore, the constant emphasis on speaking Romansh, and the perceived pressure to do so as a minority language speaker, renders it more difficult to value and involves using other resources from one's linguistic repertoire. At the same time, making Romansh a requirement in certain federal and cantonal public administration and government jobs, by introducing quotas, prioritizes 'local' recruitment and hinders migrants and Swiss citizens from other language regions alike from being competitive in the job market. On a federal level, Romansh speakers perceive a lack of understanding and condescension *vis-à-vis* their enhanced chances in recruitment situations through quotas. In the case of Grisons, prioritizing Romansh speakers can cause emigration of professionals or even 'brain drain' in certain sectors, resulting in the loss of crucial resources in a region shaped by a rather difficult economic and demographic development trajectory. As Jovin pointed out, however, quotas also serve the purpose of officializing and attributing power and justice to a minority language.

Another consequence of Romansh's minority status within Switzerland is that it is impossible for them to use it to communicate with other Swiss language regions. They generally try Swiss German first, but many switch to English for intercantonal communication with other language groups. English plays a crucial role for all students and takes up a very big part of their spare time. They all listen to, speak, read, and write in English primarily online on social media, on Netflix or on YouTube. Despite the positive associations, such as freedom, interconnectedness with the world, and innovation, the existing expectations to speak English proficiently are very demanding for some students. Jovin, for instance, revealed having a "bad conscience" (Jovin, 292) for not watching series or films in English as a form of preparation for the Cambridge Certificate in Advanced English (CAE). That said, he reported that his motivation to learn English is purely professional: "It's not about English, it's simply about having English up my sleeve for a job. Here is my diploma (--) in the end, if I can speak English or not (-), I only do it for the job or to have better opportunities" (Jovin, 302–304).

Timo shares Jovin's opinion regarding English and limits its relevance within Switzerland's linguistic landscape to the status of a mere tool. He likens the concept of ELF to Switzerland's political neutrality in which a *neutral* language, such as ELF, is compatible with its mediator position on a global geopolitical scale. Yet: "it's nothing you would associate with Switzerland's identity" (Timo, 354–355). English here is reduced to its communicative function while the national languages express the local identities and cultures.

Finally, students' lived experiences of language were both negative and positive. While language can provide a sense of belonging and can strengthen ties with a given space and group, it can also exclude individuals from the community, impact their mental health, and can incorporate symbolic violence.[1]

4.1.2 Teachers in Grisons

Like students, teachers from Grisons are exposed and accustomed to multiple languages in their daily lives. They are all speakers of at least two languages with many switching among as many as four languages regularly to accomplish different tasks within diverse linguascapes. They all speak Romansh, Swiss German/German, Italian, English, and French to a certain extent with some also speaking Spanish. Many of them, consciously or unconsciously, switch among languages since they are exposed to different languages at work and in their spare time.

Typically, at least one main regional language is spoken by everyone, depending on where individuals live in the canton of Grisons. Similar to the data retrieved from students' interviews, teachers' lived experiences of language show that Romansh as a minority language in the canton of Grisons has a binding function and connects its speakers to a community. Gita's family language background illustrates this very well. Her father, a Romansh speaker, worked in a store in a primarily German-speaking environment in Grisons, but he managed to attract many Romansh-speaking

---

1   This is explained in greater detail in section 4.5.1.

clients: "because they knew that he could speak Romansh and that's why they always came to him" (Gita, 59–60). Speaking the same language here is linked to common values as well serving as a motive for individuals to support the speech community financially. According to Gita, the reason that other Romansh speakers shopped in the store was the fact that her father shared their linguistic and cultural background.

Typically, participants are themselves plurilingual and often switch among Romansh, Swiss German, and Italian, due to migration of different language groups as well as extended family within the canton, which results in multi-faceted language repertoires. While they are generally very proud of Grisons' multilingualism, especially in the case of the minority language Romansh, the situation is more complex and complicated for Romansh speakers. As Martin explained: "We have to learn German as Romansh speakers. We can't just say no, we're not going to learn German…we are a bit under pressure" (180–182). Despite the pressure to become bilingual, the situation is perceived as yielding a positive outcome in the long run. These underlying power dynamics manifest themselves in beliefs and attitudes toward language and culture which, according to Martin, have long been established within the family context and are then sometimes reproduced without analyzing and questioning them at school. In the minority language context of Romansh in specific, Martin perceived the parents' influence as crucial regarding the transmission of Romansh cultural values and traditions. Although the school can sensitize its students, he believes that the family is responsible for the affective dimension that is linked to language acquisition.

A common linguistic practice in the trilingual canton is mutual understanding based on *receptive* linguistic competences. This implies that individuals can typically make use of one of the three official languages with which they are most comfortable and which they can expect their interlocutors to understand the most easily. Although all Grisons interviewees were plurilingual, their level of confidence was not equal for every language to which they were exposed on a daily basis. Consequently, understanding one another and speaking one's own L1 is the preferred approach to multilingualism in Grisons in order to reduce the pressure of being (or feeling) forced to speak a certain language. Speakers are particularly flexible and attentive since they regularly engage in multilingual meaning-making practices and depend on a more involved cooperation in order to guarantee understanding. Other non-regional languages are not usually included in this approach. Certain situations, however, require using different, non-local languages; this sometimes comes close to changing one's personality in a positive sense for Nicole, for instance. The feeling of transformation is even more drastic for her when speaking English – a language hugely important to her identity and that is associated with positive experiences abroad, achievements, and a greater communication space. Yet, she still describes Romansh as "the language of the heart" (Nicole, 453) and represents the common ground among its speakers, connecting them and reinforcing their sense of belonging. Although it is something very inherent, it needs to be actively employed and expressed in order not to either lose or forget it, which is not always feasible in a minority language context dominated by Swiss German.

The same is true for other non-regional languages, as was stated by Henri. HL speakers also deserve to express their languages and cultures. He believes that integration cannot work if individuals are forced to suppress important parts of their identity. A first step would be to do away with monolingual standards, which to him are very limiting and discriminatory. He goes on to explain that multilingualism should be considered the new norm since it more accurately resembles the social reality, rather than reproducing monolingual norms as more and more HL speakers come to live in Grisons. As he put it: "monolingualism is divisible" (Henri, 168); therefore, multilingualism needs to be adopted as the most appropriate, contemporary, and equitable perspective. As he advocates, only if people see the world in a more pluralist way can there be mutual understanding and respect for diversity and otherness. Yet, opportunities are lacking to practice authentic multilingualism, especially for minority languages such as Romansh or many other HLs since they (want to) adapt to (mostly Swiss German-speaking) monolingual speakers. As Gita pointed out, the linguistic situation in Grisons is reversed from the situation encountered at the national level where Swiss German is the majority language. She explained that it is considered odd to *only* speak Swiss German because of the daily exposure to both Italian and Romansh. Monolinguals are virtually considered 'non-locals' since everyone else typically speaks German *in addition* to another language. At the same time, she experiences an increasing popularity of Swiss German even as a written language in her Swiss German-speaking environment, which had long been considered a taboo.

4.1.3 Students in Zurich

The common language spoken at home by all Zurich students in the study is Swiss German/German. In addition to this language, though, students also speak Bosnian, Vietnamese, Hungarian, Italian, Urdu, Romansh, Turkish, Swahili, Macedonian, and Tirolean dialect. These HLs are connected to students' families and relatives from their own (or their parents') countries of origin. Other languages that they learned in school were English, French, Spanish, and a few took optional Mandarin classes. Similarly, English seems to correspond very well to students' spare time activities, such as watching Netflix, films, videos, series, and tutorials, chatting, online gaming, social media, reading books, (online) newspapers, scientific papers for school (especially in biology), listening to music and podcasts, bookings, programming, writing blogs or in forums, (inter)national meetings for

Fridays for Future,[2] political parties, and finally for traveling or exchange programs with English-speaking countries. Their interest in English even includes learning American Sign Language, "just because the language is so interesting," as one participant stated. French, conversely, is strictly associated with school and is used, as one student reported: "only when I have to communicate with someone who only speaks French."

More precisely, Swiss German is by far the most relevant and most commonly used language for students from Zurich at school and in their spare time. As Nicolas explained, *Züritüütsch* ['Zurich German,'] is all one needs to live there and the language in which he can best express his identity. Nevertheless, all of the participants' linguistic repertoires are very diverse and incorporate crucial links to their identity and personality that are unaccounted for in a monolingual, Swiss German-based linguascape. Arthur, for instance, perceives his identity to be made up of Macedonian, Swiss German, German, and AE. To him, Macedonian represents his roots and heritage as well as a tool to express himself:

> ...whenever I speak Macedonian and also when I'm in Macedonia, then I'm happy to speak Macedonian because it connects me to something that I can see as myself. Whereas German, there isn't such a strong connection, of course, I use it to communicate (Arthur, 40–43).

Speaking one's HL can also trigger and strengthen feelings of joy and belonging, as Arthur's quote demonstrates. Knowing where one's home is, and where one comes from, is a complicated sensation especially for (second generation) immigrants like Arthur, who engage in a continuous (re-)positioning on an identity continuum between Macedonian and Swiss. He refers to himself as a foreigner in Switzerland, which might be the result of constantly being asked about his 'true' origin:

> Yes...for example, when I speak Swiss German there is often the question if I come from Grisons. Something I didn't understand for a long time until I heard people from Grisons and they literally have this *Züri-Ausländer-Akzent* [foreign accent deviating from the one common to Zurich] (Arthur, 16–18).

According to Arthur, the legitimate and accepted accent is the one spoken in Zurich and this one only. The local Swiss German variety spoken in Grisons is already considered foreign. Along with being considered foreign, a current connotation of Grisons' accent is its 'rural backwardness' compared to Zurich's urban accent. When I asked him whether he still spoke that way, he explained that his language skills had improved immensely, but that other friends with the same language background sounded more aggressive and made more grammatical mistakes than Swiss

---

2   Fridays for Future is a global climate strike movement that started in 2018.

German monolinguals. As a *"secondo,"*[3] he is also 'detected' as a foreigner when on vacation in Macedonia since he 'deviates' from the expected Macedonian standard: "It's like the problem for *secondos* in Switzerland, it's mostly the problem that you're a foreigner here and then also in Macedonia" (Arthur, 48–49). For Arthur, speaking Macedonian leads him to his origins which cannot be found in his passport, but are rather represented linguistically: "…I am Swiss now, I have a Swiss passport, but for myself, I have to know where I come from…For me it's important to have an identity" (Arthur, 38–39). That said, this does not mean that the other languages that he speaks are insignificant. When writing lyrics for rap songs, he first chose to do so in English but then felt that the emotional connection was lacking and therefore switched to Swiss German. He explained that it was easier for him to do so in Swiss German because he wanted to express his identity and to write about personal and emotional topics. He concedes, however, that his way of speaking in Swiss German is, as he put it: "very Americanized or Hiphopized" (Arthur, 175) resulting from his passion for American music and films. Similarly, Nicolas, who considers himself a monolingual Swiss German speaker, acknowledges that his way of speaking is very much influenced by anglicisms. As he explains, his use of English within Swiss German is "not to be cool," (Nicolas, 40), but rather indicates the membership of a certain (age) group and, according to him, is the norm among his friends.

For Adya, her first and personally most significant language is Urdu. She connects it with her 'true origins': "[My parents] are both from Pakistan and I also somehow come from there and all my family is there" (Adya, 32–33). Since she was not born there herself, speaking Urdu functions as a legitimator to claim her Pakistani origin. Similar to Arthur, she states that she only *"somehow* come[s] from there," (Adya, 33 [emphasis added]) indicating that she feels as though she is in between two cultures, with the Urdu language connecting her to her family in Pakistan. Despite Urdu's importance for her family and her life in general, she is also extremely pressured by her parents to speak it. When meeting other Pakistani friends of her age, she would sometimes prefer chatting in Swiss German – a language that she shares with them; however, her parents do not allow this. English, conversely, plays an important role and brings immigrant families together. It is used as a *lingua franca* since newly arrived families and friends in particular do not (yet) speak Swiss German/German. Furthermore, Adya relies on English to write to her Pakistani family since she can neither read nor write in Urdu. As she formulated it: "It's very hard for me, I'm illiterate [in Urdu]" (Adya, 153). Identifying as illiterate in the language that she con-

---

3   The term *secondos*, for which various definitions exist, has a controversial connotation in Switzerland. It can refer to second-generation immigrants born in Switzerland or non-Swiss (by passport) adolescents living in Switzerland independent of their place of birth. Approximately 330,000 members of the non-Swiss population in Switzerland falls into this category (Maurer, 2003).

siders most meaningful in her life can negatively impact her self-esteem. She also sometimes speaks English with her friends from school, especially when they meet other students their own age from international schools in Zurich. It is spoken (and acquired) in an almost natural environment and functions as a mediator among different cultures and L1s for expats and migrant families. As Adya stated, she is very proud to speak it and to have access to such diverse people by using English without feeling the same pressure that she does with Urdu or Swiss German.[4]

Yasmin, having had positive experiences with her L1 Turkish outside her family, equates her (more diverse) language repertoire with opportunities that she would not have otherwise. The experience that made her realize this was a school excursion in Poland where Turkish connected her to other Turkish-speaking students there. This was an experience that emphasized her individual strengths and made her special when compared to her fellow Zurich students. Ever since the encounter, she has become aware of the possibility of using language as a mediator among different cultures and languages. Being able to apply Turkish in a new space with other students of her heritage cultural background made her improve her own rather negative attitude toward her language repertoire, which she felt was rather undesired and insignificant in the Swiss German context.

4.1.4 Teachers in Zurich

Similar to Zurich students, Zurich teachers are plurilinguals too, even though they do not all identify as such. The extent of their varied language repertoire changes with teachers' age and the subjects taught at school. While younger and FL teachers tend to have a more diverse language repertoire, older and German language teachers differ mainly in their daily language use. While they all share linguistic competences in Swiss German/German, English, and French, how extensively and proficiently they employ those in their daily lives varies. That said, Nesrin, for instance, speaks Bosnian as her L1 and teaches French and Italian. She believes that her plurilingual repertoire shapes her way of thinking and behavior. Having Bosnian as her L1, she is convinced that she has been unconsciously influenced in terms of how she perceives the world and how she positions herself in it. For example, she identifies strongly with the fact that Switzerland is officially a multilingual country, even though she believes that not everyone is aware of this, and its pluralism could be promoted better. Tina, a teacher of the same subjects, has also been strongly influenced by Switzerland's linguistic landscape and this led her to intensify her lived experiences of language with French and Italian during many stays within these linguistic regions as well as the choice of her study program. She is very engaged in promoting the learning of national languages at school and continues to actively use them

---

4 This aspect is explained in more detail in section 4.5.3.

in her spare time as well. Eleonore, a German teacher, shares this positive attitude toward Switzerland's multilingualism having grown up in an officially monolingual country: "I think it's wonderful how Switzerland is handling its multilingualism. I think it's very admirable and also worth protecting....I don't know what is more important than language [for one's identity]. Language is THE identity marker *per se*" (Eleonore, 95–96; 304–305). For her, being able and allowed to speak one's language equals expressing one's identity. As a speaker of standard German in a Swiss German environment, she is very conscious of her identity expression through language. The same holds true for Swiss-German speaking Patrick:

> ...so, I grew up in the canton of Bern, then I lived in inner Switzerland for 9 years and then I've lived in the canton of Zurich for 9 years and when I introduce myself to my classes and at parent-teacher-conferences, it's immediately obvious that it's not possible that I could have grown up here [canton of Zurich], but that I come from the canton of Bern. This is something you notice immediately, even after 18 years...even when I only say two sentences. This also shows somehow that this origin, this identity is somehow very strongly expressed through language and that it remains very strong... (356–362).

Elisabeth, who is also politically active on a local community level, seems to adapt her way of speaking to the role that she plays in a certain space. While the language that she connects with her identity and home is Swiss German, she finds it necessary to switch to SSG on more formal occasions and in order to make herself understood by everyone. Speaking Swiss German, according to her, is the norm however, and this should be respected as such by non-locals. Both Elisabeth and Carmen postulate that as a speaker of Swiss German in Switzerland, there is no need to speak or learn another language because of its status as the majority language and German-speaking Switzerland's nationally dominant geo- and sociopolitical position. Although it might be possible to strictly remain monolingual for German-speaking Swiss citizens (whereas even this could be refuted when defining Swiss German as a separate language from German), all of the participants are exposed to and influenced by their lived experiences of multilingualism. Sonja shares the following experience of language that she had:

> I like to remember the time when I was a child. One of my aunts used to live in Lausanne [French-speaking part]. My cousin is still there. Whenever you'd go to Lausanne, you'd simply speak French. I think, there wasn't a lot of German in return...I was ok with the idea that when I go to the Romandie as a German speaker, then I try to struggle along in French. And the same when I go to Ticino. And yet, today I feel like there is a fast switch to English. (301–307)

Despite the effort of speaking an FL, it visibly accounts for a precious experience – more so than switching to English for the sake of simplicity. That said, Sonja explains that she feels more at ease when teaching English than speaking SSG in class:

> ...I teach English, but I also studied German and I feel better when I *can* speak English in the classroom than when I *have to* speak standard German. Swiss German is fine because then I am myself somehow. These are my origins, standard German, to me, has this formality to it and English, for instance, I used it in daily life situations when I did the exchange…this shows, this is somehow, it must have a lot to do with identity and maybe also with experiences (340–344 [emphasis added]).

Sonja's experiences demonstrate how closely language is linked to identity and how associations made with and between certain languages can influence the individual's well-being when (forcefully) speaking it. The imposition of SSG in formal settings results in Sonja's preference of English and connects it to positive experiences while widening the gap between SSG and Swiss German. The context in which a language is learned also seems to play an important role. English, for instance, was learned without much pressure and continues to be applicable in authentic contexts such as music, film, and the internet; it is often automatically associated with ease, simple communication, and fun. Sonja and her colleagues are of the opinion that their students are much less aware of Switzerland's four national (and other commonly spoken) languages and that they no longer have the same lived experiences of language due to English's increasing popularity and omnipresence.

4.1.5 Students in Fribourg

Students from Fribourg generally reported that the most significant language in their lives was French. Some also spoke English, German, Cantonese, Japanese, Italian, Portuguese, and Spanish as their HL, while many only spoke French both at home and in school. Similar to Grisons, Italian was associated with and used for vacations in Italy or in Italian-speaking Switzerland. Some students also mentioned having relatives in this region. German was almost exclusively connected with school and was used only "when the context really requires it," as Lucien said. Yet, students also link German to the Goethe language certificate that they obtain throughout upper secondary school.[5] English, conversely, symbolizes the possibility to read different books, news from abroad, watch films, and to listen to podcasts and audiobooks. It is the language chosen for traveling and school exchanges with the UK and with the USA. Marie further stated that she engaged in additional self-study using

---

5   The Goethe certificate is a language proficiency certificate that attests to a certain level of knowledge in German that is provided by the *Goethe-Institut*.

online material, Rosetta Stone, or the Migros language courses. The enrolment in AL courses was justified by her in terms of the fear of not being good enough in school: "Since I didn't have English in primary school, I was scared I wouldn't be good enough in secondary school." Finally, English is considered most important for social media where it is often the most commonly employed language for communication.

4.1.6 Teachers in Fribourg

Etienne is a great example of how complex and nonlinear linguistic repertoires and how misleading the meaning of L1 and similar terms can be:

> So, literally, so, the meaning of the word strictly speaking mother tongue, the language of the mother, which is really crucial, is Swiss German for me. But that goes way back, and I was born in a bilingual city [anonymized]…and then I was born into a Swiss German family, but actually Swiss German I never really (--) I was only in [anonymized] for the first 4 years and I never went to school there. My parents moved to the USA. There, I did the first year of kindergarten in the USA and the first class of school was in American for me. So, my writing, for instance, does not correspond with my speaking because I learned how to write in the USA…somehow that sticks. Then we came back to Switzerland fairly early, but not to the German-speaking part but to the Romandie. There, I did my entire studies from almost the beginning in French. I spoke Swiss German at home, it was a static language…with many mistakes.…So German is actually a foreign language even if it's actually my mother tongue…What I like least and what I know least how to speak, is Swiss German (7–24, 52).

Etienne vividly illustrates how migrating to different linguistic and cultural spaces (as a child) can have a lasting impact on one's (academic) development and identity. Although he defines Swiss German as his "mother tongue" in the beginning, he later says that German is his L1 even though it is technically a "foreign language." Moreover, he says that he can better express himself in French, which defies simplistic and homogenizing generalizations of (one) L1 and competency. To further foster his plurilingual repertoire, he alternates among German, English, French, and Italian for reading and is exposed to several languages daily.

Jeanne's lived experiences of language as a French-English bilingual have also shaped her identity and have had an impact on her professional trajectory. For instance, when deciding to become an English teacher, her motives were influenced by her desire to find out and to understand more about her origins which had been, as she felt, a bit neglected due to the dominant French exposure. According to Jeanne, as a French speaker in the canton of Fribourg, it seems more difficult to really engage in multilingual practices since there is a (perceived) strict division between German-

and French-speaking communities and during interactions Swiss German/German speakers tended to switch to French to accommodate people. The opposite is true for the German-speaking colleagues who can switch more easily and can make use of their plurilingual repertoires. Although not every teacher speaks as many languages as David, for instance, who speaks German, Spanish, French, Italian, and English, they constantly switch at least among Swiss German, SSG, and French. Victoria learned French as an exchange teacher in Switzerland and is now fully immersed in the language, even while continuing to improve her language skills. A role model of authentic language learning herself, she believes that it is very important for students to be proud of their L1s and to integrate them into class. According to her, her students' L1s include, among others, Albanian, Bosnian, Bulgarian, Macedonian, Italian, Spanish, Turkish, Arabic, and Yoruba. She perceives the link among language, identity, and space to be very important, which can also negatively affect each other and can even lead to crises if one's identity cannot be expressed fully. As Victoria summarized it:

> There are of course also conditions external to language that ultimately lead us to our actions and identity, that construct our identity, if you will. But a great deal is also linguistically conditioned and therefore…there are also crises of identity when you live in another linguistic region…that is clearly the case (312–317).

4.2 'Monolingual Habitus' in the Education System

> Switzerland's teaching and education system mostly reproduces and legitimizes the 'monolingual habitus' and promotes a selective, ideology-laden linguistic diversity.

Although all participants have diverse linguistic repertoires, they can hardly ever use them freely in educational contexts. Thus, institutional structures, overt and covert LEPs, and the participants' own perspectives on legitimate school languages impede the adoption of a 'multilingual habitus' (Benson, 2013). The following sub-section compares student data from the three cantons before the subsequent sub-sections present the data by position and canton in greater detail.

4.2.1 Comparison of Student Data

Students are generally rather satisfied with language teaching with Zurich students most satisfied (7), very close to Grisons students with 6.75, before students from Fribourg who are least satisfied (5.25).

Figure 7: Students' satisfaction with language teaching

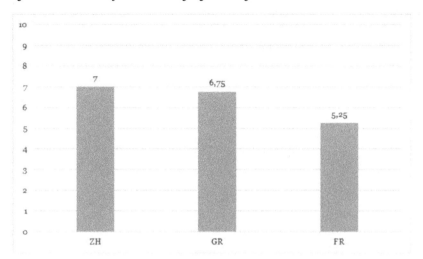

Whereas Zurich students agree that English should play a more dominant role in school than other languages spoken in Switzerland, students from Fribourg and Grisons tend to be neutral or rather disagree.

Figure 8: Prioritization of English in school

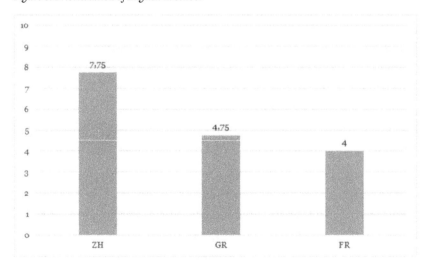

The same trend can be observed when asked about English's priority in the curriculum, which would be promoted by Zurich students while students from Fribourg and Grisons, although they also agree, are a bit more hesitant.

Figure 9: Prioritization of English in the curriculum

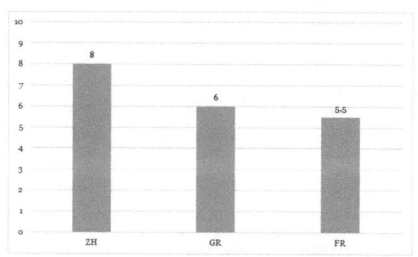

Furthermore, while Grisons students are slightly in favor of incorporating students' HLs into the classroom, students from Fribourg and Zurich are (rather) against it. Students from all three cantons are, however, open to discussing languages and cultures in school to an even greater extent.

Figure 10: Including students' heritage languages in the classroom

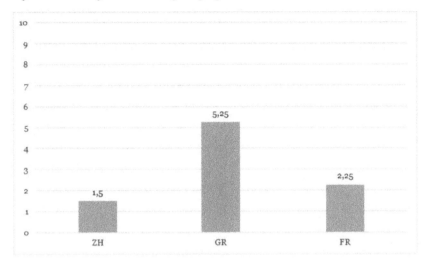

Students' self-evaluations for the non-L1 national languages are lowest in Grisons students' French competences (2), followed by Fribourg students (4) for their German competences and highest for Zurich students (4.6) for their French competences. It needs to be pointed out that many Grisons students, who report that they like French, do not necessarily take French classes in school given its optional status in the curriculum. This might distort the self-evaluation data for this cohort of the students. Students from all three cantons indicated higher competences regarding their self-evaluations in English. Students from the canton of Zurich have the highest self-evaluation (8.4), followed by Fribourg students (7) with students from Grisons estimating their English skills lowest (6.8).

Figure 11: Self-evaluations in non-L1 national languages and in English

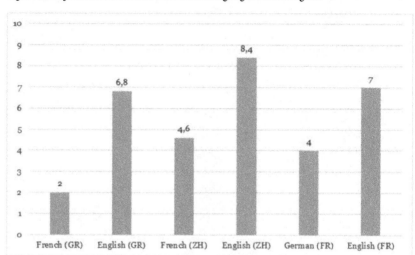

The following table shows students' grades as they reported them to be on their last school certificate. While students' grades in English are better in all cantons than in the non-L1 national languages, grades in both subjects are higher than their self-evaluations.

Figure 12: Grades in non-L1 national languages and in English

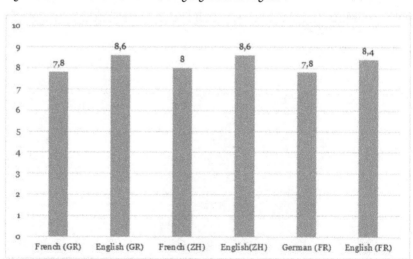

4.2.2 Students in Grisons

In Grisons, all of the participating students are speakers of at least one of the official school languages. They unanimously stated that there was no need to integrate their L1s more actively in class since both SSG and Romansh were already well represented. They explained that Romansh was very present since it is a medium of instruction for both bilingual and immersion programs. They are generally very satisfied with their ability to use their L1 at school and acknowledge the financial implication behind the promotion of a minority language. Similar to the students in Zurich, they also appreciate the opportunity to practice German in an academic context because they typically speak Swiss German outside of school. The general awareness of one's L1's positive impact on other languages seems to be present; as Anastasia put it: "First languages should also be promoted because if not, children cannot learn a new language."

Thirty-one percent of Grisons students did not respond to the question of whether they would like to change languages learned at school whereas 36% would in fact like to change as opposed to 33% who would not. The majority of students who were in favor of changing the language offered at school would like to reduce Romansh and/or German classes since they are both L1s to most. They argued that that they would benefit more if they could learn French, which is not a mandatory subject because their language skills were already high in these two languages. As Melissa reported: "I think it's sad that I have to speak in English in Switzerland because I don't know how to speak French." Others argued that French and Italian should both be mandatory language subjects. Generally, many are unhappy with the fact that their 'only real' FL is English, as Linda reported in the questionnaire:

> I wouldn't drop any languages but [would instead] introduce more. We only have Romansh, German, and English. This means that we don't really learn another language such as French or Italian. For this, you have to choose an optional class. With one or two lessons per week, it's not enough to really learn a language.

Many also wrote that Latin classes should be reduced and spent on English, Italian, or Spanish. They would feel more motivated if they could use these languages outside of school and for university, which is rarely the case with Latin. Conversely, many are also satisfied with the languages offered at school considering them to be both very important and relevant to them, especially given the focus on English.

The biggest advantage that students see in Grisons' upper secondary education system is its elaborate, high-quality bilingual immersion program. It is offered in the three official cantonal languages (Romansh, Italian, and German) and even provides specific language classes in the distinct Romansh idioms.[6] Students noticed that official Romansh classes at upper secondary level increase Romansh's value when mentioning this to non-Romansh speakers. Second, the co-existence of several idioms sensitized students to linguistic heterogeneity within the Romansh-speaking community and it improves the interaction among students. They are conscious about the fact that despite Romansh's minority status within the canton and the school, it is substantially subsidized to offer such bilingual programs especially in Romansh: "People are more aware now again of our language. The state has put a lot of money into Romansh, which I find great. And also at school, to have the possibility to do a bilingual *Matura*" (Leonie, 22–25).

In addition to this, certain subjects apply the CLIL method and are taught in English. Jessica believes that CLIL should be in English: "because it makes more sense for the future" (Jessica, 160). They unanimously agree that authentic and constant exposure to a certain language is necessary to learning it in a sustainable manner. By sustainable, André, for instance, means that language learning should also be useful and applicable after school. According to him, this is not the case for all language subjects in school: "Something needs to change because otherwise you can simply get rid of language teaching if at the end all you remember are 10 words" (André, 338–340). Students find the more useful focus on communication lacking in classes, textbooks, and in the curriculum as a whole. Students certainly seem to equate communication with a more informal way of speaking, one typically used on the internet as they mentioned YouTube or Ted talks, films, and music. Furthermore, a common criterion by which language teaching is judged by students seems to be how restrictively a given language is spoken during class, thereby denying the use of other languages altogether. The more strictly the use of a certain language is controlled and demanded in class, the more the students like it and agree with its purpose. They appreciate it when teachers – as role models – speak the language and also when they tell their students to actively and consequently use it without allowing them to switch to other languages. Students are rather disappointed when German or Romansh are 'tolerated' in an English class and when there is neither an incentive nor the opportunity to use it more actively. According to Jovin, the actual speaking time in English is very limited in class:

> [A]mong students, we also speak German….if you have a question and you raise your hand and you're allowed to ask the teacher something, then you speak English or when the teacher asks something in English. And in a class of 25 students, this happens maybe once a week, and then I say one sentence per week in English… (279–282).

---

6 Since this study focuses on the Romansh speakers in Grisons, it will not go into detail concerning the bilingual programs that are available in German and Italian.

Yet, the opposite seems true for Romansh classes in which the use of Romansh is demanded more strictly by some teachers. According to Hanna, it felt strange to speak Romansh to a friend in class, with whom she was used to speaking Swiss German, and now was supposed to change. Although she perceives it to be very odd when doing so, and is constantly reminded to speak Romansh by her teacher, she defines the school's language imposition as "logical" and "normal" (Hanna, 13–14).

André expresses his concern with textbooks' narrow focus that should be widened to include (more) speaking and online material, something more in line with students' interests. Hanna, for instance, agrees by saying that: "Actually, I'm very satisfied [with language teaching], but it's taught so much by the book, [and] curriculum" (Hanna, 170–171) indicating very little flexibility and spontaneity. Then again, almost all of the students believe that English is no longer *learned* in school. English language classes are instead seen as a support; they particularly appreciate learning new specific content-related vocabulary in their CLIL classes in which they are taught their specialization subjects such as biology, chemistry, or history in English. Jessica is very happy about having the opportunity to pursue chemistry classes in English and about how easy the transition was into English. She would have considered it too difficult had it not been for the institutional structure and for the teachers encouraging immersion programs. Yet, as Timo explains, this offer is only valid with sufficient inscriptions, which is usually the case especially for the natural sciences. Conversely, idiomatic expressions, speaking, and writing to a certain extent happens primarily online, through Netflix or YouTube videos. This is not at all the case for French. Unaware of such online equivalents in French, the students do not see much relevance in their private life.

The CAE is a crucial element provided by the school, and which cannot (yet) be replaced by students' everyday interactions in English. Everyone (except for one student) is very happy and enthusiastic about the exam linking it (almost exclusively) to better future academic and job opportunities. It is a great priority within the school where it holds a special status and represents a common objective that every student graduating from upper secondary school is expected to achieve. Conversely, Jana, for instance, perceives the prioritization of English as potentially detrimental:

> [I]n the last two years [of upper secondary school], the focus is only on the language certificate, the Advanced English, and I noticed that at the end, when you're done with the Advanced, the motivation slowly goes away. You lose the pleasure a bit if all you do is grammar and spelling. (252–255)

Jana would favor less 'drill' to pass the CAE in English and more time for literature in other language subjects. In her opinion, by wanting to cover as much content as possible in a short time, teachers neglect spending time on actual books. Additionally, all students would appreciate it if language subjects focused less on languages *per se* and more on the associated cultures. They believe that raising awareness of stereotypes and giving insight into daily life in a specific language region, and the corresponding value and belief system, can help to develop important competences. Jessica, for example, would be very interested in learning more about "the culture" and "the history" of a certain language and also about the people who speak it (Jessica, 269; 274). Zooming in on the national context, Sebastian argues for a school subject on Swiss languages and cultures: "We have a fairly high diversity also within Switzerland. That would be interesting for me to discuss this more" (Sebastian, 215–217). That said, the focus on bilingual programs in the national languages and CLIL subjects in English leaves almost no space for other languages at school. As Sebastian and Leonie state, a basic-level sensitization to and addressing other languages such as Arabic, Russian, Spanish, and Mandarin would be interesting and could also potentially be relevant for future language developments. While English is today's international *lingua franca*, it is unsure whether or not one of the other languages will become more powerful in the future, in which case it would be useful to have a basic knowledge of that language already.

Despite students' overall great satisfaction with language teaching, its biggest advantage is also one of its biggest disadvantages. While the bilingual programs and Romansh classes are highly appreciated, there is, as students reported, first, a lack of specific textbooks for language courses, but also to teach CLIL in Romansh; second, a lack of language learning opportunities apart from Romansh; and third, a sometimes forced and exaggerated emphasis on Romansh. Textbooks in Rumantsch Grischun exist, and in addition to this Romansh teachers create their own teaching material, which are made available via iBooks. Despite its innovative nature, some students perceive this circumstance as almost discriminatory because it makes them stand out from their fellow German- or Italian-speaking students who have 'regular,' that is, printed textbooks. Romansh-speaking students are envied by those and sometimes even harassed. Sebastian explains that:

> [U]nlike others, we have iPads for our textbooks because they would be too expensive to print, to work with them as print outs for four years and then we have to justify ourselves that we have an iPad especially for this. (126–129)

Timo also considers the iPads to be one of the causes for competition among those students who have them and those who do not. This competitive behavior creates tensions, barriers, and negative (learning) experiences for some students.

Another problematic development lamented by some Romansh-speaking students is the reduction of French classes to an optional subject, which had been a mandatory subject prior to curricular reforms. That means that they have to select French among several other optional subjects, unlike Romansh, German, and English, which all students in the Romansh-German bilingual program learn mandatorily. This becomes clear and is reiterated throughout Hanna's entire interview:

> I would like to learn French...I have more contact with French-speaking people and with Italian-speaking people...I think, it's also a disadvantage [for job opportunities] when I say I don't speak any French at all, I think. And it is really the case. I would actually like to speak French...this was also one of the questions in your questionnaire, if I liked how the languages were distributed in school and I do think it's a pity not to have French because it's still a part of Switzerland...If I could, I would of course speak French but then it's mostly English [in interaction with other French-speaking Swiss students]...I have had the experience where they don't know any German the same way I don't know any French (56; 61–63; 121; 134; 143–145).

Unlike Hanna, the French-speaking students that she encounters have learned German as a first FL for approximately ten years. That said, Jana, for instance, explains that she would have liked to have chosen French as an optional subject, but that the class was constantly canceled in recent years due to insufficient inscriptions (Jana, 75–76). Melina further argues that French is a very important language and is indispensable to working in the Federal Government (Melina, 101–102). However, since she is sure that she wants to be a psychotherapist, in which case French would not be an obvious advantage, she did not consider French to be important enough to choose as an optional subject. Conversely, Leonie, Jessica, and Timo believe that French would be too complicated to learn and Sebastian even argues that learning French is pointless overall (Sebastian, 194–195). These perspectives are based on minimal or no exposure to French (as a subject) since French classes are optional and other interactions with the French-speaking part of Switzerland are either limited or non-existent. This is not easily compensated by offers elsewhere since ELF is the language most frequently used by students for virtual communication and on social media.

Generally, the strong focus on Romansh, German, and English with high-level objectives and proficiency-orientation impedes one's investment of time and resources in other languages. Given Italian's importance within the trilingual canton and French on a national level, these languages deserve more space in the curricula and classrooms according to some students. Only one student said that they were interested in learning Portuguese – a language she considered to be important given that her best friend comes from a Portuguese immigrant family with whom she used to spend a great deal of time. Melina stated that although there were many immigrants in Grisons, she did not have much contact with them; this was also due to the fact that they rarely made it into upper secondary schools:

> A: They [migrant students] are not in school with you, are they?
> M: No. Not anymore, they still were in primary and lower secondary but not anymore in upper secondary. (45–47)

Despite their presence in society, Portuguese-speaking migrant students are underrepresented in (Romansh) post-compulsory education. Except for Melina, other HLs do not seem to be interesting to other students and also remain unrecognized on an institutional level.

4.2.3 Teachers in Grisons

The linguistic composition of classes in the German-speaking section is somewhat heterogeneous according to Martin, who teaches in both the Romansh- and German-speaking sections. While the Romansh section is predominantly Romansh-speaking or bilingual in Romansh and German, the school's German-speaking section includes students whose L1s are, among others, French, Serbian, Tamil, Croatian, and other Slavic languages. Roberto mentions that several scaffolding techniques can be employed in the FL classroom in particular so that students with different L1s can be more engaged and valued. For instance, he uses grammatical comparisons among different languages and draws on students' L1 knowledge to establish parallels and differences in the language acquisition process. By providing a part of their linguistic knowledge and sharing it with others, they receive recognition and demonstrate strengths which had often been totally unknown to their fellow students beforehand. Although this is already a practice in school, Martin argues for a greater awareness of the linguistic diversity and richness that exists in schools, but also for the institutionalized program offers from which more students might benefit. He has witnessed students regretting their choice of not enrolling in the Romansh-German bilingual program while Roberto sees an increase of inscriptions in Italian-German programs, primarily from non-bilinguals, to authentically learn an additional national language in immersion. These decisions are often made by parents hoping that their children will obtain better employment opportunities due to a bilingual upper secondary diploma. Similarly, expectations from students and parents are high regarding English language learning, as reported by teachers. This causes stress among those English teachers who see it as their fault if their students fail: "…they just have to pass, otherwise I'm not a good teacher" (Nicole, 289–290). The CAE is regarded (and imposed as such) as an indispensable qualification for their students' academic and professional future and it impacts the teachers' self-concept if the students' future were to be affected negatively.

On a positive note, the policy reforms come with a change in attitude toward Romansh. While it was previously commonly considered to be an informal, colloquial way of communicating in somewhat remote areas of Grisons; it is now – as an official, cantonal language – one well established as a medium of instruction. However, although it was introduced approximately 20 years ago as a compulsory subject in bilingual programs, it still does not have the same status as German, for instance, which is compulsory for all students regardless of their study program. These different restrictions not only reproduce hierarchies, according to Henri, but also their emphasis on these few chosen languages solely is rather limiting and does not do justice to the actual linguistic diversity:

> When I think about my school in [anonymized], I can have 10 languages in one class, which exist as such, but which are strictly ignored institutionally and 10 out of 20 students will probably be plurilingual, at least latently, but they will be virtually made into monolinguals through submersion (123–127).

The underlying objective, as suggested by Henri, is to "submerge" plurilingual students into the target language in order to maximize their assimilation while simultaneously suppressing their linguistic repertoires. Henri, who strongly opposes the idea of the ideal native speaker, suggests several strategies across the curriculum over time to implement a more equitable multilingual education and to do away with existing language hierarchies. In fact, he would like to develop a catalogue with examples of prototype languages so that teachers could prepare lessons based on this in order to sensitize students to different languages (or language families). He further perceives it to be essential to connect students' lived experiences of language to the content of the class and to raise awareness of the potential within the classroom. He explains that an element for comparison among the different languages could be their underlying prosodic nature, indicating that every language sounds differently. Students could explore which instrument would best represent the sounds of the new language and can listen out for words that also exist in languages with which they are already familiar. Henri further believes that being exposed to a new language through a short presentation can render visible fellow students' strengths and can result in admiration and respect for, rather than discrimination against, 'otherness.' According to him, students could also observe gestures, facial expressions, and other metalinguistic elements, which can also be integrated into music or arts classes. As he put it: "All it takes is fantasy and a bit of interdisciplinary thinking" (Henri, 232).

Gita stated that she refers to other languages in her language classes, but does not at all feel competent enough to include languages with which she is not familiar or to do so to a more significant degree. Nicole acknowledged that she had never consciously thought about including students' L1s or other languages prior to the interview. When asked about her multilingual practices in the classroom, she explained that she already uses several techniques to integrate them without even knowing that she did. For instance, she stated that she regularly asked students for equivalent words, compared grammatical structures, and she also raised awareness of parallels or differences for students to recognize connections among the languages.

Nicole also believes that a more interdisciplinary language teaching approach would be desirable, but that it would be very hard to implement due to fixed institutional structures; the strict separation of subjects, the separate German-, Romansh-, and Italian-speaking school divisions, schedules, and curricular requirements including learning objectives and materials impede more flexible, team-teaching approaches. Henri shared this impression and agreed that if the infrastructure were not as rigid as it is, then students' pluralist backgrounds could be integrated and acknowledged to a much greater extent. He further perceived the problem as residing in teachers' exclusion from decision-making processes. Gita strongly agreed and added that in-service teachers should be given a say and that this should be properly included when it comes to curricular reforms and decision-making. For her, it is incomprehensible that politicians would have the sole deciding power when it is up to the teachers to implement those decisions to the letter. Hence, whenever policy and curricular decisions are made, they are not made by a heterogeneous group of individuals, but rather monocultural and monolingual policy makers largely unaffected by the potentially discriminatory nature of those policies.

Henri is further of the opinion that English does not need such a strong emphasis in school since most students learn it automatically in their spare time, due to its omnipresence. Gita further criticizes English's non-negotiable imposition onto students. National or other HLs need better promotion by teachers and school leaders, textbooks, and curricula, especially in the context of a minority language. As mentioned previously, the fact that French or Italian have only an optional status within the Romansh program is lamented by all teachers. Henri explains the circumstances of this particular policy decision:

> Then MAR [curriculum for upper secondary education] came and everything was harmonized. Then one language needed to be dropped and for us, this is tragic and not good, French was dropped. Now it's Italian. We have the paradox that we're learning German and Romansh, but not Italian and not French. This is really sad. The potential would be there. With regard to the fact that they tried to make the system equal for everyone, they created inequality. This again is an idea that comes from monolingual thinking (423–429).

The paradox is that for Romansh-speakers, neither Romansh nor German are languages to be *learned* since the great majority are already fluently bilingual. Counting them as FLs, much like English, is a disadvantage for Romansh-speaking students since they could easily master ALs with which they are unfamiliar. Wanting to harmonize subjects and requirements, and wanting to make the workload even among all Swiss students, most Romansh teachers believe that their students have been deprived of an opportunity to easily expand their linguistic repertoire, especially considering the fact that they usually cannot use their L1 outside of Grisons. Although Gita also believes there is a rather systemic issue in language teaching, she perceives the unbalanced distribution of isolated lessons and the transitions from one school year to the next to be problematic. First, the conditions in which languages are learned in school, i.e., in short blocks of 45 minutes, 1–3 times a week, do not at all correspond to how they are acquired naturally. Second, and related to this, transitioning from one school year to the next with possible changes in class composition and responsible teachers often has as a consequence that progress in language learning is very slow and fragmentary. According to her, language learning should only begin in secondary school (not in primary) in order to avoid multiple repetitive transitions and limited progress. Her experience has shown that most adolescents in both lower and upper secondary schools have acquired efficient learning techniques and strategies and are motivated to apply those to learning languages. They are also often old enough to stay abroad for a longer period of time during which time they can learn a language intensively and authentically and, therefore, can benefit more from their language classes in school and *vice versa*. Often, however, the language that students learn voluntarily is English, but occasionally they learn Spanish.

She further believes that language teaching necessarily needs to be *multi*lingual and not *tri*lingual. Gita, therefore, teaches a module on the linguistic reality in Grisons that emphasizes its heterogeneous nature, despite the restrictive focus on the national languages plus English in the curriculum. Furthermore, the school itself is becoming more multilingual due to students with increasingly different L1s. Yet, the admission exam[7] at the beginning of upper secondary, which is a condition to even enroll in post-compulsory education in Grisons, is very difficult and almost impossible to pass with insufficient knowledge of the official languages, according to Gita. Students from migrant families in particular face these language barriers and rarely have any support to meet the requirements, which are especially demanding when it comes to academic German language skills. Gita says:

> ...there is nobody who can help them if they have problems. Most of those who are in my class, their parents can't help them. In none of the subjects. These are not academics, the parents. I find it difficult. Here, more should be done. That would be something and this has been a special concern of mine for a long time. To me, this is not tolerable that there are always so few children from other countries in our school. But as I said, there are already more than 10 years ago (222–227).

For Gita, the situation is paradoxical and incomprehensible: While the society is becoming more multicultural and more multilingual, the school continues to focus on selective, prestigious languages while ignoring important societal trends. The awareness of students' linguistic and cultural division, as a result of the selection process occurring with the admission exam, seems to be there, as Gita clearly demonstrates. She further believes that the institutional structures, the adherence to existing traditions, and finally the lack of support for students in need indicate

---

7   Gita explains that the admission exam for upper secondary schools in Grisons evaluates students' competences in German and Italian or Romansh, English, and mathematics.

that the education system reproduces the divide between high- and low-performing students. Additionally, although some private tutoring offers exist, they are oftentimes financially inaccessible for migrant students and for their parents. As a project initiated by the canton of Zurich – an upper secondary education level system renowned for its particularly difficult admission exam shows, these institutional mechanisms can be changed. Gita reported that:

> In Zurich, there is a project where adolescents come on Wednesdays and Saturdays, with an admission interview, where they have to show that they are willing to work and then they were able to at least participate in support classes…[and] 60% passed the exam (235–239).

To sum up, although bilingual programs are hugely important, especially given the minority status of Romansh and Italian, the strong (institutional and political) focus on only those (plus English) obfuscates the actual societal linguistic reality which is made up of many more languages. Yet, in fact, the language offered in school in many cases rather adequately mirrors its students' linguistic repertoires since only a small minority of students with different HLs make it to upper secondary school in the first place. Nevertheless, teachers are interested in and willing to promote multilingual education as best as they can with some already intentionally doing so and providing concrete examples of how to implement it.

4.2.4 Students in Zurich

Thirty-nine percent of the students responded that they had a different L1 than German, of which only 5% were in favor of integrating it into class. The reasons for why they would like to do so were that they were looking for an exchange with students who might have the same experiences, problems with, or feelings toward a mainly monolingual school. Another student said that it would be interesting to share one's cultural and linguistic background with fellow students, especially if this could be done using their L1. The rest of the students who speak a different L1, however, would prefer not to integrate it more actively. For instance, they said that they enjoyed speaking German in classes and also saw this as an opportunity to practice it, learning new vocabulary and phrases that they would otherwise not do, given the specific diglossic situation of Swiss German and SSG. They were happy speaking their L1 at home, with friends from the same language background, and on other private occasions. Some felt that their L1 "doesn't fit into the school context" or that "it is not worth it" because very few people speak it. They further perceived the local language to be necessarily the one taught and spoken in class. Others did not consider it to be realistic, thinking that the teacher would also have to speak the same L1 in order to integrate it.

Students were further asked whether they would want to drop a language which they were learning at school and intensify or introduce others that were not taught. While 36% of Zurich's students did not answer this question, 33% were in favor of and 28% were against changing the languages learned at school. The most common answer given was that students desired to drop French and to intensify English classes. This was justified by the fact that students had been learning French for a long time without the possibility to apply it and with very little connection to their personal lives; as Tom said: "I would get rid of French...Except for one internship, which I was forced to do as part of the curriculum, I have never used French outside of school." Furthermore, they saw greater relevance in English and in investing more hours therein to perfect their language skills. Yet, there were also students who argued the opposite, that is, who were in favor of keeping French because of its status as a national language. As three students explained respectively: "I don't like French, but I understand that it must be a part of our language learning" or: "I don't like French, but the priorities are set and I know that it is the second most important national language" or: "It makes sense to teach French because it is a national language, but I do not enjoy learning it." Other languages in which students would be interested include Russian, Arabic, Romansh, Spanish, Italian, and Mandarin. For instance, Philipp stated: "Mandarin is spoken much more commonly worldwide, and it would be really interesting. But it is of course not realistic but interesting to just imagine the situation." Some students use the same argument for Spanish saying that it is a very relevant language on an international level and is interesting for many who travel or work abroad before continuing with university. There are students who complain about the influence of politics on language learning. They believe that they have to learn Italian *only* because it is a national language and if the curriculum considered students' interests and activities, then it would offer Spanish instead. Others would like to have a choice between French and Italian, given that they are both national languages and Italian seems more useful to some in their spare time. As Marco reported: "I would get rid of French and introduce Italian. I don't like French. I could use Italian for vacation." The same is true for Romansh, a national and some Zurich students' first language.

One of the biggest differences concerning language learning between Grisons and Zurich students is that the latter mandatorily learn French alongside the only official medium of instruction, German, and the second FL English. Another difference is that no bilingual or CLIL programs are offered at this school, which is lamented by all of the participating students. They reported that, if it were introduced, then they would prefer a German-English bilingual option over a German-French option. Samira and Nicolas, for instance, believe that it would be greatly advantageous to them, especially as preparation for university:

> Generally, I find [CLIL] a very good idea, especially if you want to study at university later on. There, many lectures will be in English and I think it's good if you have the basic vocabulary in English or to understand the medium of instruction, if that is already done in school. That way you have a big advantage, of course (Samira, 94–97).
>
> What I would find interesting personally with regard to university, for example at ETH [Swiss Federal Institute of Technology in Zurich], where almost everything is in English, is that we have the mathematical concepts in English already at secondary II school (Nicolas, 102 105).

Yasmin strongly agreed because she has already chosen her future study program. As she explained, she will need proficient English skills not only to study Banking and Finance but also for her professional experiences with future clients. She is in favor of CLIL in English in order to have more academic language exposure in addition to the CAE and ELF used on the internet and among friends. In fact, her interest in and passion for English had made her consider enrolling in Zurich's private, English-only Hull's School[8] instead of the public upper secondary school. She also has many friends who are students at Hull's School and who practice its English-only policy, even outside of school and while in Yasmin's company. Yet, she changed her mind since first, she was given the possibility to take the CAE in her current school and second, she thought it was more beneficial to conduct an exchange semester or even her entire Master program in an English-speaking country. Unlike in Grisons, CAE preparation classes are not part of the mandatory curriculum for all students. They are free, additional classes on top of the regular workload and take place during lunch breaks, as students reported.

Samira, who also judges English to be much more valuable for her academic future finds it nonsensical that they are obliged to take a graduation exam in French but not in English. To make matters worse, given her specialization in sciences, she does not understand why she has *four* French lessons and only *two* physics lessons per week. According to her, this arrangement is "strange" (Samira, 265) and does not correspond to her interests and choice of specialization. If CLIL existed, then she would like to increase the lessons in sciences and therefore have those be taught in English. CLIL could offer a satisfactory solution to addressing difficult and often contested lesson planning in combining sciences lessons taught in ELF or, if possible, any other language. Although CLIL is not institutionalized as a bilingual program, Adya explains that English is used: "In biology...for instance, in order to find scientific articles, we conduct research in English in the optional subject" (Adya, 202–203).

---

8 According to Hull's School's website, the vast majority of its students are German-speaking Swiss nationals (https://www.hullschool.ch/en/).

Conversely, students like Arthur, for instance, reported watching academic tutoring videos on the internet in English, given the higher volume of opportunities it presents. However, for him, understanding the subject presented in academic English, with which he is less familiar, is a challenge. Although students encounter certain difficulties when it comes to understanding content-related information in English, Yasmin is convinced that any other language learned at school would be impossible for CLIL: "I believe for French or Italian, we are really still missing vocabulary and generally practice and exercises, for instance. I noticed this a lot in my class. French or Italian is out of question for us" (Yasmin, 255–257). Nicolas finds even more drastic words to characterize the situation: "There are so many of us who actually don't like French. For them, it would be torture" (Nicolas, 131–132). He goes on to say that "if you live in the German-speaking part of Switzerland then you're like spared a bit from French" (Nicolas, 209–210). That said, he recognizes an increasing potential in the *Romandie*, especially in the Lausanne area where the Swiss Federal Institute of Technology is located. With this in mind, French could in fact become a more important subject, even in the German-speaking part of Switzerland. Regarding his current language learning, Nicolas further explains that CLIL, except in certain subjects such as sciences, would not be extremely beneficial for the students since their private life is very much influenced by and filled with English-speaking media, communication, and activities already. Importantly, students often equated English with the spoken, informal language commonly found on the internet, in social media, and in e-games. Not everyone seems to be aware of the different registers that a language can encompass and the different functions that these can have.

Being convinced that good language teaching means implementing a target language-only policy in the classroom, students are nevertheless also interested in the wider offer of other languages. Arthur, for instance, whose L1 is Macedonian, did not learn it in school but with his parents. He believes that parallel L1 classes would have helped him to learn how to write and to practice the language on a different level than simply speaking it while on vacation in Macedonia. Knowing that there are many other Slavic languages and speakers of those at school, he suggests that a common language to be learned could be Russian. According to him, Russian classes had once been part of the optional curriculum, but were canceled thereafter. He further advocated Italian classes: "I would find it good if Italian were introduced mandatorily. After all, it's a national language" (Arthur, 289–290). Similarly, Yasmin, whose L1 is Turkish, has acquired it through her parents and does not associate it with school at all. The only time her Turkish language background became interesting in the classroom was when one of her teachers started learning it for personal reasons: "And then I talked to her shortly about Turkish, also about grammar, but other than that, Turkish is not really a topic at school" (Yasmin, 22–23). When asked whether she would prefer learning English or Turkish in school, she answered English without hesitation. Nevertheless, she went on to explain that she "would find it exciting if a project could be done in which all foreign languages spoken in class would be put together" (Yasmin, 27–29). A project, as Yasmin suggests, could at least make students and teachers aware of the linguistic and cultural diversity at hand.

According to Nicolas, optional Chinese classes are offered which is a relevant language to learn for him, given the demographic development and its importance on a global scale. He also mentions Arabic, a language not offered in school, but in which he would be very interested due to its different writing and sound system. That said, unlike Russian or Chinese, he does not believe "that [Arabic] would be much of use for later" (Nicolas, 80). Adya would also like to learn Arabic, not linking the language to future career opportunities, but to her private life. As a speaker of Urdu herself, she would like to learn to read Arabic script, which would help improve her reading and writing competences in her L1. As mentioned previously, calling herself "illiterate" in Urdu (Adya, 153), she delegitimizes her status as a native speaker, for which Arabic classes in school might compensate.

Finally, Nicolas reveals that language learning in school not only serves him on a practical level, in applying the language in a context outside of school, but that his Latin classes in specific have helped him to develop analytic skills. Latin, as he argues, is an ideal language to better understand the underlying structures of language as a system and allows for comparisons of modern FLs accordingly. Latin classes were an important element to find parallels among languages, to deduce language history and families, and to establish a basis for further language learning. A substantial part of the Latin classes is also spent on cultural history and involves teaching students about people, places, and the developments associated with the Latin language. Although Latin is not spoken anymore, and therefore taught in the school's official language, i.e., German, it has both a multilingual and multicultural character. It could even be argued that it is *more* so and more strongly oriented at combining multiple languages and sensitizing students to this diversity than modern FLs, such as either French or English.

4.2.5 Teachers in Zurich

Among Zurich teachers, one of the most important, yet "controversial topics" (Patrick, 159), according to Patrick is CLIL. Although CLIL is an increasingly popular teaching method in upper secondary schools throughout the country, Patrick perceives it to be rather unlikely that it will ever be introduced at his school in the near future. Since no nation- or canton-wide policies on bilingual programs exist, teachers are confronted with expectations from parents and students, increasing pressure from the industry, and competitive private schools. One of the major difficulties in implementing CLIL is that teachers do not usually have the necessary training in bilingual teaching. In cases where they did pursue further training, many still often lack the confidence to teach bilingually since they rarely practice the second language. As a teacher of German, Patrick is rather worried about the reduction of German lessons per week while science subjects are gaining in significance. If both German lessons are reduced and (certain) science lessons are held in English, then students will speak and write less and less (academic) German. This is particularly relevant in the Swiss-German language region in which CLIL could deteriorate the acquisition and competence of SSG, as Sonja explains:

> [I]t's probably also important to find a balance because also in history class, vocabulary is developed, the German vocabulary, if that is only taught in English then you'll maybe lose the competency to express yourself well in your mother tongue or for us rather the school language or how should I call this.... (148–152)

Growing up speaking a dialect, most students only learn SSG in school and consequently need register- and content-specific input in order to develop proficient linguistic competency. Interestingly, Sonja first refers to the language used in school as the students' mother tongue before 'correcting' herself and calling it *school language* – still hesitant about the appropriate terminology. What is certain is that unlike students in other Swiss linguistic regions, where the regional language is equivalent to the school language, Zurich students are primarily exposed to Swiss German, something which is not usually allowed in school. This complicates matters further for children with different HLs, who have to learn both Swiss and SSG in school. Adding still more languages can be overwhelming, as Elisabeth noted:

> [S]omehow they speak Serbian at home, then they should learn the dialect [Swiss German], they have to learn standard German in school, starting in grade 2 English on top of this and then starting in grade 4, French on top of that. And you see, they're not proficient in any of those languages, also not in standard German. (-) I think it's extremely difficult. (263–267)

Sufficient knowledge in SSG is, however, critical to entering either university or the job market – one of upper secondary schooling's primary objectives. In this case, CLIL could be an advantage for monolingual students more than for plurilingual ones for whom it would be an additional 'burden.' Sabine, who completed a CLIL training to teach history in English, agrees and believes that CLIL should not be imposed upon every student and that not all students would benefit from it equally. That said, she also thinks that while many of the students are very interested in CLIL, only certain students have the necessary academic skills and prior knowledge to enhance their linguistic performance. She generally likes the idea and says she that she would have liked to learn languages in school in this way herself, but language immersion programs do not have the same priority for everyone. For instance, if the applied teaching concept is oriented at communication, interaction, and students' output, then it can be hard to combine this with CLIL where students should present groupwork or must conduct discussions in an FL. Viewed like this, CLIL seems rather compatible with teacher-focused instruction for students who want to be exposed to rich, content-specific vocabulary, which is contrary to current pedagogical trends and teachers' perspectives. Generally, most participants stated that they find it important to have a good relationship with their students and to choose content according to students' interests and lifeworlds, which they consider fun; however, and as Sonja pointed out, the language needs to be one to which she can relate as well. They want to convey their subject with passion and to actively involve students in the learning process, rather than imposing their content and objectives onto their students.

Similarly, an important criterion for good teaching according to Sabine, for instance, is fun and feeling at ease. As she elaborated, language learning can be detrimental to students' mental health when they are forced to speak in front of the class, since it can result in mockery, embarrassment, or shame. Adopting a more easy-going attitude as a teacher can also help students to relax and learn a language in an almost judgement- and stress-free environment. This is of course only possible since Zurich teachers are considerably free to decide relevant content for their language classes. This means that the school's curriculum provides a certain framework or orientation and remains rather flexible and adaptable to both students' and teachers' personal needs and interests alike. All of the teachers are aware that they have a great deal of liberty to plan their lessons, yet at the same time Patrick noted that their teaching remains influenced by internal or cantonal policies and by the EDK's recommendations. Eleonore, conversely, is particularly grateful for having the possibility to design a self-study semester program for students according to her interests and theirs. Nesrin, who is a rather novice teacher, is excited about the liberty provided by the open curriculum. Nevertheless, she is also very adamant about achieving the set objectives: "Because after all, that's my job, I need to achieve this" (Nesrin, 81–82). It needs to be pointed out that all language teachers consider it important that students enjoy and feel at ease in the classroom in terms of the chosen content and the learning environment.

However, the task of creating such positive circumstances is perceived to be much easier for English teachers than for others: "Yes, well, they [the students] perceive the language [English] to be more important than other foreign languages, which they would have to learn, for instance, French…this facilitates my work with them" (Sabine, 60–62). In fact, similar to the students' perspectives described previously, teaching French to students with no or very low motivation to learn it is "apparently a torture" (Eleonore, 231). She, therefore, suggests reducing the number of years of compulsory French learning in order to "shorten the general suffering of teachers and students a bit" (Eleonore, 235–236). She further proposes investing more resources in exchange programs with the *Romandie* to create more meaningful learning experiences for students and to help them discover the utility of French, which is often questioned by or unclear to many students.

The same circumstances facilitating the teaching of English also simultaneously and paradoxically render it more difficult. Exposed to (primarily) informal language on YouTube, blogs, Netflix, etc. on a daily basis, students equate this with native-like language and undermine the value of academic English that is expected in school. This "anything goes"-approach (Sabine, 52), according to Sabine and other teachers, represents an overall tendency to pay less attention to linguistic accuracy, i.e., orthography, grammar, and registers. This is especially challenging for English teachers since they are expected to transmit and to demand the use of standard language even as students orient themselves toward social media to learn 'authentic' English.

Additionally, the students' perception of English being more important than other (foreign) languages is mirrored in the school's distribution of lessons. Teachers unanimously agree that most of the pressure was applied to French teachers since they are the first to have their lessons reduced across the curriculum. Patrick is also rather worried that the reduced German lessons, compared to an increase in English or CLIL lessons (in English), will send the somewhat questionable message of institutional prioritization of English, as mentioned previously. Tina, a teacher of French and Italian, compares the situation to a vicious circle since students' motivation to learn French as a mandatory language is very low, their language skills are continuously decreasing and the fewer hours that they are exposed to it, the less likely they will be to improve. The situation is somewhat different and less tense for Italian since it is an optional subject and students are typically interested when they initially sign up. The national teacher associations for Italian and French and the support which they obtain from them also differ hugely, as Tina explains. While Italian teachers seem to be very active and enthusiastic in organizing *settimane della Svizzera italiana* [weeks of Italian-speaking Switzerland], French teachers seem to be stuck in a similar vicious circle. The less motivated students are, and the more French lessons are reduced, the more difficult it is to find the strength to teach, let alone to have fun and feel at ease in class.

English's increasingly dominant role generates conflicting perspectives, not only among teachers but also within themselves. That is, some of the answers given were contradictory, something which hints at the difficulty of finding one's own position in this ideology-laden polarity. Sonja, for instance, realized herself that she was contradicting an answer that she had given previously and concluded that the prioritization of English over national languages was a very difficult topic with no satisfactory solution for everyone. The development is, therefore, problematic as English seems to divide the language subjects further while language policies envision the integration of those into an interdisciplinary language learning program called *Mehrsprachigkeitsdidaktik* [plurilingualism didactics]. Integrated into the school's pilot project about the future of schools,[9] the idea is to strengthen the connection among language subjects, often viewed as 'soft subjects,' as a measure to compete against the increasing proportion of 'hard science' subjects. Although it is not yet institutionalized, it has become clear that this approach can be implemented more easily in projects than in class schedules that are organized based on fixed structures and routines. One such example of inclusive multilingual learning was Carmen's week-long project in which she sensitized her students to Romansh with the help of the Lia Rumantscha[10] in Grisons.

In addition to this, Patrick pointed out that for him, the future of schools, and especially the future of language classes, will need to take demographic development into consideration. He sees a clear tendency toward increasing numbers of students with diverse linguistic and cultural backgrounds and calls for an urgent rethinking of monolingual and monocultural schools. Patrick says:

> [A]nd I think, this awareness, which (--) of this linguistic diversity, different languages, which are used [in school], are a central aspect of school, to make this clear. It's not only the four national languages, but also, I just don't know how many languages, I used to know how many languages are spoken at home in my son's school. Maybe approximately 20 if I remember correctly and I think children should already understand that this is simply the social reality and I think if we always talk about integration it's a deciding aspect that we are aware of this (320–326).

Furthermore, Elisabeth agrees that although the situation at upper secondary level is different from lower secondary, where more than 40% of the students have a migrant background, the school still needs to rethink its strategy. Similar to the situation in Grisons, upper secondary schools seem to have fewer students with a migrant background; again, this might be linked to the rather difficult admission exam or conditions. Many students who make it to the upper secondary level have Tamil, Kurdish, or Albanian origins. Although teachers seem to be commonly aware of this, it is not recognized as a 'problem' at an institutional level. Patrick, who as a German teacher remarks upon the great discrepancies between students' oral and written expression, argues that GFL classes are crucial for (but not only for) migrant students. Without proficient language skills in German, they also fall behind in other subjects since they are co-responsible for developing argumentative and analytical skills and evaluating appropriate language as part of the subjects' grade. These arguments, Patrick explains, were used to apply for and finally led to additional funding

---

9   The school has conducted a pilot project about the future of schools in which the focus is put on interdisciplinary and autonomous learning organized more collaboratively in projects instead of divided by separate lessons and teachers.

10 Lia Rumantscha is a non-profit organization promoting Romansh language and culture.

for GFL courses. The fact that language is the underlying requirement that follows all other subjects is an obstacle to those who do not have the possibility to learn it and who, as a consequence, are denied post-compulsory education. That said, an increased offer is needed to account for the increasing number of students with different academic requirements.

Alongside the lacking institutional support, some teachers, although very aware of the school's linguistic and cultural diversity, seem less convinced about the need to actively promote it in their teaching. The most common perspective is to equate applying multilingual education with speaking multiple (heritage) languages oneself in order to employ them in the classroom, in a manner similar to the medium of instruction. Sabine explains, for instance: "it is for me French, Italian, German, and Latin, to which I can refer" (Sabine, 165–166), feeling competent enough in those languages to make references or connections in her English lesson. She raises the issue of students' stigmatization due to their different linguistic and cultural backgrounds, something with which other teachers face. Although she would be willing to give students the space and allow them to integrate their L1s into the classroom, Sabine fears that this would create a bigger divide than it would serve to sensitize students or to bring them together:

> I'm sometimes a bit skeptical because the majority of the students here would talk about more or less the same culture, the Swiss German culture, and then there are 1, 2, 3 per class who would talk about a different culture and this can have an encouraging effect on the one hand. On the other hand, how should I say, stigmatizing, as different, as exotic in the broadest sense and that's why I am (--), it depends a lot on the class, how class cohesion is, how the mood is, if I were to do it.... Most of the time, I let them choose if they want to talk about themselves or if they want to do something about the village in which they live in Switzerland (171–178).

Providing an option for students to choose between their heritage language and culture and the one to which they are exposed in Switzerland is of course less imposing and allows students to make their own decisions. Nevertheless, this diminishes the chances of demonstrating individual strengths and personal trajectories to fellow students in an official classroom environment and to receive important recognition. Similarly, Sonja reported:

> If it's about exchanging opinions, this will be exciting for sure, if they grow up differently or also grew up differently or also even lived in a different country for a few years and then moved to Switzerland...I try to use that. Because I think, everyone can benefit from it. The language *per se*, I think is more difficult, it's for sure possible when I also know the other languages. So, I also know a bit of

> French, Italian, and Spanish and I also do point to those, but other than that, not so much. I find it difficult because I don't even know it myself (212–219).

A better understanding of and hands-on material on multilingual education is needed for (more) teachers to integrate other HLs and to feel confident and competent to do so, as some teachers have urged. Furthermore, such integration is impossible without adequate institutional support and training in teaching materials, textbooks, and other online resources. That said, Nesrin, who seems to base her decisions on her recent teacher education and linguistics classes, is a strong advocate of multilingual education. Not only does she refer to herself in her position as a language teacher as a mediator between the Germanic and Latin cultural groups in Switzerland, but she is also very adamant about promoting plurilingual identities. Nesrin sees an urgent necessity to act and to transmit a broader awareness of linguistic and cultural diversity in Switzerland:

> I see it in my classes that it's apparently not always so clear that other languages also exist in Switzerland. Often, it's like erased from the consciousness and only when you go to Lausanne or a multilingual area, you're suddenly aware that there are also other languages in Switzerland (158–161).

Although Switzerland is a multilingual country with four official national languages, each canton determines its/their own official language(s). Living in an officially monolingual canton, such as Zurich, can imply uncommon exposure to other languages and Nesrin suggests that schools should, therefore, raise awareness of other language groups in order to increase mutual respect and understanding. Referring to a university seminar on language and identity, which had strong influence on her, she explains how language unconsciously shapes our way of thinking and self-perception. She exemplifies this with French, where, like English, the grammatical subject (e.g., *I*) is typically in the first position in a declarative clause (e.g., *I saw you last week*). Simply analyzing sentence structures and comparing those in different languages can function as a basis to further discuss cultural values and beliefs and to critically assess stereotypes. For example, Nesrin explained that it could be perceived as "arrogant" (Nesrin, 175) in other cultures to predominantly refer to oneself and constantly repeat the subject (*I*) when speaking. Furthermore, she organizes small projects on linguistic topics such as language families through which she can demonstrate both familiarity and parallels among languages, to deconstruct the often-perceived 'otherness,' and to draw on student examples in the classroom. She noted that it was important to give students the necessary time to raise questions since learning about their HLs and their cultural origins is not usually a part of discovering their identity. Unlike other teachers, Nesrin believes that she does not have to know a language in order to integrate it into the classroom:

I've also already taken Turkish examples, I don't speak Turkish, but I have a Turkish person in one of the classes and it was important for me to show the students that the languages work differently...Then I asked the Turkish student to say a sentence in Turkish. It was about the endings. (215–220)

That said, she also shares a concern with one of her colleagues who had tried to integrate other languages into her French class and tried to make references among them, to which students responded with incomprehension. For them, it was difficult to connect different disciplines and to arrive at a more holistic and inclusive approach to learning. This shows that many are accustomed to traditional institutional structures and are in need of guidance in terms of new learning approaches.

4.2.6 Students in Fribourg

Sixty-five percent of Fribourg students either gave no response or stated that including their L1s more actively into class did not concern them, while 20% were enthusiastic about it and indicated that they would like to integrate their L1s in order to share their linguistic and cultural backgrounds with fellow students or to improve their L1 competence. For instance, Julia reported: "Yes, I would love very much to include Mandarin...as an optional class since it's a very important and very interesting language. It would help me to show others my culture and origins." Other reasons mentioned were the difference in proficiency between the official school language and the L1. It would be beneficial to have L1 classes to develop literacy skills. Ricardo, whose L1 is Italian, would like to introduce Italian instead of German classes. Since they are both national languages in Switzerland, the best option for him would be to let students decide which one they would like to learn. Conversely, 10% of students are against including their L1s. They prioritize the languages spoken in Switzerland and perceive a focus on those they view to be clearly necessary.

Moreover, a slight majority (55%) of students are against changing the languages offered at school while 25% are in favor of it (20% did not respond). The most commonly cited reason for why the languages offered should remain unchanged is the importance of both FLs – German and English – for French-speaking students in Switzerland. As two students explained it: "English is very important on an international level and for everything that has to do with accessing information. German can seem less important but in Switzerland, I think, it's important to learn it" or "...because German and English are the fundamental languages in Switzerland." Mona even expressed the desire to intensify German, due to its importance, and the time spent on learning it from an early age. Not all agree, however, and call instead for a greater emphasis on English due to its international reputation. Yet, others still would like to have Italian as an optional subject along with the possibility to choose between German and Italian. Additionally, there are also students who would like to learn Spanish in school because it is considered a "useful" and "nice" language. Students are also aware of internationally important languages, such as Mandarin or Russian, and some would be interested in learning them.

4.2.7 Teachers in Fribourg

Several of the teachers interviewed taught CLIL which, at the school in the canton of Fribourg – unlike the school in the canton of Grisons – is offered in both a national language (French or German) *and* in English. This needs to be emphasized since, as Etienne pointed out, bilingual education implies different languages depending on whether it is offered in a private or public school. Typically, a privately run school offers bilingual programs in English and in the regional language, whereas public schools tend to maximize the offer of national languages in their bilingual programs.

Teachers' perspectives on the school's CLIL programs are generally very positive. According to Victoria (290), there is no better way of teaching. Etienne adds that the ideal scenario would consist of mandatory exchanges for students *and* teachers, especially in a bilingual canton like Fribourg where this could be organized relatively easily (Etienne, 367). CLIL classes also provide the opportunity to easily draw from other languages since there is more meaning being negotiated and there is a stronger focus on comprehension. This seems to create a more open and flexible atmosphere into which multiple languages might be integrated. Etienne makes use of this when he deals with historical sources available in different languages such as Italian, Spanish, or Russian, for which he asks students' help: "I try this too and I don't even speak Russian. But students do. I always think it is great" (Etienne, 153–154).

That said, Jeanne explained that it is in fact very challenging to teach CLIL because: first, the choice of adequate textbooks and other materials is very limited; second, Jeanne says that the curriculum does not provide enough information on bilingual programs and about their specific objectives and is sometimes even incompatible with the teaching material at hand. Jeanne exemplified this with the topics 'imperialism,' 'colonialism', or 'nationalism' which are all presented differently with divergent emphases in English- and French-speaking textbooks. Given the limited offer in CLIL textbooks, based on the Swiss curriculum, Jeanne makes use of teaching material from England, thereby guaranteeing authenticity on the one hand, yet necessarily deviating from the common Swiss teaching standards and objectives for upper secondary education on the other. This raises challenging questions about whether, for instance, history taught as CLIL is primarily concerned with learning the subject in a different language or whether it impacts its perspective on *what* is being transmitted exactly. Furthermore, it renders teaching this topic in specific difficult for Jeanne, who believes that she *must* teach her lessons according to the curriculum, although she finds it "fairly strict" (Jeanne, 33): "Well, I have to follow the curriculum, it is imposed by the schools, by the institution, by the public education system" (Jeanne, 21–22). To her, following the curriculum is positive since everybody does it in the same way; this provides structure and clarity, especially for students. David, who also thinks that the curriculum "is really important" (David, 44) because of students' transition between classes and different teaching styles among colleagues, is generally very happy about a guiding structure. Defending and supporting the *status quo* and the curriculum imposed by the school, he never considered having the possibility to choose interesting content or objectives for himself: "I never asked myself the question how it would be if I could only do what I would like to do or what the students would like to do" (David, 59–60). Similarly, when asking Jeanne about her personal objectives in teaching, she was very hesitant to provide an answer. After a pause, she said: "Hmm (=) (--). For me, it is to be able to transmit my competences and my knowledge. And then that students see the importance of learning a language and that they will succeed" (Jeanne, 246–247).

Conversely, there are teachers who do not consider the curriculum to be essential to their teaching and there are those who believe that it should provide even more guidance and even a more detailed repertoire for lesson planning. Victoria, for instance, criticized the curriculum's focus on developing *competencies* such as 'critical thinking,' given that it neither clarifies how those are to be achieved nor explains what they entail in detail. As she put it: "I find these general formulations concerning competence-oriented teaching important of course, but I'm also saying that (-), you can hide very easily behind those" (Victoria, 59–60).

Luisa is still more critical regarding the curriculum and of other policies, such as EDK recommendations on multilingual education. Although the EDK's strategy encourages schools to invest in and offer mobility and exchange programs, they are not usually implemented at the school (nor is their recommendation binding in any way). In fact, Luisa has the impression that any attempts made by teachers are impeded institutionally. For instance, exchanges and excursions with other language regions are discouraged and a more flexible interpretation of the curriculum, to integrate multiple languages, is not accepted. Over time, as Luisa stated, teachers willing to foster multilingual education simply give up trying and stick to the school's regular curriculum. According to her, the regular curriculum is very traditional and this is incompatible with her personal teaching principles. Instead, she follows the CEFR, determines the specific skills which students need to achieve at a given level, and tries to emphasize the communicative aspect of language learning. This is also problematic for David who shares her idea of language being communicative, which somehow seems to be in conflict with the curriculum: "If we taught a bit more in a communicative way or if we were allowed (-), this is again about curricula, I think, this could maybe lead to students realizing that what I learn in school will be useful" (David, 243–245). Furthermore, Luisa prioritizes learner autonomy, expects students to take responsibility for their learning, and sees them as active partners in knowledge construction. That said, she explains that "I often realize that this is something that was rarely done before" (Luisa, 52–53). Students seem overwhelmed and are often unable to work autonomously, in groups, or just opt to determine learning objectives for themselves.

The curriculum, as well as the underlying institutional structures, further impede a reorganization of language teaching, which would (in theory) be supported by several teachers. Block courses of several weeks could be introduced, as teachers have proposed, based on empirical findings suggesting longer and more intensive exposure as a more efficient and natural way of learning a language. Etienne goes even further and asks: "Does it still make sense to learn foreign languages in school?" (Etienne, 350). The way languages have been and still are taught in today's schools does not correspond to students' (virtual) language use and exposure. This is why:

> I ask myself if foreign languages still make sense in the traditional lesson in class. I would also see it like this, for instance, a mandatory year abroad in upper secondary. This would be 1,000 times more efficient than grammar, pronunciation, vocabulary. (Etienne, 354–357)

Yet, as he further suggests, this line of argument is detrimental from an employee's point of view since, if put into practice, many (language) teachers could potentially lose their jobs. This demonstrates how teaching strategy decisions about language learning, as well as political and policy decisions, are interdependent and how difficult it is to align all actors' interests.

This inherent problem, although it is not expressed in the same dramatic way as Etienne's formulation, is perceived as such by almost all teachers. David, for instance, describes the situation of language learning as "this resistance against the second national language [German]" (David, 48–49), of which he – almost sarcastically – estimates that "1% of the students would call this their favorite subject" (David, 247–258). He further suggests that this resistance against the language by L1-French speakers is partly driven by stereotypes, prejudices, and hardened negative attitudes toward its speakers, the deconstruction of which should be a very important topic in German classes. David argues that regional and cultural studies informing students about daily life in other linguistic and cultural regions would be crucial to increasing motivation for language learning and for mutual understanding. The current, strong emphasis on literature, while important, is neither authentic nor very meaningful for students and often does not lead to a higher level of proficiency. In fact, as a teacher of German and Spanish, David concludes that "they have three years [of Spanish] until *Matura*, and when they do the *Matura*, the level of Spanish and German is the same, I guess at that point, they have learned German for 10 or 12 years" (David, 259–260). Learning German is seen as an obligation, for which many students do not have the sufficient motivation to succeed; this is also an aspect that was highlighted by Luisa who views it as a "desperate" dilemma (Luisa, 179). Students' lacking motivation and negative attitudes toward German impede learning and enjoying it – quite the contrary to how *English* language learning is described. Although teachers like Luisa invest a great deal of time into making GFL classes more enjoyable, she realizes that much of it derives from outside of school and other spheres of social life.

Mentions of multilingual education with a focus on HLs is only marginally present in the data, given the enormous challenges, based on the school's curriculum, CLIL, and conflictual language classes. This might be because HL speakers are typically perfectly fluent in the school's official language(s) and are, thus, well integrated; this might also be because there are only very few HL speakers on upper secondary level *tout court*, according to Etienne. Similar to the cantons of Grisons and Zurich, admission exams before the beginning of upper secondary schools select students who will complete their *Matura* and who will then, most likely, go to university. Put plainly, the selection is often made between students with and without a migration background, of which the former start working after lower secondary education and the latter continue their academic trajectory. The majority of those who do have a different linguistic and cultural background are of Portuguese origin and sometimes they speak their L1 during break as Etienne explains. However, for him it is not an option to include it or any other HLs into his German classes:

> A: And if you were to actively include it [Portuguese] into your class...?
> B: Well, in a language course, that's pretty problematic. Then, it makes no sense anymore to do German.
> A: What do you mean by 'it doesn't make sense anymore to do German?'
> B: I can't allow my Portuguese students to speak Portuguese in my German course. (143–151)

That said, as mentioned above, Etienne is happy to integrate other languages in his CLIL classes where the objective is not only to improve language skills. Nevertheless, multilingual education approaches seem incompatible with his set teaching objectives for German classes. Jeanne perceives it to be a very sensitive issue and is rather skeptical when it comes to including other languages into her classes, since the curriculum is already dense and students are already learning multiple languages. Conversely, Luisa still applies them in her classes, even though she stated that empirical studies are inconclusive as to whether multilingual education approaches improve language skills *per se*. The intention is to raise students' awareness and to foster their identity and the overall recognition of different L1s in an official setting. Yet, it depends on teachers' individual efforts and interests to create meaningful lessons and/or exchanges based on multilingual education because it is not a priority in school, in the curriculum or in textbooks. It is a great challenge to design such lessons and to find the right way to recognize the HLs in the classroom, since doing it wrong could lead to a certain stigmatization, as Luisa explained:

> ...I'm a bit scared that I rather create exactly something I don't want. In summer, I always offer so-called special days. We had to hand in a topic, and I would like to work on linguistic and cultural stereotypes. I only fear that no one will sign up. (236–239)

Even if the effort is made, and if the specific courses are available, then students' interest in these topics will generally be low. When engaging in such activities, there is also always a risk of reproducing 'otherness' and exposing students to something too personal that they might not want to share.

Another condition to fully embrace multilingual education or language learning in general, according to David, is reflecting upon one's own language repertoire:

> The problem is, (-) it's not a problem, the students also reflect little about their own languages and then it's also complicated to have a conversation [about that]...I often do this [comparing languages] with French also because it's fun to me, but I often realize (-), they all speak French as their first or second language, but often they can't compare the foreign language with the first language...they have never dealt with this [before]... (103–105; 110–113).

According to David, reflection about, and understanding of, and appreciating one's own language repertoire is crucial to further engage with other languages and cultures. Although he thinks that it is also the school's responsibility to promote HLs, additional language course offers from the country of origin are needed to foster not only oral language proficiency, but also on a written/academic basis. Similar to others, he does not consider it possible to include multiple languages into his classes because of his lacking competencies. That is, he believes that it is very challenging to make meaningful connections among languages since he does not speak the students' L1s. On the contrary, Julien and Victoria, for instance, believe that including other L1s is possible even without being able to speak them. While Julien tried to integrate Polish in German grammar classes, with the help of a student, Victoria and her students created a rap song containing French, English, Serbian, Croatian, Turkish, and German. Such language activities attribute official recognition to HLs and do not require the teacher to have proficient language skills. According to Victoria, more recent teaching approaches, such as co-teaching, theater pedagogy, and interdisciplinary self-study projects are hugely beneficial for language learning. A final concern that she shared during the interview was the canton's decision to cut funding for native-speaker teaching assistants who support local teachers in teaching language classes in their L1. This authentic, co-teaching experience was very helpful for students as well as teachers.

4.3 Language Hierarchies

Language ideologies exacerbate the symbolic power of languages and determine the 'market-value' of linguistic varieties and their speakers through hierarchies.

The following table illustrates a noteworthy result, given the study's focus on Switzerland's language learning debate caused by certain cantons' decision to prioritize English over a second national language. It shows that students from all three cantons prefer English to the non-L1 national languages of German or French, especially students from the canton of Fribourg who like English the most. French as a language subject in school is liked better by Grisons students (although it is optional for them) than by those in the canton of Zurich, whereas Fribourg students like German even less. The findings further indicate that while students from Zurich tend to agree that English should be used as an intercantonal *lingua franca*, students from Fribourg and Grisons tend to disagree.

Figure 13: Liking non-L1 national language versus English

4.3.1 Students in Grisons

In Grisons, a slight majority of students (53%) chose Romansh as their most relevant language in private life, followed by 45% of students who ranked Swiss German first. In fact, two students put Romansh and Swiss German both first explaining that it was impossible for them to decide which one was more relevant to them personally. English was ranked most relevant in one case while Spanish and Norwegian were ranked third place twice and once respectively. Forty-five percent of the students' personal rankings do not include English as a top 3 language. There were no single-language answers; 18% considered two languages relevant for their personal lives with the rest of the students choosing at least three languages.

Figure 14: Ranking the most significant language in their personal lives – GR

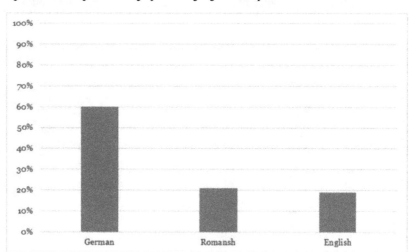

60% considered German the most relevant language, 21% chose Romansh, and 19% chose English for their professional or academic lives. French was voted second and third once respectively while Spanish was voted third twice. All except for one of the rankings included English and all except for two listed more than two languages.

Figure 15: Ranking the most significant language in their professional lives – GR

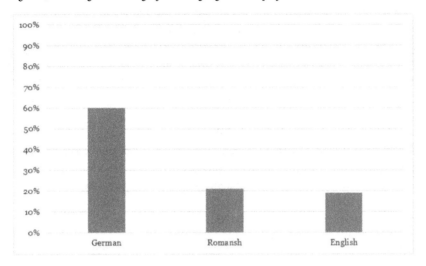

Eighty-two percent of Grisons students voted for English to be learned before French; 18% favored French. Almost all students who were in favor of French explained their answers by saying that they would rather learn French first "out of respect for the nation," as one student put it succinctly. French would automatically deserve to be prioritized over a language that is not officially spoken in any language region in Switzerland, given its high status as a national language. Another reason often cited was the similarity between Romansh and French and, therefore, the simplicity to learn it first. Nevertheless, the opposite was also stated by approximately 20% of the students who considered French to be more complicated than English and who, therefore, preferred learning English. That said, the main arguments still referred to English's popularity and importance on an international level, very similar to the ones mentioned by Zurich students. English is perceived as *the* universal *lingua franca*, inextricably linked with unlimited freedom and necessary "to be part of the world," as Enzo noted. Furthermore, English is not really considered a school subject by many any longer. It is acquired almost naturally on the side, mostly online, which makes English classes at school enjoyable and seemingly easy (especially when compared to other language subjects), as students reported.

Given Romansh's minority status, language hierarchies are a real and lived phenomenon, to which the majority of the students are constantly exposed. They exist and are experienced on both a *de jure* and a *de facto* basis. Generally, their personal language hierarchies are determined by their L1 – in this study's case, either Romansh or Swiss German; students with Romansh as their L1 consider it to be the most significant language while the same holds true for students whose L1 is Swiss

German. Importantly, *all* Romansh-speaking students necessarily also speak Swiss German/SSG, while the inverse is not considered the norm. This is exacerbated by the fact that only very few books or even any other printed or digital content exist in Romansh, so reading and writing happen almost automatically in German, as Christine explains. The hierarchy becomes even more visible "when there are many German speakers then you automatically speak German, even with people who are there and would be able to speak Romansh. (-) Because it would somehow be impolite" (Christine, 37–39). She goes on to explain that as a Romansh speaker, she has learned to adapt herself to her surroundings and to the existing language hierarchies. German is and, according to many students, should be the *lingua franca* used and understood by everyone (although this is less the case for Italian-speakers in Grisons). The overall impression is that Swiss German dominates Switzerland; yet, as Jana pointed out: "Here [in Grisons], it will be a long time until Germanization takes over, so to speak" (Jana, 194–195). This shows both Romansh's hitherto uncontested priority and importance and also an ongoing development of Swiss German/German domination which might lead to the extinction of Romansh someday.

Furthermore, the 'Röstigraben' – the German-French language border – is perceived as being too far away for students to be in physical proximity with French. Although Hanna acknowledges that French is a part of Switzerland, and she regrets not learning it in school, when asked to choose between Romansh and French as a subject, she responds: "Romansh is still more important for me" (Hanna, 49). Jana added that Italian is much more relevant in the trilingual canton than French and should, thus, be learned prior thereto.

André sees English's influence and omnipresence in a *de jure* trilingual society as a problematic development. Aware of the fact that Zurich and other German-speaking cantons have decided to prioritize English over a national language, he believes that "the importance of English is becoming too big. First one's own national language, respectively the second and then only after that English because you have to be able to communicate with our own people first" (André, 209–211). For him, the hierarchy is clear: National languages should come before English so that communication within Switzerland can be guaranteed to take place in a national language. He further added that ELF would not be successful in Switzerland since "only one language for four different cultures does not really work well because every language also has elements of this culture" (André, 291–292). He believes that federal regulations, binding for all in Switzerland, are needed in order to achieve more equitable language learning and use of national languages and to counteract the current trend of prioritizing ELF. The problem with this, as he explained, is that language learning in schools is decided on a cantonal level, even though there should be a higher national interest in Switzerland's four languages. For Jana, for instance, it would be "strange" (Jana, 181) to communicate in English and it would create an unnecessary distance among the language groups. They generally feel that communication has worked well in the past and that there is no need to change it although concrete examples of successful interaction among German-, French-, and Romansh speakers are rather lacking in the conversation.

4.3.2 Teachers in Grisons

The teachers' overall impression is that English is heavily prioritized and is endangering Romansh's already difficult minority status even more. For instance, this prioritization is materialized in the school's CAE exam and the importance given to it institutionally. As Roberto pointed out, the narrow focus on English is detrimental since it no longer qualifies as an outstanding skill. English, according to him, only serves well when coupled with other skills since the vast majority of individuals, with whom their students will compete for positions, will be as competent in English as they are. Henri compares this to an economic phenomenon with which he exemplifies the situation to his students: "…economists who always say, English is the language of the economy. No economist would say everybody should invest in the same stock. The economy would collapse" (Henri, 334–336). Thus, speaking English is not an advantage *per se*, since the competition is too big; however, combining it with other skills such as speaking Romansh, for instance, might be beneficial for students. As both Roberto and Henri have observed, however, some students are unaware of this and focus solely on English. For Henri, national languages should be prioritized over English on a moral basis. He advocates the idea of a strong cohesion in one's community: "At first, immediately the neighbor's language, that's part of it. You're not a good world citizen if you don't treat the neighbor well, that's obvious" (Henri, 271–272). Speaking one's neighbor's language can facilitate communication and demonstrate interest, openness, and integration according to Henri. Other teachers have a similar understanding of how speaking the same language can ameliorate social cohesion. As Gita pointed out, ELF "is absolutely out of question" (Gita, 409–410) as a common language for Switzerland. Unable to really justify her opinion, she would prefer improving her knowledge in other national languages instead of using ELF and calls herself "conservative" (Gita, 404).

Nicole cautions that ELF's spread is a natural development and cannot be stopped forcefully. Yet, educational policies intentionally impede full bilingual programs in English and offer them in the three official cantonal languages instead in an attempt to gain control over this development. Some teachers have argued that if CLIL were offered in English, then the risk would be too high that students would decide to no longer enroll in the traditional bilingual programs. Language hierarchies are, therefore, renegotiated and influenced by different forces on both societal and educational levels. Paradoxically, although the Grisons teachers' emphasis seems to lie on the promotion of the cantonal languages, Henri laments the non-existence of exchange at the school level:

The school does call itself multilingual, but the habitus is rather monolingual. The language that is used is German. That's the one that is expected from everyone. We have these three sections, per se, they are already bilingual, but even the exchange among these three sections, it doesn't exist. You could do so much more here" (249–253).

Thus, the hierarchy is clear with German being the most relevant language used and is expected from everyone. As Gita put it: "German is simply everything" (Gita, 312). Italian and Romansh, as *de jure* equal languages, are rather undermined and cannot compete with the majority language. From a pragmatic point of view, Gita argues that Romansh can even be said to be dispensable:

A: And Romansh?
B: To be honest? It works well without [Romansh]. Except they want to become teachers or they already know "I want to go back to my valley and open a store there or to work in an institution where you must know it". But for studying, effectively, you don't need it (317–319).

As mentioned previously, Henri believes that one of the underlying issues that exacerbates the existing language hierarchies is the lacking exchange among the school's Romansh-, German-, and Italian-speaking sections. All Grisons teachers believe that if the school reproduces the separation of languages and cultures, then students will potentially internalize these mechanisms and will act them out within society. As Henri further explained, it is up to the smaller language groups to seek exchange and to adapt to the German-speaking majority, which remains rather independent and autonomous. Furthermore, the same hierarchy exists within the curriculum. Whereas German is a mandatory subject for all students, both Romansh and Italian are optional and are, thus, indirectly labeled as dispensable.

On a cantonal level, Italian, Romansh, and German are *de jure* equal languages with huge *de facto* discrepancies. From a prescriptive perspective, the language law that safeguards the national languages' equal status is of great value in the trilingual canton. However, its implementation is not controlled, and its efficiency is questioned by many participants. Educational institutions and other national agencies such as Movetia, following a political mandate, have the task of promoting exchanges and thus of ameliorating understanding among the language regions. Such policy-based and subsidized offers show that interaction among them does not happen typically or naturally and needs to be incentivized. In those situations, Romansh-speaking students are neglected as appropriate exchange partners since it is neither learned as a language anywhere else in school nor do they learn French to really benefit from such exchanges.

As Henri further pointed out, it is only possible to mistreat Romansh and to deprive its speakers of their linguistic rights because "you don't have to be afraid that someone is going to take legal action" (Henri, 103–104). Growing up accustomed to such inequality, Henri's experience shows that Romansh speakers do not (dare to) demand their rights:

> This also has to do with the typical situation of a minority language. When you grow up, it doesn't work without German. You have this image that Romansh is like the family language, at least for some people, it's limited to friends, then the language doesn't need a public presence in this sense. Of course, politics has to intervene here, they try. But it's often in contrast to people, the people themselves. They say, no, it's actually enough for me when it's German. A small minority is very often very open toward the majority. A little submissive even. (108–114)

Henri confirmed that even though there is a certain political engagement to rearrange the existing language hierarchies in favor of Romansh, this does not come to pass because some of its own speakers are unassertive, are (superficially) satisfied with the *status quo*, and limit their L1 Romansh to private life. Others reported that Romansh is more restricted to the family context while they (unconsciously) switch to Swiss German in public space. That said, it can be further undermined even within the family context, as Nicole experienced, when there is more than one family language. In her case, Swiss German as well as Romansh were the languages spoken in her family, even though Romansh automatically lost out its place to Swiss German whenever her father, the German-speaking parent, was around. Romansh's minority position is also positive for Roberto, whose lived experiences of language are primarily shaped by being a minority speaker of Italian in Grisons and *not* Italian-speaking Ticino. Sharing the minority position with Romansh, Grisons' Italian speakers have two strong majorities – Grisons' Swiss German speakers and Ticino's Italian speakers – to which they have to stand up. Pairing up with the Romansh-speaking community, however, increases their voices and weight in discussions and decision-making with the German-speaking part in Grisons. Interestingly, Roberto perceives there to be a more fruitful cooperation among the Italian-Romansh minority and the German majority within Grisons, in contrast to the Italian language group in Ticino. Questioned in their legitimacy as Italian speakers, they are not fully accepted as members of the same language group by Ticinese, which results in rivalries and a difficult positioning of belonging.

Finally, according to Gita, all of these language hierarchies, which should not exist following the *de jure* language policies, do not yet account for the increasing number of HLs at school and within society at large. Although her impression is that German is still the language imposed onto and expected by everyone, even though there are in fact many more immigrants, a greater plethora of languages, and a more successful integration thereof.

4.3.3 Students in Zurich

All students except for two who ranked Macedonian and Romansh as the most relevant chose Swiss German/German as their number one language in their personal lives. Twenty-five percent of the students considered 1–2 languages relevant for their personal lives, whereas four out of those 25% considered 'only' Swiss German/German to be relevant. The vast majority ranked English second after Swiss German/German; other HLs spoken at home or French, a language learned in school, came third in some of the students' answers. Furthermore, a few students who differentiated between Swiss German and German ranked the other variety second while they almost exclusively prioritized Swiss German over German.

Figure 16: Ranking the most significant language in their personal lives – ZH

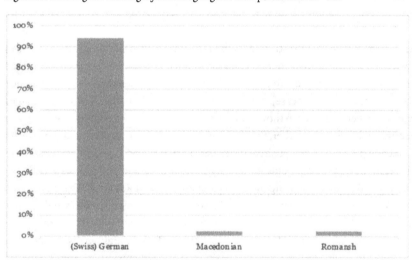

The hierarchies changed when students ranked languages according to their relevance for their professional or academic lives. Fifty percent of the students consider German and 8% Swiss German most important while 42% ranked English number one. Those who chose Swiss German/German as the most relevant language opted for English as their number two. While it is not present in all students' rankings, more than 60% ranked French third place in professional or academic contexts. Students chose at least two languages in this context, whereas the vast majority selected three languages. Generally, all Zurich students consider English to be more important than any other language (except for German) for their (future) careers.

Figure 17: Ranking the most significant language in their professional lives – ZH

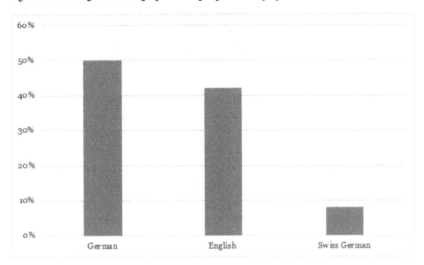

When asked whether they would prefer to first learn English or French in school as their L2, all except for 2 students answered that they prefer learning English before French. One answer was in favor of French and the other stated that it did not matter. Reasons for why they favored English were various; some even expressed their desire to stop learning French *tout court*, while others called for an earlier start of English at primary level. As succinctly summarized by Tobias: "English can be used for anything, anywhere, anytime." This is especially true for those in academic and scientific contexts in which they see their chances of succeeding greatly diminished without a proficient knowledge of English. In fact, English is no longer viewed as a specific skill, but is instead seen as a "basic requirement for anyone," as Mia reported. They perceive English as playing a major role in many spheres of Swiss society while French does not. The common attitude seems to be, as was stated by Peter: "The better you speak English, the better off you will be economically and personally." Finally, the reason why one student favored French over English was that French is a national language and is more difficult to learn than English.

Arthur, a speaker of Macedonian, is very well aware and exposed to language hierarchies and the ideologies associated therewith. According to him, most people to whom he speaks about his linguistic background are ignorant of different Slavic languages and naively group them together to simplify them. Although Macedonian is very important for his identity, he clearly prioritizes English: "I love English" (Arthur, 153). His passion for English is so great that he would like to move to the USA and have his future children grow up speaking English and not Macedonian. He feels this way due to the possibilities and prestige linked to English compared to Macedonian, which is often not even considered to be a language of its own and is instead associated with migrants of low socioeconomic status. That said, he is also concerned that English might be taking over other smaller languages. According to him, he realized too late that he was prioritizing English too heavily in school while he could have benefited from learning French and Italian. Similarly, Yasmin, whose L1 is Turkish, clearly favors English. Even if Turkish classes were offered in school, she would have chosen English because she perceives it to be much more relevant. Much like Arthur, she would like her future children to grow up speaking English since she associates it with a better life. According to her, ELF would improve communication within Switzerland if it were accepted as the common *lingua franca* and was not artificially suppressed by policies on the pretext of promoting national languages. Adya classified Swiss German as the most relevant language for her personally and professionally in the questionnaire and then explained during the interview that it was in fact English. She confessed having put Swiss German down first, thinking that it was the expected classification to demonstrate her 'Swissness.' She further revealed that prioritizing Swiss German was a role she has adapted to in school contexts in which she has the impression that this is expected of and beneficial to her. Nicolas, who considers both Swiss German and English to be his most significant languages, does not see them as necessarily competing against each other. Rather, he believes that English is very useful and indispensable for professional communication, but it is insufficient to be fully integrated in Swiss social and work life. Describing daily life at an international company in Zurich, such as Google whose working language is officially English, he believes that: "Sure, there are many foreigners…who work [there]. But finally, you won't speak English 40 hours a week because of this. The whole environment is still shaped by Switzerland and through this also the language" (Nicolas, 188–190).

He also makes suggestions on how to flatten the existing language hierarchies within Swiss society. English could lose its importance and give its place back to the national languages if more people from the different language regions played their part in understanding the other and meeting them halfway. If the national languages are prioritized, then more people will have the chance to speak their language and are less dependent upon ELF. Furthermore, this would require 'only' a passive knowledge of the other language. As Adya pointed out, however, even in a scenario such as the one described by Nicolas, there are huge discrepancies among and between each of the four national languages. The privileged position of majority languages is exemplified in the following quote taken from the interview with Samira. Applying the concept of *lingua franca*, she believes that communication in Switzerland would function best if everyone adopted one common language, in this case, German. Samira says:

> B: I think we should rather determine one of the four languages that we already have and not take on English in addition to this.
> A: And which one would that be?
> B: Well, since I don't speak Italian or Romansh, I think German or French. I also think that most people in Switzerland can speak German or French (120–126).

This example shows the extent to which monolingualism is still considered the norm and displays a homogeneous linguistic landscape that is more efficient for communication. Since she possesses language skills in German and French, she believes that one of those should be determined as the *lingua franca*. This simplistic deduction is made from a point of view that represents the privileged, majority language group's position.

4.3.4 Teachers in Zurich

Some teachers believe that multilingualism is not even necessarily a topic in the German-speaking part of Switzerland. Carmen, for instance, argues that the primary requirement to participate actively in society is to speak Swiss German/German; this implies that the co-existence of multiple languages and cultures may not be such a strong Swiss identity marker after all. The existing language hierarchy is nonetheless clear: Professional as well as private life is essentially based on Swiss German/German. As Nesrin put it: "I believe you simply have a great advantage if you already know how to speak German, when that's already a given" (Nesrin, 416–417). While the first place in the socially existing hierarchies is, thus, occupied by Swiss German/German, all teachers agree that English has become indispensable in society, media, education, and particularly in virtual lifeworlds. When contrasted with French, English is simply more embedded in Zurich's social reality than other (national) languages that status and relevance of which are generally regarded as rather low. Patrick, having grown up close to the French-German language border, laments this situation, recalling daily practices immersed in two languages and cultures as an adolescent and the positive impact that they have had on his life. He witnesses that the value of multilingualism and multiculturalism within Switzerland has deteriorated. He considers it to be very essential to be aware of the different linguistic and cultural traditions in Switzerland and their impact on national cohesion. Monolingual cantons in particular, and in those further away from the French- or Italian-speaking parts, have devalued the national languages and virtually replaced those with English. Patrick also sees it as the school's responsibility to reduce the existing language hierarchies as well as the tensions exacerbated through the language learning debate:

> I have the feeling that the Romandie registers this indifference of many German-speaking Swiss toward French with no small amount of indifference. I have the

> feeling that it's a bigger issue in the Romandie than vice versa because the German-speaking part of Switzerland is simply the majority. And I think the German-speaking part does have a certain responsibility to pay attention to other languages as well and not just look at these pragmatic arguments. And the school in particular has a central task, not only as a servant of the economy. I believe that schools should definitely be able to set other priorities as well. (287–294)

The choice to introduce English before another national language seems to be motivated economically, whereas Patrick sees a potential danger in internationally, market-oriented LEPs which ignore sociopolitical aspects on a national level. Additionally, schools face increasing accountability and have to justify their curriculum to more and more stakeholders. One of their primary concerns regarding upper secondary education in the German-speaking part of Switzerland is students' training in English as a preparation for international competition. Sabine argues that skills in ELF are most likely sufficient unless the company or institution has strong ties to the *Romandie* or France. This has become the new norm over the past decades, thereby inverting the prioritization of formerly national languages to ELF. Nesrin suggests that "we don't have to artificially counteract this [the dominance of English]" (Nesrin, 322), but cautions that in certain positions and contexts, these hierarchies exist and prioritize national languages over ELF, which can also prove problematic.

That said, although English is prioritized, FL teachers doubt that this has a significant impact on the majority of students' language skills. They unanimously agree that students learn English very quickly. The language hierarchy is, thus, rather ideology-laden since, as Sonja explains, the prioritization of English over French "is a bit of an insult to a part that also belongs to Switzerland" (Sonja, 239). Even from a competence-based point of view, more emphasis and resources would be needed in order to put another FL learned at school on the same level as English. Students seem to perceive the existing hierarchies but, as Patrick has experienced, are unable to first, deconstruct them and second, to see beyond English's utility and omnipresence. The educational policy decisions further reproduce these hierarchies and incorporate the neoliberal position that is oriented at international, economy-based exchanges in ELF. Given their majority status among the national languages, Swiss German/German speakers have the choice of which language they would like to prioritize, according to Sonja. A nation-wide solution that combines everyone's interest is, however, very complicated to find, as Sonja explained:

> I believe that's one of these decisions which can probably never be made satisfactorily because either you say, we want to remain competitive internationally, then it's clear for German-speaking Switzerland, that's English…But if we say, to keep the feeling of nationalism and language diversity, then it would be French. Although (-) then the Ticinese would have (--), then they wouldn't be

happy either because the first foreign language would be French and not Italian (256–262).

This passage demonstrates that the question of language order almost automatically implies the teaching of English and French when in fact Italian (or other languages) could also qualify as a compulsory language subject. Since two FLs are taught mandatorily in Zurich, the choice is habitually made in favor of French and English. As Tina explained, French has a larger speech community than Italian, which serves as a sociopolitical and economic argument. The subjects taught and the hours allocated thereto can also impact upon teacher education and the choice of study programs for future teachers. For instance, given the fewer employment possibilities with a major in Italian, Tina chose to prioritize French herself although she would have preferred Italian. Second, given Swiss German/German's powerful position in Switzerland, it is in their students' best interest to invest in another "very dominant" language (Patrick, 241) to compete on an international level.

That said, Sonja would understand if other parts of Switzerland also prioritized English over German. In fact, if all Swiss students started learning English first, then they would have the same language order in school and, thus, would have the same first FL which they could use to communicate more easily. Sonja suggested that ELF can reduce power dynamics and linguistic insecurity: "...so at least they both speak a foreign language...and are on equal footing. This to me is somehow also an advantage" (Sonja, 106–109).

Few include Italian and even fewer Romansh when talking about national languages. According to Sabine, Romansh does not necessarily deserve to be treated equally to the others since the relevance outside of Grisons is very limited and the pressure to include as many languages as possible is already high with French and English. The same is true for HLs, which are situated at the lower end of the language hierarchies. Elisabeth, referring to a professional experience that she had with an Albanian family, believes that HLs are important and should be spoken at home. However, she stated that she tended to:

> ...find it just as important that they, if they want to stay in Switzerland, necessarily also optimize German to the extent that they, as you were asking before, possibly (--) I have to formulate it differently, that German is not an obstacle for their professional career. (432–435)

Stressing the importance that Swiss German in particular has in all social spheres, Elisabeth believes that migrants coming to Switzerland and intending to stay need to classify Swiss German at least as importantly as their L1:

> I really think, one's own language identity, the one you are born into, that you grew up with, that is important. But when you live in a different country

you simply have to adopt a second language identity. That's my clear position. Otherwise, it doesn't work. (458–461)

This quote demonstrates that first different language hierarchies exist for private and public spaces and that they are accepted according to different criteria developed by each individual's stance and underlying ideology toward each language. Second, it shows that language ideologies, as in this case, by teachers and backed up by LEPs, can have a positive or negative impact on students' integration, well-being, and educational trajectory depending on what language they speak.

4.3.5 Students in Fribourg

A slight majority of Fribourg students (55%) ranked French their number one language in their personal lives. Other languages that were ranked as most relevant were English, Italian, Cantonese, Spanish, and German. Japanese was ranked second and Portuguese third by two students respectively. All except for one considered (at least) one of the canton's official languages – German or French – to be very important to their personal lives in addition to other HLs. English was a top 3 language for 75% of the students. Unlike the students in Zurich, there were no single-language answers for their personal lives; all students chose at least two languages of importance for their personal lives.

Figure 18: Ranking the most significant language in their personal lives – FR

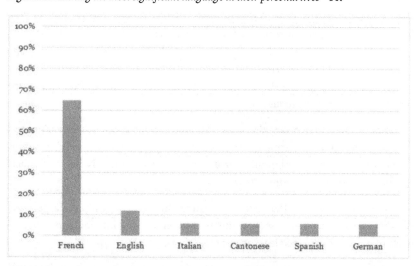

Professionally, 65% considered French to be the most relevant language. The rest ranked German or English as more relevant for their professional lives. More precisely, 65% prioritize German over English for their (future) careers. There was one single-language answer for students' professional/academic context, which was French.

Figure 19: Ranking the most significant language in their professional lives – FR

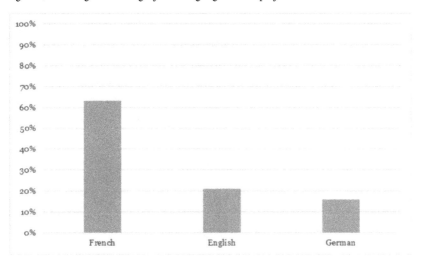

Unlike Zurich and Grisons, 70% of Fribourg students would *not* prioritize English over German if they could. They believe that English is easier to learn, which is why it should *not* be taught before German so that more time can be spent on learning the more difficult language. The main argument is based on the French-speaking part's dependency on German-speaking Switzerland economically and politically, however. Students express concerns that if German lost its place at school, that "it would separate us more from the German-speaking part of Switzerland." They further state that "without German, everything is pretty hard to achieve in Switzerland." For instance, they explained that if they wanted to become a teacher, then they would need a relatively high (B2) level of German to enter teacher education schools. They perceive German to be very important for almost any profession after graduating from upper secondary school. Many students do not feel the need to change anything because "it works well the way it is" and "the tradition has always been like this." They are less interested in changing the *status quo*, especially given the fact that German is Switzerland's majority language. Those students who would rather learn English before German, which make up 30% of the answers, argue that it is an internationally important language that can be used anywhere. While German is very specific to the Swiss context, they perceive English to be equivalent to globalization and life without borders. Its ostensible neutrality is appealing and makes it more interesting to learn.

4.3.6 Teachers in Fribourg

For teachers in Fribourg, language hierarchies are a social reality to which they are exposed daily when working in a space in which two otherwise geographically separate language groups come together and interact. These language hierarchies, as Jeanne believes, are shaped by underlying forces that partly result from the canton's linguistic composition. Contrary to Switzerland's overall linguistic landscape in which Swiss German/German dominates French, the latter is the majority language in the canton of Fribourg. Victoria deduces that the tense situation between the German- and French-speaking population is the result of historically evolving "German-French crises" (Victoria, 188). She explained that:

> [F]or instance, in Ticino, (-) so the Italian-speaking canton, the way of dealing (-), the natural way of dealing with the French and the German language is much more equitable, it's much more given than, for instance, in the French-speaking canton where German MUST be learned or in the German-speaking cantons where French is learned. There, such a friction becomes noticeable for me and I think it would be pretty good if you counteract this. To reduce prejudices, etc. and that you don't consider the other language as a competitor but as an enrichment (190–197).

These tensions are also noticeable even if, as Luisa summarized it, the *status quo* is French and is undoubtedly the school's most important language. That said, it is undeniable that German is crucial, especially in professional contexts, as Victoria pointed out: "Everyone who works in a reputable profession can speak both languages, well or very well. I believe that this is already almost a requirement" (Victoria, 139–141). Jeanne explained that the existing language ideologies, and some of the tensions, result from demonstratively taking advantage of the French majority position and intentionally treating Swiss German/German as inferior, possibly in response to the situation on a national level.

Language laws and other cantonal policies do not depict social reality, according to Etienne, even though both languages are *de jure* equal. He argued that first, the already existing laws for equal treatment are neither implemented nor controlled. Second, they discriminate against significant languages within society such as Portuguese, Turkish, or Serbian, thereby reproducing language hierarchies: "Of course, they are not indigenous languages, but even the word indigenous gets a new meaning in today's society" (Etienne, 124–125). That said, by excluding those languages from his classes, he establishes a clear hierarchy himself, in which German not only has a privileged position but is in fact the only accepted language. As an experienced German teacher, he has witnessed the resistance and difficulties that some students have learning GFL, leading him to question its meaningfulness altogether. To him, it is much more sensible to accept ELF as the medium of communication within Switzerland, to overtly accept the language hierarchy that already exists covertly, and to reduce classes in national languages. He argued that it would be more efficient and less of a burden for students and teachers if English could be introduced before German. He further argued that German and higher levels of English should be made optional while ELF classes should be mandatory to guarantee (and possibly expand) communication with other language regions. Luisa is also rather skeptical when it comes to arguments presented by policy makers and politicians in favor of national languages, such as mutual understanding and social cohesion. According to her, these are used as a pretext to pursue romantic ideals of the so-called *Willensnation*, a well-functioning nation-state comprised of four different languages and cultures united by will. This is seemingly a necessary policy strategy to cover voices of dissent: "Actually, very little holds it [Switzerland] together and it's actually a miracle, the so-called special case Switzerland, really an exception. Very special. I also don't know what holds us together culturally" (Etienne, 276–279). As Luisa pointed out, as long as everyone is satisfied financially and the society is generally well off, then no more profound questions are asked which would challenge the *status quo*. The language learning debate, however, does exactly this and calls into question the public perception of the harmonious, solitary *Willensnation*.

Other teachers generally described ELF's omnipresence in Switzerland and the danger it represents for the national (minority) languages as a big loss. For Jeanne, it is very regrettable that certain Swiss cantons prioritize English over French, which would not be possible if LEP decisions were made federally. She is of the opinion that the 'language question' should be answered unanimously and should be implemented equally in every canton. David considers the language order in favor of the national languages to be an advantage for students, noting that is not at all acknowledged by them as such. Then again, Luisa believes that the language order is irrelevant since students' preference of English is becoming stronger, even despite the school's emphasis on the national languages. Nevertheless, Jeanne is pleased with both the canton's and the school's policies respecting Switzerland's linguistic composition. Contrarily, David perceives the 'over-emphasizing' of German and English or Spanish and the neglecting of some students' L1s as a huge problem. Without social or official recognition, students' L1s are further devalued within the school and by themselves. That is, on the one hand, students who happen to have English or Spanish as L1, are asked to integrate it actively into teaching and are praised for their language skills; on the other hand, though, speakers of Portuguese, Albanian, Czech, or Croatian are punished twice: Not only are their L1s undesired at school, thereby making it impossible to showcase their AL skills, but their L1 also places a burden on them by depriving them of the status of 'true' (monolingual) native speakers of French. According to Victoria, these different values and perspectives on languages exist since they are always linked to spaces and people. She does not believe that ELF can ease the tensions between German and French or among their speakers since no language is neutral and those that already exist need more social and institutional recognition.

4.4 'Native-Speaker' and 'Standard-Speech' Ideologies

> The concepts of '(non-)native speaker' and '(non-)standard language' express romantic and rationalist ideals and are reproduced and legitimized by the education system.

The study's data analysis revealed that participants almost equally aim at a native-like language proficiency when learning or teaching a language. This is illustrated by the fact that they (almost all) strongly agree to prefer AE or BE over a 'Swiss variety of English' in the classroom or in textbooks. The underlying standard speech ideology is, however, less explicit for Swiss German versus SSG. Many are torn between Swiss German as an important identity marker and SSG as a valuable language, both academically and professionally.

4.4.1 Students in Grisons

Sub-hierarchies including native speaker and standard speech ideologies exist among students in Grisons for German, English, and Romansh. SSG expectations in school can be challenging for Romansh speakers in specific, who are also exposed to Swiss German in Grisons' society in addition to their L1. For Jessica, these expectations and the lacking practice of SSG make her afraid of presentations in class. She is stressed about making grammatical mistakes or having to look for words that would delegitimize her German language skills and embarrass her in front of the class. The following extract, taken from the interview with André, illustrates this complex situation further:

> B: ...we always only speak Swiss German.
> A: This is for you of higher value then than Schriftdeutsch [written German] or Schuldeutsch [school German] (-).
> B: Yes, it's much more complicated to speak.
> A: Because you never learned it except in school?

B: Yes, and in school, we never really spoke it. With a teacher or a presentation or two at most.
A: But you have it as a subject in school, right?
B: Yes, we have it in school, so, in school, you learn standard German, written standard German of course. You speak it a little but it's a written language.
A: And if you were to go to Germany, how would you speak?
B: Well, Swiss German. (85–104)

It is very clear from André's explanations that Swiss German is the more important language, and that SSG is almost entirely reduced to its written function. Furthermore, André does not consider SSG to be more valuable because it corresponds to the fixed standards. Instead, he would rather speak Swiss German even in Germany, a country often associated in Switzerland with dialect-free standard speech. Others confessed that they are ashamed and very self-conscious about their German skills, which often do not correspond to the prescriptive standard speech conventions, in their own assessment. Paradoxically, although they feel more at ease using Swiss German, they can still sometimes better express themselves in SSG since the vocabulary is more varied and also covers more formal registers. Most agree that it is, therefore, sensible to teach SSG and not Swiss German because otherwise they would not have any exposure at all and would lose out on an important skill. Others, however, would favor Swiss German in school instead, justifying it with the special status that it has within Switzerland.

Concerning students' sub-hierarchies of English, they seem heavily influenced by (social) media, the film industry, and sometimes by the reputation of the countries themselves, but also considerably by the varieties used by their English teachers. For instance, Jessica justifies her preferred English variety: "…because our English teacher only speaks AE with us and then you've internalized this" (Jessica, 144–145). Students also associate AE with an interesting and fascinating language that might lead to a new life far away and in a culture different from the one they know. Hanna, who has visited the US before, says: "I believe, I can identify more with them [Americans] because I've already been there and I've tried to adopt the language" (Hanna, 203–204). According to her, the best way to speak English is to make proper distinctions among the varieties and to stick to one. This is the experience that she has in school where the textbooks showcase BE, while her teacher speaks AE. Christine, conversely, chose BE since it is the variety used by her teacher and she thinks that it is the one that is expected to be used in school. Timo differentiates between English used in school and in his spare time. While he considers BE to be the standard variety for school, he prefers and uses ELF especially in online communication. As Timo explains, it was particularly due to his ELF practice that he improved his English, not the BE he was taught and learned in school:

> [F]or almost two years I played this game almost every night; there were Polish people, English people from all over the world people came together, a couple from India and you really had to communicate with them, make plans, really every day actually 2–3 hours, I spoke English. I then noticed my progress myself, I felt more confident. If you can use it a lot, *especially because we didn't have any native speakers with us*, so real English people, but a Polish person with his English and the Swiss person, then everyone is on the same level. Then you dare more easily to simply start talking…They [Indians] spoke English very well, but with a strong accent and that's why you also dared. In school it's BE; everyone is familiar with it, that's high level… (244–266 [emphasis added]).

While Timo approaches English from a rather pragmatic point of view, Jana and Melina disagree. For Jana: "…the goal would be to, when you graduate university, to be perfectly proficient. I mean, absolutely perfect" (Jana, 148–149). Melina, very aware of the difficulties that come with speaking English to native-like level, says that: "I actually try to speak BE as well as possible. It isn't all the distinct vowels that I use, rather in an attenuated way, but I just try [to speak] as well as possible" (Melina, 280–282). Generally, students were very aware of and adamant about the language levels, creating sub-sub-hierarchies based on their proficiency, such as classified in the CEFR within the sub-hierarchies of different varieties of English. A common goal for all of the students was achieving level C1 in a 'school-accepted' variety – AE or BE – while some even aimed for (and achieved) level C2 (described as 'native-like' by the CEFR).

Finally, the political decision to create a Romansh standard language out of three (but not all five) Romansh idioms causes systemic sub-hierarchies and controversy among their speakers. For instance, as Timo explained, educational policy makers decided to fund textbooks in the standardized language RG, but not in specific Romansh idioms. That said, many students are in favor of RG, support prioritizing a standard language for school, and use their own idiom as a family language. Unlike with German or English, where a historically established and ideology-laden distinction between the standard and non-standard variety exists, most students' concern was a different one. As mentioned previously, Romansh speakers are singled out at school due to their use of iPads and self-created teaching materials in the given idiom. Some argue that RG could unify Romansh-speaking students and end the special treatment, as a result of the absence of missing textbooks. Others say that RG should be limited to writing and that one's own idiom could still be used for verbal communication. This would be problematic for students enrolled in the Romansh-speaking program who do not speak it as their L1, however. For those, RG is often the only option to learn it since it has standardized grammatical rules and a dictionary.

4.4.2 Teachers in Grisons

The data collected in teachers' interviews revealed that the language sub-hierarchies that exist on a societal level are exacerbated and legitimized in the education system. Martin's experience, for instance, is a strong indicator of this. He explains that in order for his wife to become a teacher in a Swiss public school she first had to learn Swiss German, even though she was already a proficient speaker of both SSG and Romansh. While this was incomprehensible to Martin, Henri argued that many teachers in Grisons would in fact like to teach in Swiss German, not in SSG. Roberto, who teaches in the Italian-German bilingual program, agreed that emotions can be much better expressed through dialect. For him, as a native speaker of Italian and often surrounded by Swiss German in society, speaking a dialect also comes with less pressure. He feels less insecure when speaking Swiss German than when speaking SSG and, simultaneously, feels a stronger connection to his students. Within his native language Italian, he also differentiates between the standard language and the dialect. Growing up as a speaker of Italian dialect, he considers it "the language of the heart" (Roberto, 26). Whereas Roberto's perception of his dialect is both positive and emotionally enriching, Henri cautions that these native speaker and standard speech ideologies have a felt negative impact on individuals. The existing stereotypes and prejudices associated with certain accents influence how speakers are both viewed and valued in society. He believes that accents that deviate from a certain norm are responsible for why individuals themselves are devalued. He cites the example that somebody from upper Surselva, a valley region in Grisons, is said to be "a second category person" (Henri, 344). This is due to its former economically weaker position and strong focus on agriculture. That said, he witnesses a certain generational change that is impeding the reproduction of such stereotypes. Henri further believes that certain standard accents carry prestige, but those people who recognize certain varieties or accents as being more prestigious than others "out themselves as highly superficial" (Henri, 348). He argued that such sub-hierarchies and ideologies are inappropriate, particularly in Switzerland, a country heavily shaped by the dominant, non-standard Swiss German. On the contrary, "when somebody shows up with his *bühnendeutschen Akzent* [professionally trained standard German accent in actors], that's rather negative" (Henri, 357–358). According to him, standard language is not considered to be as important as it is in Germany. Generally, the comparison between the linguistic situation in Germany and Switzerland is a recurrent theme. It often results in a rather inferior, submissive positioning on the part of Swiss-German speakers having to justify themselves for being more proficient in Swiss German than SSG.

When asked about their linguistic repertoire, Martin, for instance, did not name English as part of it. At a later stage during the interview, he then revealed that he specifically did not mention English because he does not feel entirely comfortable speaking it and would not feel competent enough to teach bilingually. The Cambridge First Certificate in English (B2 level), which he completed after a stay abroad, certifies an advanced level with which he feels at ease. Not only does it function as 'proof' of his English competency, but its issuer – Cambridge Assessment as part of the University of Cambridge – also attests to the knowledge of a prestigious variety. Nicole, already fascinated by the BE accent during her own schooltime, recalls feeling ashamed for trying to sound native-like. She explained that not many were able to imitate the accent 'correctly' and wanting to do so made her stand out. After her training to become an English teacher herself and after multiple stays abroad, she feels rather proud to be recognized by English native speakers as one of them. She explains that she has appropriated the language, which is inextricably linked to her own way of speaking and even her identity. Although it is important for her to speak a native-speaker English as a role model for her students, it is not a primary teaching objective to make them sound like her. That said, as the findings above suggest, students are influenced by the variety spoken by their teachers and sometimes even intentionally adopt it to achieve 'true native-like proficiency,' something about which teachers might be unaware.

4.4.3 Students in Zurich

Given its importance and omnipresence in the canton of Zurich, the uncontestably highest-ranked variety is Swiss German, or more precisely, the local variety thereof. That said, Adya, for instance, received compliments for her standard German accent in school, which for her was a very positive experience.

For Arthur, the native-speaker and standard speech ideologies to which he is exposed in Swiss German/German and Macedonian have had felt consequences on his identity and sense of belonging. As mentioned previously, he is not accepted either as a native speaker in Macedonia nor in Switzerland since his language skills are compared to a monolingual standard. In his case, it seems that Macedonian influences his German language skills and vice versa. His desire to be a native speaker of AE is so big that he learns expressions used by "Americans, be it Kanye West or Whitney Houston [or] Michael Jackson" off by heart (Arthur, 158–159). He believes that if somebody is really interested in a language, then they will learn how to speak it in a native-like fashion. Although his own goal is to be a full native speaker of AE, he doubts that he could ever lose his accent entirely. That said, he also believes that accents indicate someone's origins and can, therefore, be a legitimate accessory to a language. According to him, there are certain contexts which require a higher proficiency in the standard language: "When I see someone like Ueli Maurer [Swiss Federal Councilor] [in] the interview with CNN, where he embarrasses himself in English...this is how the international community simply sees us then" (Arthur, 350–352). Others are less focused on AE, but also list BE and Australian English as desirable, native-speaker varieties. According to Adya, other English varieties such as Indian English are discussed in class, but these have apparently not yet obtained the same legitimacy as the 'Inner Circle' varieties. Conversely, Nicolas has a more pragmatic opinion: "…proficiency is always good, there's nothing against being able to speak a language really well, but to expect this from every citizen in the world, no" (Nicolas, 161–163). For him, prioritizing a certain native-speaker variety, such as BE, would automatically endanger people's other L1s. The already existing predominance of English would only be exacerbated if individuals were expected to achieve native-like competency.

4.4.4 Teachers in Zurich

Similar to the teachers in Grisons, Zurich teachers generally do not view native-speaker proficiency as their primary teaching objective. Sonja witnesses an increasingly diverse linguistic landscape on a global scale and argued that "…they [students] have to deal with so many accents. Whether they muddle through with a Swiss German accent or not, I find, that's not such an important goal I pursue" (Sonja, 54–56). When it comes to her own English language skills, she considers it important to be proficient, alluding to a native-speaker competency. She would like her students to be exposed to a "hopefully good pronunciation…so that they pick it up automatically" (Sonja, 63–64). She believes that textbooks should primarily make use of native speakers. More precisely: "They don't have to necessarily always be speakers or AE, but I find it nice if they are native speakers. So that they [students] really have this as their primary goal, a certain accent will remain anyways" (Sonja, 65–67). While she does not attribute much importance to native-speaker varieties, arguing that this is more compatible with the diverse linguistic landscape at first, she then stated her preference for exactly those over non-standard English varieties. This contradiction illustrates the complex underlying ideology and how entrenched the native-speaker concept is in language teaching. Sabine further explains that the native-speaker ideology is inherently part of the education system. One of the most important admission conditions for Swiss teacher education in order to become a language teacher is a stay in a country in which the language is spoken as official L1. The idea is to acquire the language from those native speakers as proficiently as possible so that they can then transmit this linguistic resource to Swiss students. Sabine then also justified and legitimized her own English language skills with multiple stays abroad pointing out that she learned English with Australians, Americans, and Brits. Thus, while she speaks BE and explains that "native speaker is my goal but it's not my goal that the students copy this exactly from me," (Sabine, 33–34) she also accepts AE: "If they decide for various reasons to adopt or to train an American accent, due to stays abroad or watching films, then that's totally fine of course" (Sabine, 34–36). This passage shows once again that the two most commonly used English varieties – BE and

AE – are retained and reproduced through the education system. Other less common varieties are rather lacking in school and are not mentioned at all. Patrick, who has not had as much exposure to English, believes that language hierarchies exist in favor of prestigious varieties and do not play the same role in all social spheres. For instance, he perceives ELF to be widely accepted and sometimes even preferred on a professional basis in Switzerland. As he explains, this is true because English functions primarily as a transmitter of information in these contexts.

The social and emotional components of professional interactions still largely draw on Swiss German. That said, Patrick is very adamant about speaking SSG in class and that judging students' exposure thereto as very important. Sonja agreed, recognizing a potential problem in immersion programs since students might become less proficient in SSG, given that it is primarily associated with school and rarely used outside thereof. Swiss German, and more precisely the local variety and accent that its speakers have, is a means to identify oneself and to be identified as a legitimate member of a certain speech community. All teachers agree that Swiss German is by far the most common and natural way of communicating in the canton of Zurich and is a necessary condition to participate actively in social life. For Elisabeth, Swiss German gives her an additional voice in the classroom, one that has a more profound impact on students. Switching between Swiss German and SSG, she can emphasize content differently, ease tensions, make jokes, point out the seriousness, and create proximity or distance. When asked if everyone was able to follow classes if part of it was in Swiss German, she said that virtually everyone did with few exceptions. She recalled a Polish student who did not understand Swiss German "but she didn't resist. Then she would have been an outsider" (Elisabeth, 31).

Additionally, there are exchange students who are treated differently linguistically depending on where they come from. For Elisabeth, it goes without saying that she speaks SSG with *international* exchange students, who typically stay for one year and are only familiar with the standard variety, if at all. For exchange students from the *Romandie*, who stay three to six months, the expectation of their (advanced) SSG skills and social integration is higher. While Elisabeth and fellow students speak SSG at the beginning, they also speak Swiss German since "otherwise, social life in Switzerland simply doesn't work enough" (Elisabeth, 43).

Finally, Swiss German is not openly part of the curriculum, yet the sole focus on SSG is problematic for Elisabeth: "And the students who come from primary school, they are altogether extremely conditioned to speak standard German in school, also in group activities" (Elisabeth, 50–51). SSG is the state-imposed language and is perceived as such by almost all participants. Eleonore, a speaker of standard German, notices different behavior and expectations by both students and parents. First, she considers herself to be more tolerant toward students' academic language skills in German, taking the view that most students only really learn SSG when they enter school into consideration. Second, students, have the impression that, due to her standard German background, she is stricter when it comes to mistakes and assessments. Third, parents' attitudes reveal the underlying language hierarchies vividly. Greatly satisfied with their children's exposure to 'authentic' and 'real' standard German, they believe that their children will benefit from it more in their future since it is the (more) prestigious, internationally used variety.

4.4.5 Teachers in Fribourg

The overall language learning objective does not seem to be native-like competency, but rather the completion of a certain proficiency level that is determined by the CEFR and by the curriculum. One of the recurrent challenges, which German teachers and learners face in particular, is Swiss German's high status and wide-spread use. It is a very controversial topic, so much so that not all teachers are ready to openly talk about it: "It's difficult for me to comment, I'm not a German teacher. I find it difficult. I don't have an opinion on this" (Jeanne, 180–181). For David, these ideologies are very hard to understand and impact his teaching. While he strives to promote the exchange among students across the language border, his experience shows that many French-speaking students would rather go to Germany than to the German-speaking part of Switzerland. For them, the language that they learn in school is more closely linked to the one spoken in Germany than the local dialects found in Switzerland and are often considered to be the 'real' German. Luisa even questioned the concept of *language* altogether. More precisely, given that Swiss German and SSG fulfil different functions and are used in different contexts, they might very well be defined as two different languages. Victoria's teaching experience reveals that, although many students have a migrant background, they are not used to seeing one in their teachers. Rather, they are typically accustomed to French-speaking or French-German bilingual teachers with a Swiss cultural background. Whenever she speaks French, students react to her accent and basic speaking skills exposing her as 'non-native' and view her as 'deviating' from the norm. Accents can, thus, create otherness and make people vulnerable if they do not meet the native-like standard. As mentioned previously, speaking a low-valued HL (such as Albanian or Czech) can also result in the devaluation of their proficiency in the local language for migrant students. That is, some teachers reported that some of their bilingual students considered themselves or are portrayed by others as less 'pure/legitimate' speakers of the local school language, which can result in questioning their language skills overall.

4.5 Symbolic Violence

> Linguistic prejudices and discrimination result in symbolic violence to the detriment of speakers' well-being, self-confidence, the development of their linguistic repertoires, and successful language teaching in schools.

Some participants' lived experiences of language show that well established, discriminatory stereotypes, and prejudices can turn into symbolic violence and can stigmatize individuals. They are also a substantial barrier in language learning in schools, which could make a meaningful contribution to deconstructing and reducing them. Instead, they provide the institutional space for them to be reproduced, something that is detrimental to individuals' (linguistic) well-being and self-confidence and to Switzerland's intercantonal cohesion and understanding.

4.5.1 Students in Grisons

More Romansh speakers were confronted with linguistic prejudices and discrimination than Swiss German speakers among the students interviewed. The general tendency as reported by students, however, is that those are decreasing for the new generation of Romansh speakers with more equitable cantonal language policies and support positively eroding this negative trend. That said, certain ideologies and systemic inequities persist to the detriment of minority language speakers. Leonie, for instance, learned growing up that Romansh speakers are associated with "peasants" and "hillbillies" within Swiss society (Leonie, 33), even though she says that such terms have never been used with her personally. Jessica believes that Romansh speakers are mocked for speaking a minority language that is not valued to the same extent as the other national languages and for speaking Swiss German/SSG with potentially more mistakes than those who have it as their (sole) L1. This led her to speak more Swiss German, even though she notices that mainly Swiss German speakers do not know about Romansh or, if they do, that they do not accept it as a legitimate national language. Timo shares the same perspective:

> [T]hat's impressive for most that you do the *Matura* bilingually, that it's heavily promoted because it's not known at all that the language is still alive and that it's taught in school. For many it's just (-), in Zurich they think that only the old peasants in the mountains speak it... (66–69).

Others also mention that the ignorance *vis-à-vis* their L1 within Switzerland, or the arrogance perceived in the case of Zurich in specific, can be hurtful and illustrates that they feel rather powerless due to their speech community's small size. André and Sebastian regret that political discussions constantly exclude Romansh and its speakers and that they would not even be able to follow those if it were not for their bilingual language skills in German. There are almost no translations into Romansh and this creates a dependency on learning German and disregards their legal status of equal languages on a cantonal level. As André describes it, he does not necessarily feel disadvantaged since he can follow the news and media thanks to German, but it makes him "a bit upset" (André, 306). He goes on to say that "every time it's German, French, Italian. The worst, I find, is rather a press release with the national languages and ENGLISH" (André, 306–308). He implies that English, despite not being an official language in Switzerland, is sometimes taken more seriously and put in a powerful position of news and information circulation. Addressing foreigners and/or those unable to speak one of the national languages, he finds it unfair that the local population is deprived of their right to information in their L1-national language. On an individual, personal basis, it makes them feel less valued than Swiss German speakers. That said, André specifically stressed that linguistic discrimination was much worse 20 years ago and has already been heavily reduced by activist groups for linguistic rights, policies, and by substantial financial support.

Although linguistic discrimination seems to be decreasing, the experiences Romansh-speaking students shared are still alarming. In addition to the sometimes already difficult status they have due to Romansh, they are also discriminated against for not speaking French. As mentioned previously, French is not a compulsory language to be learned in Grisons' upper secondary schools despite the wide-spread assumption that all Swiss students learn both German and French. This assumption then also leads to discriminatory experiences such as the one Hanna had with a French-speaking student during a national sports tournament:

> [O]ne time, somebody asked me, you can't speak French? No, I don't have French in school, which is actually a bit of a disadvantage because I just have Romansh. Then I said, no, I have Romansh instead and then he said, you can't make use of THAT language anyway (38–42).

Melina said that instead of taking such comments personally, "Romands don't like to speak German although they actually can. So then I don't know that we should accommodate them although they can speak German and that would be so much easier" (Melina, 233–235). Others who have barely any experience with learning French in school believe that the language was too complicated to learn, its pronunciation was impossible to acquire for German speakers, or simply stated that "I really don't like French anyways" (Jovin, 148). Leonie, for instance, has the impression that "it's almost easier if a French-speaking person learns German than the other way round" (Leonie, 176–177). Thus, not all students feel responsible for not speaking French and instead find reasons elsewhere. Leonie further talked about stereotypes that exist about the *Romandie*. A common one is likening the *Romands* to the French and believing that people in France "eat frogs and such things" (Leonie, 52).

4.5.2 Teachers in Grisons

As the only trilingual canton in Switzerland, Grisons holds a special position within the otherwise dominant, officially monolingual linguistic landscape. The participants argue that plurilinguals are discriminated against since this *de jure* monolingual habitus is still widely accepted as the norm outside of Grisons. The social expectation still seems to be, as some teachers suggest, that an individual must have *one* L1; being bi- or trilingual is considered abnormal. Gita herself experienced shame for also speaking Romansh, not just Swiss German like everyone else. That said, not speaking Swiss German implies a loss in value of the speakers themselves. Growing up, she was forced to speak Swiss German with her mother, arguing that speaking Swiss German like anyone else would save her from embarrassment and linguistic insecurity. This led her to appropriate Swiss German and to neglect Romansh. Similar to the students' accounts who perceive a general attitude change toward Romansh, younger teachers seem less affected by such symbolic violence.

4.5.3 Students in Zurich

Although migrants from the Balkan region are well represented in the canton of Zurich, Arthur reported that speakers of Slavic languages stand out since they have a more aggressive pronunciation in German and make many grammatical mistakes. In his opinion, the canton of Zurich is responsible for many existing linguistic prejudices within Switzerland since it holds a special position, both politically and economically, and claims to have the 'purest' variety of Swiss German: "I certainly think that especially in Zurich, that Zurich looks down a bit on other cantons, especially on the cantons with a different language" (Arthur, 372–374). This condescending behavior becomes visible through the treatment of the French- and Italian-speaking parts of Switzerland as 'illegitimate.' More precisely, he explains that they are typically referred to simply as 'the French' or 'the Italians' respectively, alluding to the language they share with the neighboring countries. Arthur shared an experience that he had with his brother when watching Swiss news: "...'hey, look these French people.' They are actually not French. Or also in Ticino, 'haha the Italians with the Coronavirus', are not Italians in the end. We're not Germans either" (Arthur, 369–371). While his brother calls them 'French' and 'Italians' respectively, Arthur perceives this to be inappropriate and likens it to their situation and the wrongful comparison with Germans. He also noted that in the end, despite the common language with the neighboring countries, they are still Swiss and belong to the same country. For Samira, learning French is not only a burden, but is also linked to cultural miscommunication and misunderstandings. While she thinks that "French sounds a bit stupid" (Samira, 61), she is fed up with *Romands* who visibly do not make any effort to speak German when they come to the German-speaking part of Switzerland:

> We also had to learn French and the Romands almost force us to speak French. I've already met many people from the Romandie who came to Zurich and continued to speak in French. They should just speak German if they already learn it in school. (140–144)

One solution, according to Samira, would be to agree on one intercantonal language and to guarantee the teaching of it in school so that no extra effort or adaptation would be required of anyone in such encounters. Although this is a potential solution for intercantonal communication, the language for intra-cantonal communication in Zurich is undoubtedly Swiss German. Many participants from the German-speaking part show very little tolerance toward individuals who are not (yet) speakers of the local variety. In Adya's case, this resulted in discrimination against her lacking Swiss German skills and the forced learning thereof. During the interview, Adya spoke twice about an experience that she had at school when preparing for an internship, which is a mandatory part of the curriculum:

> A: With friends, in school, you speak Swiss German?
> B: Yes, but only since the second upper grade. Basically because my teacher forced me halfway because Swiss German would have been better for the applications when I was at job interviews or the introductory internship. Before, I had always understood it, in school, during the breaks, everyone speaks Swiss German all the time, of course. I never spoke it myself, I was used to speaking German and then I had to change my habits in the second upper grade and now I speak Swiss German with my friends and at home and at school (-). (61–69)

Later in the interview, when she spoke about her rankings within the questionnaire in which she classified Swiss German as her most important language both personally and professionally, Adya justified herself for so doing:

> Because I live here in Switzerland and with my friends and because of this application for the introductory internship. That's why it's relatively important, simply because I live here…So I think, it's simply good when people know that you (--) I've grown up here, you can't really tell when you see me for the first time. My hip-hop teacher was always confused and he always talked German with me and I talked to him in Swiss German…I think they've inculcated me with that, I shall simply speak Swiss German so that you also recognize that I'm completely integrated here (284–300).

Both passages depict that speaking Swiss German for Adya was not a result of her own free choice. It was (unconsciously) forced onto her, thereby also impacting her personal life since she completely switched from standard German to Swiss German in all social spheres thereafter.

4.5.4 Teachers in Zurich

Interviewing students and teachers in Zurich revealed that certain linguistic prejudices are well-established and span across generations. A commonly cited stereotype was that although *Romands* learned German in school, they did not make much effort to actually speak it with them. The common impression was that it was up to the German speakers to speak French and not vice versa. Eleonore's experience with today's students shows that the lack of knowledge about life in the *Romandie* is still prone to the reproduction of stereotypes. Students asking her: "Is there also TV in French in Switzerland?" (Eleonore, 247–248) is an example of such obliviousness and demonstrates the missing interaction, especially among young Swiss people from different language regions.

Other prejudices, mentioned previously in the students' interviews, regarded the value that was attributed to the many different Swiss German varieties. Similar to the stereotypes existing around the distinct Romansh idioms, the Swiss German varieties spoken in the more rural parts are typically associated with the remote lifestyle of the mountains. Sabine also explained that her dialect is often referred to as 'nice' or 'cute' implying a less serious language and potentially even speakers. In Zurich, she is often asked where she originally comes from, often alluding to her non-local way of speaking. At the same time, this very accent is seen as a legitimator by which to obtain access to the speech community in her home village. However, since she has lived and worked in the canton of Zurich, she has adopted certain linguistic features of the Zurich variety, which have not gone unnoticed by inhabitants of her home village: "…people I grew up with who confirm 'oh you now have adopted this Zurich dialect,' a bit like betrayal…they don't consider it so positively" (Sabine, 332–335). The feeling of betrayal is likely to be exacerbated by the fact that the linguistic features that Sabine integrated in her more rural variety are taken from a prestigious, more urban Swiss German variety; this, in itself, is another linguistic prejudice. These existing prejudices, and the way they are triggered through the different accents, delegitimize Sabine's belonging to a speech community and make her justify herself for her own idiolect in both spaces.

Eleonore, who grew up speaking a dialect-free, standard variety of German, conversely, has accepted to be 'detected' as 'German.' Having lived in Switzerland for many years and having attempted to learn Swiss German unsuccessfully, she perceives a certain lack of integration, which would usually be established through the local dialect. She thus feels rather foreign, even though she is not discriminated against for speaking German. Her children speak Swiss German and do not accept her as a legitimate speaker of 'their' language. Generally, the norm is to speak Swiss German, which is not only the most common way of communicating, as well as a very powerful marker of belonging, but it can also function as a tool to exacerbate linguistic prejudices.

4.5.5 Teachers in Fribourg

Living in a canton through which the French-German language border runs, participants have a much more direct exposure to the two national languages and cultures. Jeanne is, therefore, convinced that the canton of Fribourg is an excellent example of lived bilingualism much in contrast to other regions in Switzerland. Although confessing to never having spent much time there, she believes that those cantons close to the borders with Germany, Italy, Austria, and France neither take Swiss multilingualism very seriously nor practice it on a daily basis. While Jeanne has a rather positive attitude toward Fribourg's bilingualism and biculturalism, other colleagues are more concerned, with some even considering the underlying reason for unsuccessful FL learning being linguistic prejudices. According to David, there are many historically established prejudices against German as a language but also its speakers, which makes GFL classes much more difficult than, for instance, EFL classes. A deconstruction of such prejudices would be necessary and helpful to improve motivation for and interest in language and culture. His French-speaking students are convinced that their fellow students in the German-speaking part do not like them, that they cannot communicate due to the dialect with which the *Romands* are unfamiliar and that they would be lost if they were to participate in an exchange, for instance. Other common stereotypes found among Romands are "that the German-speaking Swiss are boring, very narrow-minded, somehow very efficient, in a positive sense, but somehow no fun, boring and especially I think, the language is the border" (David, 184–186). While these are superficial and general stereotypes, they are continuously reproduced and negatively impact language learning in which a certain openness toward, and an interest in other, languages and cultures is key. David perceives there to be a mental border that students do not want to cross, making use of the argument that they would need to speak Swiss German to be understood and accepted, which they do not learn in school. However, he notes that it is used more as a justification than an actual reason to keep interaction going among different language groups at the lowest level possible. Similarly, he believes that such prejudices also exist within other parts of Switzerland while there is no comparable 'language problem' since French is spoken in the standard variety only.

Although David perceives the prejudices as less developed against the German variety spoken in Germany, Luisa sees the origin of the existing stereotypes exactly there and as something that is inextricably linked to its political history. She experiences very negative attitudes toward German on the part of students and their parents and believes that this is due to the reproduction of negative attitudes toward the German language and culture within the family setting. The unquestioned reproduction of stereotypes and prejudices is exacerbated by the lacking interaction and, according to Luisa, results in fear of otherness. The following passage illustrates her own lived experiences of language supporting her perceptions:

> When I used to commute to Neuchâtel, Romand students refused to sit next to Swiss German students, they prefer standing. Parents who wrest the *20-Minuten* [Swiss newspaper freely available at train stations] from their children because it's in the other language, in the sense of "you don't understand that anyway" (202–205).

This example shows that although interaction between French- and German-speaking Swiss students would be possible, due to the cohabitation in the same canton, these underlying, deeply rooted stereotypes prevent them from doing so. As Luisa explained, socialization processes, influenced by parents' negative attitudes toward GFL and the culture and people more generally, are detrimental to students' learning and might cause (or reinforce) segregation between the people of the two languages and cultures in the long run. Despite German's mainly negative perception, Luisa estimates that a little minority of students is nevertheless interested in GFL classes. Although she does not know exactly why this is the case, she speculates that they might link German to their future professional opportunities and better understand the learning thereof as a benefit for them than others might prove. A positive teaching experience that she had, which helped to reduce some of the students' stereotypes already, was an exchange day with Swiss German-speaking students. Her French-speaking students concluded after the encounter that they were nice and that they had a great time together. It is surprising then that the connection between learning German and using it within the Swiss German context is barely visible in the GFL classes. Other participants perceived learning German to be an imposition on *Romand* students. The language classes cannot be neutral since they seem to be strongly linked to stereotypes and prejudices against Swiss German/German speakers based on the political history that is primarily associated with Germany. Not only do they influence cohabitation, mutual understanding, and cantonal or social cohesion, but even on a school level, as teachers argued, there is very little exchange and communication between the two language sections. Some suggested that change should start at the school level before attempting to reduce tensions among Switzerland as a whole.

Discussion

The findings presented in this study's previous sections indicate that multilingualism is a majorly important phenomenon within Swiss society that both impacts upon and is impacted by individuals' experiences, interests, positioning, recognition, and opportunities as well as LPP-, LEP-decisions, strategies, and laws. This study has demonstrated how multilingualism has become instrumentalized through neoliberal forces that promote English's popularity and necessity, through the romantic forces keen on maintaining a traditional focus on the four national languages, and through social justice forces advocating for the amplification of HLs. The study has offered a deepened understanding of how linguistic practices and their embeddedness in overt and covert policy decisions and speakers' ideologies about languages can ameliorate social relations and might increase linguistic and cultural equity.

This section will discuss the study's results in concert with its underlying theoretical framework. It addresses the lived experiences of language and identity, the monolingual habitus in multilingual education practices, language hierarchies and symbolic power, as well as native-speaker ideologies in four sub-sections. The findings sub-section on symbolic violence (4.5) is subsumed under 5.4.

5.1 Sameness and Difference in Identity Expression through Language

> "Even after 18 years...even when I only say two sentences...this origin, this identity is somehow very strongly expressed through language."

The study's analysis of participants' lived experiences of language and linguistic repertoires has shown that languages, experiences, and identities are inextricably linked and are interdependent. Individuals' linguistic identities are (de)stabilized and transformed through experiences and social interaction, in which speakers position themselves through language(s) *vis-à-vis* and are positioned by their interlocutor(s) and a given linguascape. This positioning is often especially challenging and disadvantageous for plurilinguals who can rarely employ their entire linguistic repertoires and, therefore, are constantly forced to suppress parts of their identity in order to assimilate to or accommodate the local speech community (Hu, 2003b). Adapting one's own way of expression, thereby adopting a different role in a given social context, can also have an impact on one's norms, habits, values, and actions and thus can deeply affect individuals' self-perception and self-esteem (Lahire, 2011). According to Foucault (1982), this positioning process of discovering who we are is a

> form of power…which categorizes the individual, marks him by his own individuality, attaches him to his own identity, imposes a law of truth on him which he must recognize and which others have to recognize in him. It is a form of power which makes individuals subjects. There are two meanings of the word 'subject': subject to someone else by control and dependence; and tied to his own identity by a conscience or self-knowledge. Both meanings suggest a form of power which subjugates and makes subject to (p. 781).

Thus, existing power and hegemony mechanisms dictate how individuals' identities are shaped or 'subjectivated' (Foucault, 1982), rendering it extremely difficult, if not outright impossible, to follow Gramsci's (1971) call for truly and consciously 'knowing thyself' in such conditions. The continuing, unquestioned acceptance and reproduction of Switzerland's restrictive monolingual and standard speech norms, despite the official multilingual language policies and practices, further pressures plurilinguals to construct certain hierarchies within their linguistic repertoire. Forcing individuals to determine one language – and only one – as their L1, for instance, also results in inner conflicts and dissatisfaction when their reality is much more accurately described as a more complex, "translingual continuum" (Anderson, 2018). This is the case for Swiss German speakers who are constantly pressured to adapt their way of speaking to speakers of other dialects or languages and social contexts in which they are confronted with feelings of insecurity and inferiority. It is also particularly detrimental to individuals with a migration background who are (unconsciously) coerced into adopting local linguistic and cultural norms to fully integrate while their "attachment to multiple sociocultural spaces" (Zakharia, 2016, p. 141) is ignored or, worse, actively punished. Full integration, implying individuals' assimilation to Swiss language and culture and the (partial) suppression of their own, is embodied in policies at the federal, cantonal, and municipal levels and is expected as such from the society. As the results indicate, however, being able to apply the entirety of one's linguistic repertoire and one's ability to live one's cultural heritage is indispensable to knowing oneself, one's home, and origins, and is hugely important for identity construction.

Swiss language practices and policies exemplify the view that languages and cultures continue to be associated with a fixed (albeit imagined) geographical region or nation-state (Anderson, 2006; Becker, 2022). That is, despite Switzerland's official status as a quadrilingual country, it can be argued that it is much better described as monolingual or restrictively multilingual in certain social contexts since languages are tied to cantonal policies and geographical spaces, and usually do not transgress historically established borders (see for instance the 'Röstigraben'). The French and German language groups are usually separated, even within the bilingual cantons, and multilingual encounters are therefore rather rare. The 'imaginary' link between language and space has yet further consequences for HL speakers in Switzerland. First, speaking a HL in the new country of *residence* legitimizes one's 'true' roots and compensates for the fact of not living in one's country of *origin*. However, this can result in a great amount of pressure and conflict when expectations and cultural attachments differ among first- and second-generation migrants, for instance, as Adya's lived experiences of language illustrated. Second, being constantly torn between two (or more) linguistic and cultural identities complicates the sense of 'true' belonging. HL speakers typically experience difficulties feeling and being accepted as a 'true' local (Levitt & Jaworsky, 2007) when identifying with multiple languages, cultures, and spaces. Arthur's lived experiences of language, for instance, incorporate a constant negotiation of his self-perception and sense of belonging, which is based on how others perceive and position him through his way of speaking. Measured against a hypothetical monolingual native-speaker standard, Arthur's linguistic repertoire neither fulfills the requirements for Macedonian nor for Swiss German, since it is always in flux and adapting to communicative contexts. The inextricable link between authentic language and belonging causes linguistic insecurity and restrictions for individuals' personal and professional trajectories. As Blommaert (2010, p. 6) noted: "Mobility, sociolinguistically speaking, is therefore a trajectory through different stratified, controlled and monitored spaces in which language 'gives you away.'" Oftentimes, people have to justify their additional linguistic and cultural resources (sometimes perceived as 'deviant' from the locally expected standard) with which other monolingual and monocultural individuals are unfamiliar. Whenever the participating minority language speakers had the opportunity to employ their linguistic repertoires, outside their accustomed monolingual barriers, they experienced it as very enriching and beneficial for their well-being and self-esteem, something that was also observed by Abendroth-Timmer and Hennig (2014). In fact, using hitherto censored resources within their linguistic repertoires from public settings helped us to perceive the minority language speakers – and their skills in multiple languages in particular – as intercultural mediators who are able to deconstruct borders and connect people and spaces, as described by Byram (2009). This quality is primarily attributed to ELF, which is crucial in bringing people with diverse backgrounds together. Some participants identified so strongly with (certain) BE or AE speakers that they would have liked to *pass* as them (Motha, 2014) and to exchange their own linguistic repertoires, provided that they could be perfectly proficient in English. Yet, English is often simplistically considered a *neutral* language, something that is very compatible with Switzerland's traditionally perceived, ostensible *neutral* geopolitical position; this necessitates ignoring the fact that neither are, of course, and that English hegemonizes the local linguistic landscape and participants' perspectives. Nevertheless, despite English's lack of neutrality and its impact on national and heritage languages in Switzerland, it still provides a pragmatic alternative to emotionally charged and often inefficient communication strategies and practices in (two) national languages. All of the participants were very familiar with and already actively employed English in leisure, fun, and real-life activities; as many participants reported, this also indicates that it is becoming a language of identity for them. This is increasingly the case for younger generations whose lived experiences of language are much more significantly shaped by English and less so by Switzerland's non-L1 national languages. Some younger people are less aware of the rich linguistic diversity and identify less as plurilinguals in the sense that is promoted by Swiss LEPs or the CoE.

This development is particularly consequential for Switzerland's minority language groups such as Romansh speakers who identify with their L1 very strongly and are more dependent upon a common linguistic awareness and promotion at a national level. In fact, condescension, mockery, or disrespect toward their "language of the heart" (Nicole, 453) due to its perceived low prestige and minority status, as some have experienced, negatively impact speakers' (linguistic) identity, self-confidence, and bodily well-being (Abendroth-Timmer & Hennig, 2014; Kramsch, 2009). As the CoE suggests, such "a diversified experience of otherness" (CoE, 2001, p. 34) also contributes to identity construction and is in line with the poststructuralist approach of individuals forming themselves and being formed in discourses. Another consequence is that group identity among Romansh speakers can be so strong that it creates a certain dependence or fixation. While it is reinforced by common traditional activities, such as parades and village fairs celebrating Romansh language and culture, it is felt even more strongly outside of Romansh-speaking territory. This can go so far as to limit one's social interactions to Romansh speakers only and can result in isolation; conversely, though, Romansh in such cases serves as a common ground and connector among its speakers. In Bourdieu's (1991) terms, Romansh, like any other language, has the ability "to *make and unmake groups*" (Bourdieu, 1991, p. 221 [emphasis in original]) and to produce sameness and difference, which in return contributes to the construction of individuals' identities (Bucholtz & Hall, 2005a; 2005b).

Finally, this is particularly true in the German-speaking part of Switzerland where Swiss German is directly linked to participants' identities and a crucial requirement to participate in social life. Speaking (a local variety of) Swiss German, thus, determines whether individuals are accepted members of the majority language group or whether they might be marginalized. The latter are thereby marked, while the former "gain a special, default status that contrasts with the identities of other groups, which are usually highly recognizable" (Bucholtz & Hall, 2005a, p. 372). Conversely, without Swiss German, its speakers feel deprived of the possibility (and right) to fully express and to *distinguish* themselves in settings which impose SSG by law (such as schools, for instance). Distinction refers to "the mechanism whereby salient difference is produced" (Bucholtz & Hall, 2005a, p. 384), here between SSG and Swiss German (speakers) to indicate legitimate group membership, which "involves the pursuit of socially recognized sameness" (Bucholtz & Hall, 2005a, p. 383). As Bucholtz and Hall (2005a) also note, however, the mechanism of sameness and difference "most often operates in a binary fashion, establishing a dichotomy between social identities constructed as oppositional or contrastive. It thus tends to reduce complex social variability to a single dimension: us versus them" (p. 384).

5.2 Pressure toward Monolingualism

> "Ten out of 20 students will probably be plurilingual...but they will be virtually made into monolinguals through submersion."

Switzerland's education system simultaneously reproduces and legitimizes the monolingual habitus and celebrates a selective, prestigious linguistic diversity based on language ideologies (Berthele, 2020), even despite efforts and resources put into language teaching at the upper secondary level. Institutional structures, LEPs, and existing language ideologies impede an equitable approach to language learning by homogenizing students' (and teachers') diverse linguistic and cultural resources and imposing upon them objectives that are unsuitable for many students' identities and lifeworlds (Delpit, 2006). The priority given to and the policies promoting the school language (French, German, or Romansh), English, and a second national language exclude HLs and restrict the linguistic offer and attribute valuable linguistic capital to a few chosen, prestigious languages (Bourdieu, 1991). As Henri put it succinctly: "[T]hey tried to make the system equal for everyone, [but] they created inequality" (Henri, 427–428).

Problematically, not only are most HLs censored from institutional settings, but so are many HL speakers *tout court*, thereby resulting in a 'selective and elitist student body' (Apple, 2012; 2019). That is, while the upper secondary schools only allow a few chosen languages in specified educational settings, they sadly (but realistically) account for the underrepresentation of students with more diverse linguistic and cultural backgrounds. This situation is due to the generally low number of students with migrant backgrounds in post-compulsory education, even though the number has been steadily increasing at a societal and at primary and lower secondary level.

Typically, those students with a migrant background who enroll in upper secondary education schools are proficient in the school language with many of them having been born in Switzerland to migrant parents. Nevertheless, they are submerged into and assimilated through the local language and culture under the pretext of equalizing socioeconomic opportunities and full integration, by which some of the participants in this study were also deceived. For instance, some associated the languages used and taught at school with universal prestige, professional benefits, and important (and expected) markers of their 'Swissness.' Others considered their HL inappropriate in official school contexts or believed that it was not worth spending time on their L1, which indicates that 'curricularizing heritage languages' (Valdés, 2017) is not simply just a matter of a well-intended policy framework. Although the majority of HL-speaking students superficially fulfill the linguistic requirements, in actuality they typically lack academic language, self-esteem, and parental and financial support compared to majority language-speaking students as numerous studies and participating teachers in this study have shown (Cummins, 2018; Delpit, 2006; Bankston & Zhou, 2002).

The admission requirements in the official school language have an impact on students' academic performance in all subjects, so that those who have more exposure are also advantaged in other areas. Swiss national and commonly taught FLs are a substantial part of the mandatory upper secondary admission exam and this indicates that multilingual education is key in (post-)compulsory schooling and is hardly compensable for newcomers without these linguistic competences. Put more plainly, students can be denied access to upper secondary, and thus university education, if they lack (high-level) language skills in two national languages plus English. Evidently, as some teachers' experiences exemplify, there is a huge discrepancy between the policy documents and their implementation. To wit: Even if migrant students pass the admission exam, many continue to be disadvantaged since they often come from a low socioeconomic background with less financial and emotional support.

While the selective emphasis on national languages is detrimental to plurilingual students' more diverse linguistic repertoires, it does raise the status and recognition of minority languages such as Romansh at an institutional and societal level. The fact that Romansh is used at upper secondary level and for the completion of the *Matura*, which is in itself viewed as rather prestigious and elitist, reinforces its appreciation particularly among non-Romansh speakers. Yet, despite the extensive offers made in Romansh, students are still envied and discriminated against by others because they lack basic (printed) teaching material and are provided with iPads instead. As García and Lin (2017, p. 12) observe, this seems to be a general problem for education in minority languages since "it does not make economic sense to publish material in small languages." Romansh-speaking students are aware of and appreciate the institutional effort made to teach their L1 at upper secondary level. Furthermore, many of them are grateful, like many Zurich students, that they can also use SSG in an academic context. Given that it is rarely spoken outside of school, but remains required and evaluated in written exams and presentations, students in fact rely on standard language policies and their implementation by teachers to improve their SSG language skills. Delpit (2006) believes it to be the teachers' task to familiarize students whose L1 is a 'non-standard' variety with the standard language and to give them the opportunity to learn and practice it since it continues to be an important requirement for academic and professional development.

In Grisons, a remarkable balance between L1 (Romansh) and L2 (German) is established through intensive bilingual programs aiming at an equal promotion of two cantonal languages while French, "the second most important national language," as one student reported, is consequently reduced to an optional subject. As a result, many Romansh-speaking students who wish to learn it, do not have the chance to do so (successfully) and seem disadvantaged if their career choice is not already made and they might only realize after graduating that they would have needed French. In case optional French classes take place, that is if enough students inscribe, the time allocated to it is very low with 1–2 lessons per week and hence is likely to be insufficient to learning a new language. As Stotz (2006) cautions:

> [W]e need a discourse of persuasion which allows individuals themselves to see more clearly the choices they have and the sorts of resources they would like to build up in order to be able to do the things they want in the spaces they will occupy professionally and privately (p. 262).

Students hardly have the time to *use* the language individually or with fellow students, even in their compulsory language classes that have more lessons per week. In fact, this is one of the reasons students are against including multiple languages into the classroom and, thus, are against inclusive approaches in which several languages (or linguistic features across those) are learned together as a whole. They fear that if more of students' HLs were integrated, then even less time would be spent learning and actively using the target language.

However, a certain shared understanding among students and teachers seems to be that (academic) competences in one's L1 are crucial to acquiring any AL, which is why their adequate integration into teaching is justified. According to Benson (2009), these transitional models in which the use of L1 in educational settings prepares the transition into the use of the L2 are "most successful when a good foundation of language and literacy is developed in the mother tongue" (p. 67). While a few HLs are indeed promoted until lower secondary level, although this depends on the organization and subventions primarily by the country of origin and the parent, there are no LCO classes at upper secondary level in the form of external classes. In support of the EDK (2004) recommendations, this study argues that LCO classes should first be institutionalized within public schools and then also expanded to upper secondary level. This would allow for a greater independence from external subsidies and a greater customized offer of HLs spoken by the school's students.

The lack of qualified LCO teachers at the specific schools was often cited as one of the main reasons for the limited offer, which sheds light on a more profound issue regarding (Swiss) teacher education and in-service teachers. As Makarova and Birman (2016) point out convincingly, given that schools are crucial sites for minority students' acculturation, teachers are key actors and can facilitate this process by officially recognizing heritage linguistic and cultural backgrounds and identifying special needs. However, as they also show, many teachers are ill-equipped to teach in increasingly diverse classrooms. In fact, the majority of the participating teachers in this study have a Swiss background, and therefore represent a homogeneous, institutional force to which students with migrant backgrounds can hardly relate. That said, some teachers had more diverse linguistic and cultural backgrounds and could more easily identify with a more heterogeneous student population. As several of the participants (Henri, Luisa, Victoria, and Nesrin, for instance) and Kubota (2010) importantly observe: "In order to truly embrace racial, cultural, and linguistic pluralism and to make the campus a societal role model for students, schools...should make an effort to hire more non-White teachers from diverse cultural and linguistic backgrounds" (p. 109).

Innovative ideas such as virtual LCO courses were generated during the interviews, which could serve as a (temporary) solution until such a time as the policy framework for teacher education is modified accordingly. Although the idea evolved out of the discussion about how to raise awareness of Romansh and how to enable its teaching across Switzerland, it is as well applicable to the context of HLs. Given that some HLs are less common than others for which on-site classes can be more easily organized, offering those online for minority languages within a network of participating schools seems a timely and exciting alternative; this is especially so considering that students, teachers, and institutional structures alike have become more flexible and open to blended learning solutions, due to the Covid-19 pandemic. Importantly, such (online) LCO classes should also attract non-HL speakers whenever possible in an effort to sensitize students to the linguistic and cultural backgrounds of their fellow students. LCO projects or lessons can also be integrated into regular language classes and given the possibility to conduct those virtually, they can reach a wider audience and can optimize limited human and financial resources. This could also contribute to a more holistic and equitable understanding of language teaching in schools and might reduce students' concerns that if HLs were more present in the classroom, then they would automatically learn or practice less the target language.

This is particularly true regarding students' fear of missing out on opportunities to improve their English, which trumps both the development of diversity-engagement and intercultural competences. For many, one of the primary objectives of upper secondary education is increasing proficiency in English for future academic and professional opportunities. Yet, for others, English plays such a crucial role in their private lives already that they no longer see English classes in school as being the key context to learn and practice the language authentically. This is much more commonly achieved in virtual, English-dominated worlds of e-gaming, social media, or when watching (American) series and films within a global online community. Importantly, many students simplistically legitimize their digital exposure to (native-speaker) English as the sole true, authentic variety (for a critical response to the connection between authenticity and native speakers see Myhill, 2003). Consequently, this defines and raises students' expectations *vis-à-vis* teachers' language competences and use within the classroom and their own level to be reached at the end of upper secondary education. At the same time, as teachers reported, there is an increasing tendency to focus on informal, oral communication, in which less attention is paid to accuracy, thereby leading students to adopt the same (informal) register even in more formal, academic contexts. This creates tensions between students and teachers since they are (also) evaluated for their academic language skills, incorporated through standard speech and prescriptive grammatical rules and that are often flagrantly violated by 'true native speakers,' and students consider these people to be the legitimate model speaker(s). Problematically, many participants in this study were often unaware that the concept of a *model native speaker* is socially constructed and that all speakers of any variety speak their very own idiolect more or less similarly to the prevalent standard, as already observed by Davies (2003) almost 20 years ago.

An important common objective for both students and teachers is the CAE exam that, as part of the University of Cambridge, certifies that students possess a high competence level in (British) English; it also exemplifies the pressure to prepare for and to pass such an exam. As the results of this study demonstrate, this can lead to students feeling guilty for not using their spare time to watch films in English as a form of exam preparation. Problematically, students failing the CAE exam can have a negative impact on teachers' professional identity, for instance, when they associate 'insufficient' exam results with their 'insufficient' pedagogical or language competences. While many students are only interested in obtaining such a certificate in the hope of fulfilling requirements imposed by future employers in well-paid jobs or (prestigious, international) universities, schools contribute to the reproduction of the native-speaker ideology and sustain an industry based on exactly those same expectations. That said, public upper secondary schools are faced with increasingly more competitive and accessible private schools, the curricula of which are based on native-speaker English instruction and exams, university preparation, and bilingual programs. Certain public schools have adopted market-oriented mechanisms and teaching offers such as CAE exams in order not to widen the gap between public and private schooling, but to provide equal opportunities to all students. However, as pointed out by Ricento (2015a), by the time English as a desirable skill is made accessible to the greater public through schooling, its value already decreases and needs to be compensated with other (elitist) qualities and competences.

Similarly and according to Ricento (2015b), English-based CLIL is heavily linked and contributes to the knowledge economy. Nevertheless, it is (in GR and FR) or would be (in ZH) highly appreciated by students since it combines non-language subjects with the learning of an FL and is seen as a perfectly suitable preparation for university. As they indicated, the language, or more precisely, the register, acquired through CLIL also differs enormously from the more informal one to which they are already regularly exposed. Students, therefore, feel more motivated to learn academic English through content, similar to what they expect from university teaching. Typical language classes at upper secondary level should also focus less on teaching grammar, vocabulary, and literature, and more on intercultural competences and the hands-on application of languages in culturally diverse contexts, as advocated by some teachers and students. The emphasis should be put even more heavily on communication and interaction and less strongly on following the structure dictated by the teaching material and curriculum. Learning about and familiarizing oneself with cultural aspects of daily life in other (Swiss) language regions (Delpit, 2006) is essential for successful, meaningful intercultural encounters as an ideal supplement to, but not a replacement of, linguistic exchanges. In such encounters, not only is the knowledge about, but the culture itself is co-produced, which can result in "'friction': the awkward, unequal, unstable, and creative qualities of interconnection across difference" (Tsing, 2005, p. 4). It can also lead to a more profound understanding and appreciation of the existing cultural and linguistic diversity within Switzerland, given that, as Nesrin reported, "it's apparently not always so clear that in Switzerland there exist also other languages" (Nesrin, 158–159).

One suggestion made by Sebastian was to devote a specific class to Switzerland's (national) languages and cultures in order to promote and raise awareness of the locally existing diversity. Many participants indeed pointed out the lack of interaction and communication among the language regions, which could thus be improved, and the negative impact of existing stereotypes on language teaching, which could be addressed and deconstructed in class. Kubota (2010) cautions that "it is thus important for teachers to acknowledge the complexity and fluidity of racial, cultural, and linguistic categories, and liberate themselves from a fixed worldview conditioned by stereotypes" (p. 106) and calls for a non-essentialist understanding of race, culture, and language. Adopting a critical multicultural perspective, teachers can likewise raise awareness of the social field's underlying power dynamics in which individuals position themselves and are positioned thereby. According to her, "relying on a color/difference-blind approach of equal treatment for everyone would merely perpetuate the existing relations of power" (Kubota, 2010, p. 106). Being (made) aware of these power dynamics can turn the feeling of otherness and marginalization into 'strategic essentialism' (Spivak, 1993) which intends to capitalize on difference as a valuable shared identity marker for historically disadvantaged social groups and to increase their political representation. Critical examination is required to guarantee equitable expression of individuals' 'multi-voicedness' (Bakhtin, 1981), given that a strategic essentialist approach might create a forced and artificial homogeneity within each social, cultural or language group. This is crucial since, as Bakhtin (1981) argues, "all languages of heteroglossia, whatever the principle underlying them and making each unique, are specific points of view on the world, forms for conceptualizing the world in words, specific world views, each characterized by its own objects, meanings and values" (pp. 291–292).

In the case of Switzerland, as Stotz (2006) argues, stereotypes and associated power hierarchies are part of Switzerland's self-constructed political identity. As he put it: "Squaring political power and evening out perceived or real grudges among the German-, French-, Italian- and Romansh-speaking groups has occupied the agenda for a century and a half" (Stotz, 2006, p. 249). Importantly, although many were aware that multiple stereotypes existed and were used among the four language regions, they – some consciously – continued to employ the same narrative to describe their interactions, relationships, and 'the others' in general. The situation was particularly tense regarding the teaching of French in German-speaking Switzerland and the teaching of German in the *Romandie* and among their speakers respectively. Motivation decreases and tension increases here, given that some students view these classes as an obligation without any concrete benefits (compared to English) and some teachers choose French or German (merely) because of the job security based on political incentives to promote national language learning. That said, language teachers were worried about imposed reallocations of German and French hours to informatics and science subjects.

The language debate has revealed power issues among the different language groups which had long been ignored by incorporating globalizing and localizing forces through the learning of English and a second national language. As Stotz (2006) summarizes it succinctly:

> The discourse of communicative globalization has exposed the traditional scarcity of interaction between compatriots and the use of additional languages by a few, tendentially elite groups or bilingual families. The tense relationship between national languages locked into their territories, evoking a condition of isolation and separateness, and a language, English, which many people see as offering economic and symbolic advantage gets played out by the cultural and educational politics of language, with schools having to bear the brunt of the struggle (p. 261).

Raising awareness of intranational linguistic and cultural diversity in specific classes could reduce historically established tensions and prejudices, might open the way to a more tolerant and diversity-engaged teaching, and could increase students' motivation to learn another national language. Arguably, the decision to prioritize English over French in some German-speaking cantons exacerbated the tensions further, rather than alleviating them, and is paradoxical if mutual understanding and social cohesion on a national level are key objectives in Swiss language teaching. As Stotz (2006) suitably observes: "In a country with firm linguistic borders and a territorial notion of language, school language learning appeared to be, speaking with Foucault...a disciplining exercise in the service of national cohesion" (p. 252).

Importantly, a class on Switzerland's linguistic and cultural diversity could provide a *holistic* picture of the social reality, including HLs, and should not simply reproduce the already existing emphasis on the national languages as dictated by cantonal and educational authorities. Such an inclusive approach would also be supported by some students and teachers, even while others remain critical. However, equity can only be achieved when *all* languages and cultures are recognized as Delpit (2006) cautions, and the culture of power is shared by everyone. Translanguaging as an inclusive teaching approach aiming at social justice and the recognition of all languages and linguistic practices should serve as a model to prepare schools for the increasing diversity of the 21st and indeed the 22nd century. As García and Lin (2017) summarize it succinctly: "The continuous hierarchization of people who speak different languages means that bilingual educators have to *be vigilant to work against the power and hierarchization* of the language practices of dominant groups" (p. 11 [emphasis in original]).

5.3 Language Hierarchies within the Hegemonic *Willensnation*

> "[The prioritization of English over French] is a bit of an insult to a part that also belongs to Switzerland."

Multiple language hierarchies exist within the Swiss linguascape, thereby leading to advantages for the majority language group in the form of the effortless accumulation of linguistic capital and disadvantages for minority language groups through discrimination and exclusion (Bourdieu, 1991). Importantly, majority and minority language groups differ at national and cantonal level, due to the territoriality principle and the historically established geographical dispersion. That is, while SSG is the official majority language, it is the minority language within the canton of Fribourg and which, as this study's findings suggest, sometimes result in an act of defiance by demonstrating reversed superiority and power. As Altermatt (2005) summarizes his research on bilingualism in the city of Fribourg: "The German language, the German-speaking minority and bilingualism...are not duly taken into account by the authorities, not really recognized, and not specifically promoted") (p. 79 [my translation]). Conversely, SSG is also the dominant language at a cantonal level in the trilingual canton of Grisons, with Romansh and Italian sharing the language minority positions, resulting in additive multilingualism (Benson, 2009) particularly for Romansh speakers who grow up bilingually.

Romansh speakers cannot choose *not* to learn SSG, due to their L1's minority status, even though this results in high-level language competences in two languages. Rather, as this study has shown, the majority of Grisons students prioritizes SSG over their L1, Romansh, in a professional context. There are also teachers who, by believing that the *status quo* stands for "German is simply everything" (Gita, 312), reproduce the language hierarchy in favor of SSG and its speakers.

Many do not consider their linguistic rights endangered or disrespected because this situation has been normalized by social practices and ingrained as such in people's minds. In fact, in Gramsci's (1971) terms, the non-dominant groups have adopted the dominant group's worldviews, thereby leading to incoherent actions and beliefs to the detriment of their own linguistic and cultural repertoires. Thus, although language policies establish *de jure* linguistic equality among the three cantonal languages in Grisons, Romansh speakers have learned through discriminatory lived experiences to be submissive and to adapt their language practices in official spaces or to majority language speakers. For instance, as reported by Christine: "when there are German speakers then you automatically speak German. Also with people who…would be able to speak Romansh. (-) Because it would somehow be impolite" (Christine, 37–39). That said, there are voices of concern about a potential "Germanization" of Romansh-speaking Grisons (Jana, 194) to the detriment of minority languages. These circumstances indicate that the language law, aiming at equality among the three cantonal languages, has not been successfully implemented, is not controlled, and its misuse has not been sanctioned (Spolsky, 2009). Contrarily, as argued by Coray (2009), the "Germanization" is positively associated with socioeconomic progress by many in a historically rural and underdeveloped area of Switzerland. Learning the languages of one's 'neighbors within the same country' is also presented as a crucial requirement for social cohesion and ought to be prioritized "out of respect for the nation" or justified by participants themselves "…because you have to be able to communicate with our own people first," as advocated by some participants. Problematically, many minority speakers have come to accept and recognize the symbolic power as legitimate through a seemingly invisible process, thereby giving up their chance of *de facto* equality and restricting their L1 to informal contexts, apparently voluntarily (Bourdieu, 1991).

French and German are rather strictly separated in bilingual Fribourg, not only by geographical boundaries but also by mental ones (Becker & Magno, 2022) resulting in a tense and ideology-laden co-existence of two monolingual language groups on a societal level. On an individual level, participants' personal language hierarchies depict a more plurilingual reality and include many different HLs. At the same time, French-speaking students are coerced into learning German, otherwise they would be even more isolated from the national majority language group and the socioeconomic opportunities linked thereto. In fact, all Fribourg students (except for one) believe that their competences in the local national language (French) are not enough to be competitive in the Swiss job market. As one student formulated it concisely: "Without German, everything is pretty hard to achieve in Switzerland." As a result, the majority of Fribourg students and teachers report being satisfied with the current LEPs that introduce German before English and do not want to prioritize the latter as other German-speaking cantons have done. Moreover, there are students and teachers who take pride in the (traditional) LEPs and the respect these are believed to demonstrate toward Swiss traditions and the other language regions, ignoring that Italian and Romansh are hardly ever involved in these discussions, thereby reproducing language hierarchies themselves. As some non-Romansh-speaking participants explicitly stated, Romansh does not qualify as relevant enough to be integrated into language teaching outside of Grisons and other HLs would only overwhelm students with their (already dense) curriculum.

Nevertheless, some call for a federally binding, homogeneous policy decision in response to the language learning debate. It has been argued that a national LEP should make the learning of the two dominant national languages mandatory for all Swiss students, although it is highly doubtful that such (forced) LEPs can completely erase underlying power mechanisms and even have the potential to establish equitable language learning. This is particularly so considering that it was through an almost autonomous initiative by Zurich's former Minister of Education, Ernst Buschor, that the traditional language order was reversed. This study's findings also indicate that many students (and some teachers) perceive GFL classes as a tedious obligation, justifying them almost solely with neoliberal arguments such as better socioeconomic opportunities. The findings further suggest that these arguments are insufficient for successful language learning and result in low motivation and academic achievements. Hegemonized by the majority language group and their historically established dependence on it, their own will and understandings have become obfuscated and uncritical (Gramsci, 1971). Thus, given the French-speaking part's financial, political, and economic dependence on the dominant German-speaking part, they also cannot choose *not* to learn German. In fact, many of the French-speaking participants were against expressing dissent regarding LEPs since it would involve questioning the *status quo*, with which many are satisfied since "it works well the way it is" and "the tradition has always been like this," as one participant stated. Caught in a *culture of silence* (Freire, 2005), minority language speakers uphold the *status quo* in the hope of socioeconomic advantages than (re-)discovering, claiming, and expressing their own voices as active and legitimate participants in social decision-making processes. Importantly, this demonstrates that actors from bottom-up (minority language speakers) also prioritize upholding the *status quo*, rather than becoming 'agents of change' as a way of practicing democracy (Ayers et al., 2017).

That said, there are participants who are against romanticizing the national languages of a quadrilingual *Willensnation*, which problematically contributes to a glorification of traditions and homogeneity while ignoring the increasing *de facto* influences of linguistic and cultural diversity through global flows (Hardt & Negri, 2000). Alternatively, as Heller and Duchêne (2012) observe sharply: "[W]e seem to be nearing the limits of linguistic national…regimes to organize our lives, finding systems breaking up into circulating flows, local agentivity poking holes into institutional reproduction and the boundary between authenticity and artifice breaking down" (p. 19).

LEPs prioritizing the national languages merely do so to reinforce the *status quo*, almost without any real-world purpose for their learners given the separation of the language regions and the lacking interaction at a federal level. As summarized by one participant: "Actually, very little holds it [Switzerland] together…it's actually a miracle…" (Etienne, 276–277), although disagreements among the four language groups are rarely openly expressed or debated. As long as the country can rely on a thriving economy, and provided its traditions and social practices are respected and unquestioned, there is no need to breach the (artificial) peace. As Stotz (2006) argues convincingly drawing on Giddens (1991):

> The failure of language policy and the confederate discourse on multilingualism in Switzerland to create a clear mission and a rationale for action is not the result of bad intentions or sheer neglect, but it is the outcome of a reliance on traditional values and hegemonies. The territoriality principle, the ostensible care for autochthonous minorities, the shared history of half a millennium of relatively peaceful bi- and multilingualism and the division of power into even smaller relations due to subsidiarity: all of these factors have worked together to form a complacency liable to underestimate the dynamism of late modernity (p. 261).

The situation is particularly challenging for HL speakers in the *Romandie* (and the Italian-speaking parts) who have to learn both French and SSG for private and professional reasons and who cannot benefit from their rich linguistic and cultural repertoires, given their L1's exclusion from LEPs and laws. Thus, although language laws and policies provide a legal basis for linguistic equality among the national languages, they also discriminate against 'less prestigious' HLs spoken by a substantial proportion of the Swiss population, thereby reinforcing language hierarchies. That said, hierarchical discrepancies among students' HLs also exist. While students whose L1s are Spanish or English can in fact benefit from and showcase those in school since they are considered prestigious; speakers of Albanian, Croatian,

Czech or Portuguese are silenced due to the perceived low linguistic capital.[1] The lacking social recognition that is mirrored in the language hierarchies is reproduced through institutional structures within language teaching, since English and Spanish are actively included while others are 'locked out' (Becker & Knoll, 2021; Abendroth-Timmer & Fäcke, 2011).

English's high linguistic capital is promoted through LEPs and embraced by many stakeholders, even though English as a non-national language may not (yet) be included in language laws. In fact, Swiss-based multinational organizations and companies, as well as their employees, would benefit if their voices and concerns could be represented through ELF as an official language. That said, participants adhering to romantic ideals of Switzerland's *quadri*lingualism and more conservative traditions also expressed their vehement disagreement with ELF as "absolutely out of question" (Gita, 409–410). Even internationally oriented students shared this opinion, believing that the national language still determined the (*de facto*) language practices dominating (*de jure*) English language policies in Swiss-based multinational companies. The reasoning is justified by attributing higher legitimacy to historically "indigenous languages" (Etienne, 124), upholding the problematic modernist agenda of national identity construction through the *one language, one culture, one nation paradigm* (Pujolar, 2007). Similarly, migrants who happen to speak one of the national languages are attributed different (better) statuses than those who do not. This, as Fraser (2003) argues convincingly, "institutionalizes patterns of cultural value that pervasively deny some members the recognition they need in order to be full, participating partners in social interaction...constitutes an obstacle to parity of participation and thus an injustice" (p. 49).

Consequently, following the 'logic' of language ideologies and hierarchies, HLs and their speakers, who rarely have the same privileges as elitist expats in high-income positions, have even less of a chance of integration into existing LEPs and laws (Moyer & Martín Rojo, 2007). This study supports Brown, Koreinik, and Siiner's (2017) call for a reconceptualization of state-imposed LPPs as "a more diverse, democratic agent" (p. 3) to minority language communities and other (international) stakeholders that extend historically established (nation-)state borders and programs developed by majority language speakers. This can contribute to amplifying HL speakers' agency and voices in the LPP decision-making processes, given the restrictive national language policy framework and the high expectations from the local population regarding their linguistic competences. That is, HL-speaking migrants depending on the local job market are imposed stricter

---

1   The prestige and linguistic capital that is linked to a certain language is always context-dependent. While Spanish is considered a prestigious and popular language in Switzerland, for instance, certain Spanish varieties associated with HL speakers can be stigmatized in the USA (García & Lin, 2017).

(linguistic) requirements for integration given their intentions (or need) to stay more permanently compared to (English-speaking) expats, who typically live in Switzerland only temporarily. Put otherwise, personal ideologies and intolerance toward diversity are hidden behind superficially 'well-intended' advice for migrants' better integration and socioeconomic success by expecting migrants to acquire and to employ the new local language just like (or better than) the dominant language speaker group. For instance, Elisabeth formulated it like this when talking about a potential promotion of an employee with a migration background: "if he does not urgently push his Albanian language identity a bit into the background and speaks more German, he will never become her successor" (Elisabeth, 452–453). As Heller and Duchêne (2012) put it more sharply:

> If you don't speak the language of the nation, and speak it properly, you show that you lack the ability to reason and the strength to prevail that citizenship requires; you therefore can't claim access to political and economic power. If you haven't learned it, it is because you lack the competence to do so, for either moral or physical reasons…If you have, you still need to constantly prove yourself against the measure developed by the dominant group, who use agencies of the state…to describe what counts as linguistic competence and the means to identify it (p. 5).

Such perspectives on migration, and the expected behavior of migrants, illustrate that these individuals and their life trajectories are often misunderstood and pressured to assimilate, judging the local language and culture as more relevant and powerful than the ones with which they are already equipped. As Levitt and Jaworsky (2007) caution convincingly, however:

> Migration has never been a one-way process of assimilation…but one in which migrants, to varying degrees, are simultaneously embedded in the multiple sites and layers of the transnational social fields in which they live. More and more aspects of social life take place across borders, even as the political and cultural salience of nation-state boundaries remains clear (p. 130).

Interestingly, language hierarchies are not detrimental *per se*, as evidenced by participants' heteroglossic language repertoires and their lived experiences as individuals with migration backgrounds. Rather, the fact that languages are ranked according to their perceived prestige and linguistic capital within a hierarchical social construct provides the basis for minority language speakers to challenge their position and to engage in advocacy. For instance, Arthur is very proud of his Macedonian roots, yet he experiences condescension when his HL is not differentiated from other Slavic languages, making him believe it is not worth the effort. This illustrates that, although the underlying idea of deconstructing languages as mere social 'inventions' to critically reconstitute their social, cultural, and political implications and power dynamics (Makoni & Pennycook, 2007) is intriguing, disadvantaged HL speakers rely heavily on the concept of *languages*. More precisely, by critically assessing their HL's position within the society, they can raise awareness of inequitable treatment. Social justice, thus, becomes much more achievable if their HL can be named and pinpointed than if all named languages were to be dissolved into languaging practices (García, 2009), 'disinvented' or 'deconstructed' (Makoni & Pennycook, 2007), which would obfuscate underlying power issues (Grin, 2018; Marácz, 2018).

In these circumstances, ELF should (and does) act as a mediator and leverages individuals' voices that are hindered from learning or using the local language(s) and silenced by restrictive, discriminatory language laws, policies, and practices (Shohamy, 2006; Tollefson, 2006). Similarly, many participants support the prioritization of English over national languages in an effort to increase equitable participation in and exchange among all national language groups and to decrease the German dominance. As Sonja formulated it poignantly, "...so at least they both speak a foreign language...and are on equal footing. This to me is somehow also an advantage" (Sonja, 106–109). Furthermore, some cantons' decision to introduce English before French is seen as an overt acknowledgement of the covert language hierarchy that has been developing over the last three decades.

Importantly, the language order in which national languages (primarily German and French) are prioritized over English represent just as much of a language hierarchy; however, this is legitimized by the national, (restrictively) multilingual discourse on traditions, hegemonies, and the nation-state. Thus, despite ELF's handy function of acting as a mediator among diverse language and cultural groups, it might more closely resemble a superficial communication solution than actually resolving intercultural misunderstandings and ideology-laden power issues. Yet, only by openly and intentionally promoting differences instead of suppressing, denying or artificially tolerating them can ideologies, prejudices, and inequitable power relations be reduced.

ELF's uncritical glorification as *the* stepping-stone to bright socioeconomic opportunities, a key to accessing social media and virtual lifeworlds, or viewing it as 'a panacea' (Phillipson, 2009) *tout court* is detrimental for HLs. Problematically, many HL-speaking participants are deceived by English's popularity and alleged necessity and consider it a more important asset than their own linguistic and cultural heritage. Similar to the French-speaking minority and their dependence on the German-speaking part of Switzerland, the latter are mesmerized by an Anglo-American hegemony that is infiltrating the local language ecology and causing the linguistic capital dispossession of national languages (Phillipson, 2009). Hence, schools should adopt a critical multiculturalist stance and question, instead of reproducing, neoliberal mechanisms and undergirding hegemonial, economic interests and requirements (Kubota, 2010). As Motha (2014) argues, the aim is to avoid becoming socialized into a public school system in which adults teach children to unquestioningly accept associations spun between English and opportunity, cosmopolitanism, and wealth in the social imaginary and to develop deep-seated desires for English and all that it has come to represent, and in which adults purport to be teaching neutral worlds, structures, and processes (p. 133).

Finally, if the existing language hierarchies were transparently analyzed and deconstructed, then students would be more aware of their choices and associated power dynamics regarding linguistic capital and diversity in a restrictively multilingual society. This could contribute to a much-needed paradigm shift from 'ignored bilingualism' (Hélot, 2007) of individuals' non-dominant HLs to the normalization of a 'multilingual habitus' (Benson, 2013) with fewer discriminatory language hierarchies and ideologies or at least higher awareness and a better understanding thereof. Such a paradigm shift should imperatively also encompass legal protection and the social recognition of sign languages as well as easy languages in an effort to include as many underprivileged individuals as possible and to broaden everyone's understanding of inclusion.

5.4 Symbolic Power and Legitimacy in the 'Native-Speaker' and 'Standard-Speech Ideology'

> "I felt more confident...especially because we didn't have any native speakers with us, so real English people."

Similar to the findings discussed in the previous section, language sub-hierarchies rank linguistic varieties and their speakers according to their prestige, legitimacy, and 'native-speakerness' and are reinforced by the education system. These language sub-hierarchies also position linguistic varieties on a continuum of romantic and rationalist ideals (Geeraerts, 2003). The 'romantic' pole, which showcases identity expression and 'pride of membership' (Heller & Duchêne, 2012), represents participants' HLs, personal ways of speaking (idiolects), and local/dialectal varieties. The adjacent 'rationalist' pole stands for official, standard(ized) languages such as German, French, Rumantsch Grischun, or internationally dominant ones such as AE or BE, which provide their speakers with access to official, public spaces, sociopolitical, economic opportunities and power from which primarily dominant groups can 'profit' (Heller & Duchêne, 2012). These two poles of 'romantic' and 'rationalist' ideals or 'pride' and 'profit' are necessarily linked and, as Heller and Duchêne (2012) argue, their interwovenness is increasing: "'Pride' no longer works as well as the sole trope of nation-state legitimization; rather, the state's ability to facilitate the growth of the new economy depends on its ability to legitimize the discourse of 'profit'" (p. 10).

The study's findings revealed that participants are constantly torn between these two poles or societal forces, having to negotiate between their (linguistic) identity, the expression of their own voice, and a sense of belonging on the one hand and emancipation, participation, and socioeconomic opportunities on the other. Put differently, they are caught in a positionality struggle between tradition and globalization (Hua & Li, 2016). Great tensions exist regarding Swiss German, its questioned legitimate status due to language policies and laws prioritizing SSG, and its discriminatory nature *vis-à-vis* other (national) language groups, given Switzerland's diglossic situation. The situation is particularly challenging for Romansh speakers in Grisons who also grow up speaking Swiss German in contrast to Swiss German speakers who typically do not acquire Romansh in return. Exposed to Romansh and Swiss German in society primarily, they are required to employ SSG in educational settings in which their language skills are often assessed based on a dichotomous distinction between 'standardness' and 'non-standardness' (Delpit, 2006). Importantly, the same goes for minority language-speaking *teachers* who might be less familiar with the standard form, yet experience even more pressure to speak 'correctly' and to represent the state's authority and policies appropriately (Foucault, 1982; 1991; 2007). As the study's findings suggest, this leads to embarrassment and shame for some participants when, as Delpit (2006) has pointed out, the classroom should provide a safe space and "the opportunity to practice [standard language] *in contexts that are nonthreatening, have a real purpose, and are intrinsically enjoyable*" (p. 54 [emphasis in original]).

Contrarily, as one participant's experience exemplifies, making Swiss German an (unofficial) employment requirement for German-Romansh bilingual teachers is just as discriminatory and potentially even less comprehensible since, according to the language laws, it is not even a legitimate language in official, institutional contexts. Such protectionist behavior fosters the symbolic representation of a regional identity and cohesion through the "ideology of dialect" (Watts, 1999) and increases certain individuals' authenticity over others, based on arbitrary linguistic markers. Changing the school's LEPs to also allow Swiss German as a medium of instruction, which some teachers would in fact prefer, would correspond better to the local linguistic landscape and to many individuals' language repertoires, but is officially unauthorized given the language laws' restrictive nature. This study argues that the feeling of inferiority and deficiency that many Swiss German speakers unnecessarily experience regarding their own constant comparison with standard German norms and speakers could be reduced if Swiss German and SSG were viewed more as a continuum and less like a dichotomy. As the findings indicate, the participants' language practices are far more complex and do not neatly fit into the categories of standard versus non-standard speech. More precisely, speakers switch between SSG and Swiss German depending on the context and their communicative needs, thereby maximizing their linguistic repertoires and drawing on different registers, vocabulary, and grammar (Petkova, 2016).

In addition to the hierarchies that exist in Grisons regarding Swiss German, language ideologies also impact how Romansh's different idioms are socially perceived and ranked regarding their prestige and power. As the results indicate, one's position in the language hierarchy seems to correlate with one's socioeconomic and family background. Moreover, language ideologies also reproduce historically established stereotypes of rural versus urban population and corresponding speech varieties, automatically categorizing individuals living in rural Grisons as "a second category person" (Henri, 344). Convincingly, Henri argued that the act of recognizing different values in local varieties is in itself "highly superficial" (Henri, 348) and, thus, contributes to an illegitimate legitimization. This process was appropriately described by Bourdieu (1991) as 'misrecognizing' symbolic power and, in so doing, 'recognizing' it "as legitimate…[while]…fail[ing] to see that the hierarchy is, after all, an arbitrary social construction which serves the interests of some groups more than others" (p. 23). Problematically, such a hierarchy is not only created by speakers' ideologies, but is also institutionalized in language status planning (Hornberger, 2006) to officialize RG as a standardized language of the three (but not all five) Romansh idioms, thereby (de)legitimizing idioms and their speakers.

Züritüütsch ['Zurich German'] is often perceived to be the most prestigious one and it is commonly promoted as such by its speakers. As Siebenhaar and Wyler (1997) caution, however, while this may contribute to popularity and to a feeling of dominance, particularly within their own speech community, it is often interpreted as arrogance and presumption outside of Zurich. Postulating that "social life in Switzerland simply doesn't work enough [without Swiss German]" (Elisabeth, 43), Swiss German speakers exacerbate the figure of the native speaker and those standard speech ideologies predominant in society and educational settings that are detrimental to many. The complexity is well captured in Adya's lived experiences of language. She is complimented for her standard German accent in school, which is a result of exposure to speakers from Germany and causes an inner conflict of feelings of pride and betrayal since it makes her stand out. Problematically, it also puts her fellow students, who do not have the same German accent, in a position of inferiority since their German exposure is mostly based on a Swiss accent. Moreover, not only is the language hierarchy reproduced in an educational setting, and thus officialized, but the study's findings also revealed that certain students and parents in fact favor a standard German accent in teachers and that exposure is needed to the even more 'authentic' and 'prestigious' variety than Zurich German or even SSG. At the same time, students, teachers, and other stakeholders advocate English-based CLIL, which would in fact reduce the hours of SSG exposure, which is typically seen as one of the main responsibilities of schooling and which is thought to be essentially necessary for almost all other school subjects, university, and professional contexts (Grütz, 2018; Sieber, 2013).

Conversely, some teachers ignore the standard language-LEPs and rely on Swiss German in their classes instead; this, consequently, creates in- and outgroups between those who share the same linguistic and cultural background and those who do not (Bourdieu, 1991). Furthermore, in addition to those ignoring such LEPs, there is a certain activism among some participants to counteract and defy standard language-LEPs, calling one's adherence to the state-imposed language "conditioning" (Elisabeth, 50). Importantly, not all teachers were aware of their actions, especially when students were regularly enrolled local students and were not part of a school exchange, for instance; some in fact became aware of discriminatory practices during the interview itself. Similar to what has been stated above, not distinguishing between students' linguistic and cultural backgrounds and adopting a colorblind approach might appear well-intended on the surface, but it neither recognizes nor fosters diversity (May & Sleeter, 2010). Instead, it is an attempt to homogenize the classroom's diversity and to impose the same requirements for everyone, thereby ignoring the crucial difference between equality and equity. Intriguingly, a distinction is made between international and national exchange students. While standard German is spoken with the former, given that they are believed to have no exposure to Swiss dialects whatsoever, expectations differ with exchange students from the French- or Italian-speaking parts of Switzerland. Swiss German is also spoken with the latter, again under the pretext of well-meant intentions of more authentic integration, during their stay in the canton of Zurich.

However, both scenarios face a dilemma. On the one hand, it seems as if integration without Swiss German is virtually impossible and teachers and fellow students alike almost artificially adjust themselves to the international students. Their special treatment, while considerate and well-intentioned, might not lead to the same degree of inclusion, acceptance, and well-being of the foreign students. On the other hand, French- and Italian-speaking Swiss students are most likely to be just as unfamiliar with the Swiss German dialects as the international students. They are exposed to Swiss German sporadically at most (with some exceptions) and learn GFL often with Germany-centered teaching material.

The study's findings further revealed that for some participants from the *Romandie*, Swiss German, and the perceived negative impact it has on intercantonal communication with different language groups, is a very controversial, emotional, and partly taboo issue. The use of Swiss German in interactions with *Romands* is largely considered condescending since they learn standard German in school and are typically not exposed to it otherwise. Participants' teaching experiences have shown that individuals are not willing to talk about it openly and express their dissatisfaction, partly because it is a taboo issue and because it has developed into a fear of even coming into contact with Swiss German speakers. Students' preference of going to Germany, instead of the German-speaking part of Switzerland, to conduct school projects and the unquestioned reproduction of stereotypes to support their arguments are typical examples of this gridlocked situation. The prestige and authenticity incorporated by the variety spoken in Germany is also much more promising in a context in which the language is learned primarily for socioeconomic purposes. Arguably, *Romand* students' familiarity with Swiss German varieties and their significance for their speakers is at least just as important since it can contribute to a better understanding among Swiss citizens – literally and figuratively.

Interestingly, ELF has been suggested as providing a neutral medium of communication, particularly among different Swiss national language groups (Durham, 2014), which is much complicated by the use of the different local varieties of Swiss German that are mostly incomprehensible to and often interpreted as an insult by the French- and Italian-speaking parts (Ribeaud, 2010). As this study's findings suggest, however, the native-speaker ideologies are reinforced by how much prestige and power is attributed to 'Inner Circle' varieties by students, teachers, and by other stakeholders. These ideologies (re)produce sub-hierarchies of languages, typically ranking AE/BE at the top, given that prestigious, standard varieties continue to be an (unreachable) objective for many English learners (Cook, 2007). The findings further indicate that students are susceptible to these varieties because they attribute authority and (linguistic) legitimacy to their role-model speakers, who are either English-speaking actors, musicians, Internet celebrities, or their English teachers with a native-like AE or BE accent. As Jana summarized her perspective on the native-speaker ideology: "[T]he goal would be to, when you graduate university to be perfectly proficient. I mean, absolutely perfect [in AE]" (Jana, 148–149).

Influenced by neoliberal ideology, proficient linguistic competences in English are considered indispensable human capital to qualify as a successful participant in the knowledge economy and to take advantage of the associated economic benefits (Ricento, 2015b). The Swiss education system, including the organization of national teacher education, contributes to a systemic reproduction of the native-speaker ideologies in language teaching. The (teacher) education system incentivizes its applicants to completely adopt the target language in order to pass as native-speaker role models for Swiss students by making stays in countries in which the language is spoken as a first/official language and/or C2 (highest CEFR proficiency level) certificates a mandatory requirement to even start teacher education in language subjects. As the study's findings demonstrate, teachers in fact appropriate the English language. They further move from passing as a native speaker to developing agency and a strong connection to their own experiences and linguistic identity (Norton & McKinney, 2011). This is particularly the case for Swiss German-speaking teachers who discover another (perceived to be) legitimate voice in their linguistic repertoire through English, which is often impacted by feelings of inferiority due to standard speech ideologies in SSG. The need to justify the proficiency of their own language skills by those stays abroad, by the exposure with local native speakers persists, however, thereby also reproducing the problematic static connection between a certain nation-state, e.g., England, and the locally spoken legitimate variety, e.g., BE.

Similarly, the CEFR applied in schools to foster and evaluate students' linguistic competences "by promoting methodological innovations and new approaches to designing teaching programmes, notably the development of a communicative approach" (CoE, 2021, n.p.) can be said to pursue the same neoliberal objectives (Kubota, 2015). Although hidden within an ostensible innovative and communication-oriented language policy framework, in order to normalize plurilingualism and to foster linguistic exchanges among speakers of different L1s, it reproduces native-speaker ideologies and fixed measurements by ranking one's competences on a scale from A1 (Basic User) to C2 (Proficient User) (McNamara, 2011). Textbooks also heavily rely on 'UK models of English' (Syrbe & Rose, 2018) which, as a general guidance in terms of pronunciation in specific, is largely appreciated by the participants. This is paradoxically the case for some teachers who claim that they reject such native-speaker ideology, thereby contradicting themselves. Although the pressure is already high among participants to pass the CAE (C1) exam, the admiration for those students who attempt to pass the C2 exam, which officially certifies near-native-like English proficiency, is even greater. As it is advertised on the Cambridge Assessment's website: "A C2 Proficiency qualification shows the world that you have mastered English to an exceptional level" (Cambridge Assessment, 2021). This not only creates in- and outgroups among students (Bourdieu, 1991) who obtain the Cambridge C1 or C2 certificate – although the actual difference in competence is probably negligible in the study's context – it also attests to many participants' strong desire to pass as an English native-speaker, which in itself is a mythical concept (Davies, 2003). As Motha (2014) argues convincingly:

> The wish to pass or necessity (or perceived necessity) of passing can be connected to the meanings and degree of undesirability associated with the category 'nonnative'…[it] can be read as denial or even loathing of one's own linguistic identity, intertwined as it is with one's racial and colonial identity, processes of passing simultaneously represent a challenge to linguistic essentialism and ideologies surrounding meanings of English and nativeness. Just as the concept of racial passing is reliant on Black and White being conceived of as completely distinguishable, fixed, and concretely defined, linguistic passing requires a separability and fixity of the categories 'native' and 'nonnative' (p. 94).

Adya's problematical lived experiences of language, for instance, incorporate the phenomenon of (perceived) necessity of passing that is embedded in what Hua and Li (2016) have coined 'nationality and ethnicity talk.' According to them, this kind of discourse "is essentially an act of identity calibration and involves categorization and positioning of self and others and stance-making" (Hua & Li, 2016, p. 450) in an effort to answer the question 'Where are you really from?' (Hua & Li, 2016). Although she receives compliments for her standard German accent (see above), she is also categorized as 'non-native' in terms of her (lacking) Swiss German competencies in both school and private contexts. Importantly, although the passing is imposed onto her, she portrays it as only "halfway forced" (Adya 63–64), having already internalized the 'native-speaker logic' and defending the perceived 'well-intended advice' from her teacher and dance instructor. Arguably, her linguistic passing is also linked to racial passing for her to 'fit in' better into Swiss society. As a Pakistani person, her physical appearance does not match the stereotypical 'average Swiss' person. To compensate for this, and to prove her 'localness' and legitimacy as a Swiss national, she now speaks 'Zurich German' and suppresses the German variety that she used growing up. This discriminatory behavior is justified by her teacher by claiming that it is beneficial for her professional future and successful integration. The same ignorance could hold true for her dance instructor who, considering her to be 'foreign,' speaks German although she uses Swiss German not to stand out (even more). Describing her experience as an "inculcation" (Adya, 299), it becomes clear that she was not free to choose her linguistic repertoire/identity and that she was discriminated against due to her physical appearance and her way of speaking. She felt like she had no other choice than to assimilate and to acquiesce to the existing (language) ideologies because she was forced into this position by her teacher, a representative of the education system in a position of power, and by her dance instructor, a role model and authority figure as well.

The native speaker ideology is not only reproduced in the form of institutionalized symbolic power and violence, but also (unconsciously) in participants' leisure activities and interests. As the example from Arthur's lived experiences shows, native speakers are personified in "Kanye West or Whitney Houston [or] Michael Jackson" (Arthur, 158–159), for instance, and their way of speaking is used to deduce authentic expressions and accents. Such simplistic categorizations of native speakers ignore the wide range of different levels of linguistic competencies among speakers and the question of (formal, informal, academic, etc.) register and contextual appropriateness (Agha, 2005). Conversely, there are participants who draw a line between professional and private contexts that require different English varieties with different standards. Timo's lived experiences of language indicate such a distinction which, although still problematical, increases tolerance and participants' exposure to a broader variety of accents and ways of speaking:

> [F]or almost two years I played this game almost every night, there were Polish people, English people, from all over the world people came together, a couple from India...I then noticed my progress myself, I felt more confident. If you can use it a lot, *especially because we didn't have any native speakers with us*, so true English people, but a Polish person with his English and the Swiss person,

> then everyone is on the same level. Then you dare more easily to simply start talking....They [Indians] spoke very well English, but with a *strong accent* and that's why you also dared. *In school it's BE*, everyone is familiar with it, that's high level.... (244–266 [emphasis added])

ELF applied in a translanguaging framework, with influences of many speakers' L1s, is an equitable communication tool in online gaming settings which reduces pressure and linguistic insecurity in non-native English speakers who rely on it to engage in innovative meaning-making language practices (García & Li, 2014). That said, Timo's quote also reveals that Indian English, for instance, which is the official language and L1 of many, is considered to have a strong (that is deviant) accent from the 'Inner Circle' varieties, which nevertheless triggered a feeling of equality and membership among non-native speakers of English.

Finally, ELF is considered to be inappropriate in official educational settings where the *status quo* is BE, a prestigious, elite variety transmitting value of authority, tradition, and order. For many other participants, ELF and other translanguaging practices also qualified as empowering mechanisms, providing an almost value- and judgment-free space with as few linguistic norms and rules as possible, but still retaining the maximum of interpersonal encounters. This should be the objective of inclusive multilingual education, in which awareness and promotion of diversity finally replaces monocultural and monolingual superiority and hegemonization. As Mohanty (2009) summarized it sharply:

> MLE [Multilingual education] is not just about building a bridge or many bridges; it is about developing a mindset to overcome the barriers between 'monolingual stupidity' and 'multilingual promise', barriers between a legislated and contrived unity and a naturally flourishing diversity. It is about building a better world, a world of diversity. It is about our survival (p. 14–15).

To conclude, this section's intention was not to provide a definite answer to the rather provocative question of English as a *mediator* or *troublemaker* since languages, the interactions among those, their speakers, and situational contexts are always in flux and are renegotiated so that they should always be seen as resources, not as fixed entities that can take over others. It is up to us to maximize the potential of the entire linguistic and cultural diversity that exists around us and not to limit it to ostensibly prestigious and powerful languages. We must also be careful not to neglect the symbolic power and opportunities often linked to those. Just as every individual is unique, so too are their linguistic repertoires, which makes any attempt to homogenize diversity superfluous.

Conclusion

Switzerland's multilingualism is a complex social phenomenon, which is inextricably intertwined with the country's historical past as a *Willensnation*, engrained in its constitution and public policy framework, and experienced in intercantonal social practices ranging from politics to multimedia. Switzerland's linguistic landscape has been substantially shaped by an increase in diversity over the last few decades, despite its long-established multilingual tradition and its very good international reputation for equal LPP (Kużelewska, 2016). One heavy influence comes from the growing popularity and use of English in the Swiss public sphere, virtual contexts including social media, and communication among speakers of different (national) languages. Additionally, migrants from a myriad of different cultural and linguistic backgrounds have gained in significance against the backdrop of increasing diversity and led to an increase from 3.7% in 1970 to 22.7% in 2019 (FSO, 2021) in the permanent resident population who speak non-national languages. This development presents a particular challenge for the education system since it is confronted with neoliberal mechanisms that are mobilized through English and ideology-laden curricula reforms on the one hand and by a growing student diversity without a corresponding increase in diversity- or inclusion-engaged teaching approaches, staff, or infrastructure on the other.

It has been my objective to elucidate the different societal forces that affect Switzerland's multilingualism and the implications for the education system from a critical social perspective by uncovering underlying power relations and hidden hegemonic mechanisms that are often obfuscated and invisible to those individuals who are directly affected by them. Therefore, the education system's local agents, i.e., students and teachers, were chosen as voices for this study. This study advocates a bottom-up policy decision-making process in which all actors are equally involved, and from which everyone can benefit equitably, by emphasizing the perspectives of students and teachers. In this section, I address the study's research questions and examine potential implications for theory, policy, curricula, and practice. Importantly, while this is this manuscript's last section, it is also a new beginning by which to re-engage with my participants' narratives and experiences, re-explore their language biographies, and revive their voices based on different (research) questions, specific social debates, and issues or ongoing policy reforms.

6.1 The Language Learning Debate as Starting Point

This study – at least the preliminary ideas and theoretical considerations – began with personal experiences that I had when moving to Switzerland just over four years ago, my first time ever living in an officially multilingual country. I quickly learned that *de jure* language policies were adopted differently in real-life interactions, that bi- or multilingualism could refer to the separate co-existence of two or more languages with little exchange among the multiple languages, and, perhaps most importantly, that I myself had held ideological beliefs about certain languages/varieties to which I had not been exposed previously. The more I read about Switzerland's multilingualism in the media or scholarly literature and the more I talked to local people, the more I noticed that there was one particular debate – the language learning debate – which mobilized the education policy decision to prioritize English over a national language to address sociopolitical issues of dominance and dependence. The debate I was witnessing echoed Blommaert's (1999) observation that

> debates develop against a wider sociopolitical and historical horizon of relationships of power, forms of discrimination, social engineering, nation-building and so forth…the outcome of a debate directly or indirectly involves forms of conflict and inequality among groups of speakers: restrictions on the use of certain languages/varieties, the loss of social opportunities when these restrictions are not observed by speakers, the negative stigmatization of certain languages/varieties, associative labels attached to languages/varieties (p. 2).

It was my intention to better understand and to disentangle the language learning debate, its underlying power mechanisms, consequences for certain groups of speakers, the education system, and its actors, and to amplify the voices of those affected by, but who were often excluded from, the debate.

These questions were addressed by talking to actors in the field of (language) education and were based on a theoretical framework that combined the concepts of *power, language,* and *education, critical multiculturalism, plurilingual identities,* and *unequal Englishes*. 94 questionnaires were completed by students and 34 in-depth interviews were conducted with students and teachers; this enterprise was embedded in a phenomenological research design (van Manen, 2017) with an emphasis on individuals' lifeworlds, their perspectives, practices, and experiences and was conducted with the objective of raising awareness of this crucial topic and its implications. The findings derived from the data are summarized in the following four sub-sections and each address the study's research questions:

- Linguistic repertoires, lived experiences of language, and identity expression through language in restrictive multilingual contexts;
- The reproduction of the 'monolingual habitus' in Swiss upper secondary schools;
- Language hierarchies;
- Symbolic power and legitimacy in the native-speaker and standard-speech ideologies.

6.2 Linguistic Repertoires, Lived Experiences of Language, and Identity Expression through Language in Restrictive Multilingual Contexts

This sub-section addresses primarily the first research question concerning how students' and teachers' linguistic repertoires are constituted and how they are employed to position individuals and groups within (restrictive) linguascapes. Since linguistic repertoires are closely linked to individuals' lived experiences of language, this sub-section also partly covers the second research question: What are students' and teachers' lived experiences of language? This question is further elaborated in sub-section 6.5.

All of the study's participants are speakers of multiple languages, although some either do not identify as such or are unaware of their habitual multilingual practices. As a result of the discussion in which my participants and I engaged, some of them indicated that they had become more aware of their language skills and practices, which can increase their self-esteem and confidence as the data and the existing literature suggest (Abendroth-Timmer & Hennig, 2014; Delpit, 2006; García, 2009). The perceived linguistic insecurity regarding their entire repertoire partly originates from their lived experiences of language often within restrictive linguascapes that impede the use of other languages than the local/official one based on language policies, laws, and ideologies. It further renders it more difficult, if not impossible, for some plurilinguals to fully express their identity when certain parts of their linguistic repertoire receive devaluation or even outright discrimination. At the same time, some participants felt more 'complete' or 'at ease' in settings in which they could freely use their linguistic repertoires and capitalize on different personality traits linked to each language. Languages, dialects, and other ways of speaking are hugely important to position oneself and (are actively and proudly used to) indicate membership of a certain speech group. This is especially true for minority languages, as was reported to be the case for Romansh, the Italian dialect spoken in Grisons, and for the various Swiss German varieties which all functioned as a means to distinguish speakers from the surrounding language majorities, thereby creating a greater sense of community.

The multi-faceted and non-linear nature of linguistic repertoires, influenced by migration and globalization processes, also suggests that they are always in flux, are co-constructed in interaction with others, and underlie a constant negotiation of skills, ideological constraints, and contextual or social cues. They "come to the fore, then return to the background, they observe each other, keep their distance from each other, intervene or interweave into something new, but in one form or another they are always there" (Busch, 2017c, p. 356). Suppressing certain parts of one's linguistic repertoire which are and remain ever-present and inter-dependent on other parts to make a whole, necessarily impacts upon individuals' subjectivity, perception of the self, and well-being. As expressed poignantly by Patrick, "even after 18 years...even when I only say two sentences...this origin, this identity is somehow very strongly expressed through language and...it remains very strong" (360–362).

6.3 The Reproduction of the 'Monolingual Habitus' in Swiss Upper Secondary Schools

This sub-section addresses the study's third research question about students' and teachers' perspectives on Switzerland's multilingualism and its multilingual education.

Monolingual language practices and LEPs are the norm in all three participating schools, despite the bilingual immersion programs, CAE exams, and most students' and teachers' awareness of the existing linguistic and cultural diversity within the classrooms. Certain selected (non-national) languages, such as English or Spanish for instance, are allowed within controlled settings such as specific language or CLIL classes. HLs, conversely, are sometimes institutionalized in LCO classes at lower secondary level, but not at all in post-compulsory education. The data also showed that it is not only the lacking offer or infrastructure for HL inclusion that is problematic; rather, the *de facto* exclusion of students with diverse linguistic and cultural backgrounds due to – among other forms – existing language barriers to gaining entry to upper secondary education, for example, reveal a more profound systemic issue. Many also considered their L1 inappropriate and bothersome in official school contexts among the participating HL-speaking students and this indicates that a more profound attitude change is needed in order to increase minority language speakers' confidence and to decrease feelings of insecurity and shame. Furthermore, such change is likewise needed in the policy sector, given the prevalent perspective that it is "totally impossible to believe [all the HLs] will be integrated into school" (Jacqueline, 175–176). While providing institutional space and recognition for all students' diverse linguistic and cultural backgrounds is certainly a complex endeavor, it is the only way for schools to achieve equity, capitalize on everyone's potential, and to provide valuable and meaningful learning experiences. The case of Romansh as a national, minority language, as described by my participants, clearly exemplifies how attitudes and policies mutually influence each other at both school and society level. It illustrates how thorough acquisition planning (Hornberger, 2006) can lead to official language rights, political and financial support for language promotion and education, and an increase in recognition of Romansh and its speakers. At the same time, pro-Romansh LEPs in Grisons, as summarized keenly by Henri (427–428), "tried to make the system equal for everyone, [but] they created inequality." French is a national language that is considered important by Grisons students, but is reduced to an optional subject for students enrolled in the German-Romansh bilingual program, which can decrease their chances of Switzerland-wide employability and can exacerbate intercantonal communication.

Conversely, many participating students viewed stronger English language skills as the primary objective for language classes at upper secondary level, which would adequately prepare them for future academic and professional challenges. In fact, many teachers also regard the CAE exam preparation as a greater responsibility than other curricula objectives, given that it leads to a prestigious certificate which has become viewed as a standard requirement for university or job applications. Although the exam is not mandatory in all three of the participating schools, the situation puts pressure on both students and teachers, to wit: it causes feelings of guilt in some students for not using their spare time to prepare for the exam and feelings of failure in some teachers for not achieving their pedagogical objectives. Moreover, although the CAE certificate attests that students have a high level of English language skills (C1), the data showed that those students taking the Cambridge Proficiency of English exam (C2) were admired (even more) by many students and teachers. Conversely, this also created tensions and discomfort in other teachers since they are expected to have a C2 level certificate to *teach* English; having both teachers and students 'officially' share the same language level is what undermined their authority.

Finally, school language teaching in Switzerland has been a crucial, but sensitive, topic for a long time. As Stotz (2006, p. 249) formulated it: "Squaring political power and evening out perceived or real grudges among the German-, French-, Italian- and Romansh-speaking groups has occupied the agenda for a century and a half." It is commonly seen as the education system's responsibility to pave the way for national cohesion and harmony through the learning of the national languages. At the same time, despite the covert and overt tensions, dissatisfaction, and inequity, Elmiger (2021) rightfully observes that "one can sometimes get the impression that at the school level, the field of foreign languages is too well ordered to be questioned" (p. 12 [my translation]). This order has been disturbed, however, with the language learning debate partly triggered through the introduction of English before a national language in some cantons.

6.4 Language Hierarchies

Language hierarchies are the central element of the study's fourth research question, and it deals with how students and teachers (de)construct and legitimize them. The data indicate that language hierarchies are a constructed social phenomenon that exist on different levels. They are reproduced and legitimized at a societal level through political decisions, individuals' perspectives and ideologies, and through public discourse. The same is true for educational institutions in which they are reproduced and legitimized through LEPs, curricula, and through their actors' perspectives and ideologies. Problematically, these hierarchies not only rank languages, dialects, or other ways of speaking, but also their speakers. As Arthur explained, for instance, being a speaker of Macedonian, a language which is generally considered with low prestige, often automatically labels him as someone from a low socioeconomic background. At the same time, all participating HL speakers prioritized the local national language over their HLs, due to its perceived higher status and linguistic capital (Bourdieu, 1991). Many of those further considered ELF to be more important to their personal and professional lives, which in some cases created more profound inner conflicts of cultural or linguistic identification. The interview with Adya, for example, revealed that she was not only aware of these language hierarchies, but that she even used them to her advantage. Given Swiss German's societal importance, and the commonly perceived interwovenness of language and integration, she has adopted Swiss German as her most significant language to demonstrate her 'Swissness.' The majority language position is reinforced by perspectives such as: "German is simply everything" (Gita, 312) or "if they [migrants] want to stay in Switzerland, [they] necessarily [have to] also optimize German..." (Elisabeth, 432–433). As Heller and Duchêne (2012) observe critically: "If you don't speak the language of the nation, and speak it properly, you show that you lack the ability to reason and the strength to prevail that citizenship requires; you therefore can't claim access to political and economic power" (p. 5).

The German-speaking dominance or "Germanization" (Coray, 2009) is also felt by speakers of other national languages, interpreted by Victoria as "a friction" (Victoria, 194), which is particularly strong between the French-and German-speaking groups in bilingual Fribourg. These ideologies and tensions can be explained, Jeanne believes, by a reversed intentional demonstration of power capitalizing on the French-speaking dominant position in the canton, which is habitually perceived as undermined at a national level. The overall impression is that "German MUST be learned" (Victoria, 193) and prioritized over English, even though it is not liked by students. Many Fribourg students and teachers believe that they would decrease their chances of employment, given the *Romandie*'s dependency on German-speaking Switzerland, without strong German language skills. These arguments are seen as pretext or a mere uncritical reproduction of the *status quo* by others since students' language skills are typically higher in English than in German and social reality already demonstrates that ELF is the preferred choice for communication among speakers of different L1s in both private and professional contexts. Schools, and therefore their actors, are instrumentalized in order to maintain traditions and to improve social cohesion while Etienne, for instance, "do[esn't] know what holds us together culturally" (Etienne, 279). In fact, many German-speaking participants believed that ELF could reduce power dynamics and linguistic insecurity in communication among the different language groups, a common denominator impossible to achieve otherwise given each canton's (potentially) different implementation of LEPs. Yet, as Sonja summarized succinctly, these cantonal discrepancies and the lack of a Swiss-wide approach to reducing such language hierarchies impede the possibility of a satisfactory solution being generated that pleases everyone:

> I believe that's one of these decisions which can probably never be made satisfactorily because either you say, we want to remain competitive internationally, then it's clear for German-speaking Switzerland, that's English....But if we say, to keep the feeling of nationalism and language diversity, then it would be French. Although (-) then the Ticinese would have (--), then they wouldn't be happy either because the first foreign language would be French and not Italian (256–262).

Finally, this quote, despite mentioning "language diversity," in fact only focuses on *national* languages, thereby exemplifying a prevalent language hierarchy, that is: the exclusion of Romansh. As the data indicate, Romansh speakers are often exposed to such discriminatory hierarchies and (are forced to) commonly defend their linguistic rights as a language minority on a cantonal and national level. That said, they (as well as the Italian-speaking minority in Grisons) can use their low position within the language hierarchies to advocate for their rights, raise awareness among speakers of other languages of potential unequal language policies, laws, and practices, and can receive more political and financial support. This requires strong conviction from the Romansh speakers themselves who are often accustomed to accommodating other language speakers (particularly German ones) since they are all bilingual in both Romansh and German. The same holds true for LEPs and the curriculum in Grisons schools which prescribe German as mandatory language for all students while Romansh and Italian, the canton's two other official languages, can be learned optionally. Yet, although language hierarchies often devalue minority languages, and are thus detrimental to their speakers, they are always in flux, socially co-constructed, and can be used as leverage to advocate for disadvantaged social groups' political representation, in changing the *status quo*, and to increase social equity as a form of 'strategic essentialism' (Spivak, 1993).

6.5 Symbolic Power and Legitimacy in the 'Native-Speaker' and 'Standard-Speech' Ideologies

This sub-section primarily addresses the study's fifth research question concerning how students and teachers (de)construct and legitimize (existing) sub-hierarchies within certain languages and further exemplifies students' and teachers' lived experiences of language as part of the second research question (see also 6.2).

Language sub-hierarchies as social constructs capture well the different positions linguistic varieties and other ways of speaking along with their speakers have based on the perceived prestige, legitimacy, and their resemblance to an (imaginary) 'native-speaker' and 'standard-speech' yardstick (Bylin & Tingsell, 2021). The findings can also be presented as a continuum (see below) of romantic and rationalist poles (Geeraerts, 2003) with the former expressing identity and pride and the latter profiting from linguistic capital (Heller & Duchêne, 2012). Importantly, this does not exclude the possibility of employing Swiss German varieties or Romansh idioms, for instance, to gain profit, too.

Romantic/Pride		**Rationalist/Profit**
Heritage/minority languages		Standardized national languages
Swiss German dialects		(Swiss) standard German
Romansh idioms		Rumantsch Grischun
	ELF	American/British English

Switzerland's linguistic landscape has become the site of a positionality struggle between tradition and globalization (Hua & Li, 2016) with an increasing complexity in linguistic diversity and interests. In order to acknowledge all the different idiolects on the continuum which defy simplistic categorization on either pole, active promotion of linguistic and cultural diversity is needed for which a critical deconstruction of the 'native-speaker' and 'standard speech' ideologies is key. The data show that this criticality is often lacking. There are students who, for instance, take American hip hop artists as their role models for the English language without fully understanding the different registers and contextual cues (Agha, 2005). There are others who see perfecting their English skills as the main purpose of education:

"...the goal would be to, when you graduate university to be perfectly proficient. I mean, absolutely perfect [in AE]" (Jana, 148–149). Such native speaker ideologies often delegitimize Swiss English teachers who pursue different pedagogical objectives regarding accuracy and academic speaking and writing styles, although they simultaneously also reproduce the native speaker ideology based on a more formal register of AE or BE. On a policy level, admission requirements to Swiss teacher education institutions such as stays abroad or Cambridge proficiency certificates systemically reproduce the 'native-speaker' ideologies and incentivize pre-service English teachers to adopt an 'Inner Circle' variety to later pass on to students. At the same time, certain students are pressured by the high language expectations in AE/BE and feel much more comfortable in contexts where ELF is used as a common communication tool. The study has found that the reproduction of the 'native-speaker' ideology and the language sub-hierarchies, which favor prestigious varieties, can hegemonize speakers of other languages and social practices and impede meaningful, value- and judgement-free communication, thereby engaging everyone's potential. ELF and other translanguaging practices serve exactly this purpose and are not only applicable in international communication, but are very much appreciated as a mediator even in Switzerland's intranational communication. It provides a legitimate voice to all those who cannot fully use their language of choice due to sociopolitical constraints or underlying standard speech ideologies, which is often the case for both speakers of heritage and minority languages and for Swiss German varieties; the latter of those in particular cause tensions among the different language groups and are deeply embedded in power dynamics (Ribeaud, 2010), which can potentially be reduced through a non-national language such as ELF.

That said, existing beliefs that represent the majority language speaker position such as "social life in Switzerland simply doesn't work enough [without Swiss German]" (Elisabeth, 43) cannot be addressed simply by switching to ELF in order to avoid conflict. Adya's lived experiences of language, for instance, exemplifies the view that the 'native speaker' ideology can also refer to dialects and oppose the 'standard-speech' ideology. In her case, as she was told by her teacher, instead of speaking standard German – one of her L1s – she should adopt Swiss German to showcase her 'localness' and integration often questioned due to her 'non-typical Swiss physical appearance.' Swiss German can, thus, be used to strategic, profitable advantage to increase academic/employment opportunities and to pass as a 'true' Swiss person while reducing "undesirability associated with the category 'nonnative'" (Motha, 2014, p. 94). At the same time, others envy her for her standard accent in German, which is still often considered more prestigious by many especially in educational contexts, thereby again forcing her to adapt her linguistic repertoire to social expectations and ideologies. Exchange students are also impacted by the use of Swiss German in class, since it plays a central role in rapport building among teachers and students and is the natural way of communicating for its speakers, even though it is excluded on a *de jure* basis. For those who do not speak it, however, it can label them as members of the outgroup (Bourdieu, 1991) and can render integration more difficult. More transparent LEPs and equitable language practices are needed that recognize all students' and teachers' ways of speaking, paying particular attention to 'non-standard' idiolects that are officially censored from educational contexts. For instance, providing institutional space to Swiss German can not only reduce feelings of inferiority and deficiency, which many people experience when comparing their way of speaking with standard German norms and speakers, but it can also foster better understanding for exchange and/or *Romand* students who learn the standard variety exclusively. The situation is similar for the different Romansh idioms, three of which have been standardized into RG while the other two have been excluded. Despite the systemic hierarchization of individuals' ways of speaking through status planning processes (Hornberger, 2006), the distinction of more or less prestigious varieties also impacts their position within society at large. Those living in more rural areas in Grisons, whose ways of speaking resemble less the (artificial) standard(ized) language, are often considered to be "a second category person" (Henri, 344).

Finally, instead of viewing languages, dialects, and other ways of speaking as hierarchies, they are better understood as existing on a continuum and as movable. Language practices in an increasingly diverse society are more complex and translingual and, thus, defy simplistic dichotomous categorization as '(non-)standard' or '(non-)native.' Raising awareness of the potential sociopolitical, economic, and/or mental consequences of such existing social constructs is a responsibility of the education system, however, and should be taken seriously (Delpit, 2006).

6.6 Theoretical Implications

A general remark is needed on terminology. Throughout my theoretical framework, data analysis, findings, and the discussion, I make use of concepts and terms that are used because of a lack of better terminology or because they are established terms in the literature, which remain no less inappropriate. These include, for instance, native speaker, standard speech, the somewhat forced distinction among individual's L1, L2, etc. when one's linguistic repertoire is much better described as a dynamic continuum, national/foreign/heritage languages, or ELF. By defining these concepts with a fixed name, I contribute to the reproduction of categories that do not authentically depict social reality's complexity and that might be considered inappropriate by individuals for whom I use the terms. A theoretical implication should be to deconstruct such terminology more thoroughly, given the (discursive) power of categories (Butler, 1997), and to commonly decide on adequate descriptions and terms with participants or ethical advisors for future research. These implications might be limited to the theoretical/empirical context and gradually change mentalities and habits of the wider society since these categories typically fulfill practical or pragmatic purposes in everyday social practices.

The study's underlying theoretical framework consists of different theories, frameworks, and concepts to situate my study and to embed my research questions. It positions language and education at the interplay of different influences and mechanisms such as neoliberalism, power, social justice, hegemony, critical multiculturalism, LPP, identity, and applied teaching approaches. These were considered indispensable to capturing the multi-faceted nature of both language and education, the different functions and constituents, and actors involved on the societal and educational levels. Despite the multiple foci and different international theoretical and applied orientations, the theoretical framework seemed partly insufficient to capturing the complexity on a *national* level. A framework combining all these aspects with a focus on its national linguistic and educational landscape would be beneficial, given the plethora of details regarding Switzerland's education system, the different education levels, cantonal discrepancies, curricula reforms in some regions and not others, policy documents in four national languages, and political involvement through referenda. This would allow for an investigation of intranational aspects further and comparatively among more cantons, language regions, mono-/bi/trilingual cantons, influx of HLs, and its policy framework from a historical or contemporary perspective and would allow us to then engage in further comparative studies in international contexts. At the same time, adopting a national lens when globalization and migration processes make social life increasingly diverse, dynamic, and complex might perhaps be counter-intuitive. Yet, although education has no boundaries, national education systems continue to impose limits and restrictions and, thus, serve as different research sites, which can be used to learn from each other until boundary-less, equitable education is achieved. That said, a more nationally focused theoretical framework should not replace the one used here since, from a post-structural perspective, concepts such as *identity*, *language*, and *power* are always in flux, constantly being (re-)produced through discourse and space, and can continuously be re-appropriated by individuals as agentive subjects. Thus, research that combines international and interdisciplinary perspectives with a *national theoretical framework* can contribute to new policies and practices that are necessary for the future of education.

6.7 Implications for Policy, Curricula, and Practice

> The school is a large ship which, no matter how fast it cruises, is difficult to maneuver: each attempt to reorient its trajectory can only be envisaged in the long term, because often a change of course – even a small one – is only translated into reality slowly and gradually. (Elmiger, 2021, p. 100 [my translation])

While implications for policy and practice are often listed separately in other research, I intentionally combine both aspects here and add specific implications for school curricula within the study's focus on upper secondary education. I consider it to be more appropriate to highlight the necessary paradigm shift of common, bottom-up policy decision-making processes with all actors involved.

Important policy strategies as suggested by the EDK (2013) ten years ago without sufficient implementation to this date – also endorsed by this study as recommendations – include:

- the active promotion of students' plurilingualism through excursions in neighboring language regions or countries, use of teaching material in different languages, project-based learning for students of the same HL, inclusion of the community and parents as speakers of HLs, culinary/cultural/musical activities associated with different languages, co-/team-teaching with other language subject teachers, book/film clubs for different languages, etc.;
- the facilitation of collaboration among language teachers to enable team and integrative language teaching through interdisciplinary study programs for all language subject teachers and the introduction of modules on multilingualism and migration for all pre-service teachers;
- the expansion of CLIL particularly regarding authentic and tailored teaching material to take local/national curricular requirements into consideration, authentic and rich target language input, and appropriate teacher preparation and compensation;
- the development of an internet platform to organize school exchanges.

It is crucial not to neglect these ongoing challenges when they are redebated in current curricular reforms among other urgent social issues such as digitalization, climate change, or the ongoing Covid-19 pandemic as critically important educational topics for future generations.

Generally, objectives for post-compulsory language teaching need to be revisited. While detailed objectives based on the CEFR exist regarding language proficiency, more profound questions concerning students' actual language *use* outside of school need to be asked. Are students trained to study or work in a different language region? Do they learn how the different cultural mentalities represented in Switzerland actually work? Are they meant to create meaningful encounters with peers from another language region and accommodate them by speaking the other's language? Should everyone in these encounters be able to speak their national L1, thereby practicing receptive multilingualism? To what extent do schools see themselves or are seen as responsible for teaching their students the basics to ensure national cohesion, peaceful cohabitation, and mutual understanding? How can the teaching of national languages, English, and other languages create synergies instead of competition? It is essential to discuss these questions, to which no satisfactory answers have yet been found, before adopting new policies or curricula and thus continuing a way of language teaching that has only been moderately successful in output and has done so "more out of obligation than conviction" (Elmiger, 2021, p. 110 [my translation]).

While schools have increased their offers of bilingual programs over the last decade, there is more to be done on a systemic level to provide this to as many students as possible in an equitable way. Thus, it should not be up to individual school leaders to decide whether such programs are to be implemented at their school, how many financial resources allocated, and which teachers charged with carrying them out. Rather, such decisions should be made at the cantonal level at least in order to have consistent programs in case students have to change schools, to efficiently manage human and financial resources, and to collaborate with the canton's teacher education institutions to fill the demand for bilingual teachers. The majority of bilingual programs are also conducted in the local national language plus English. While this is sensible, to a certain extent given that many university study programs (at MA level) are offered in English, students are already very used to and exposed to English in (almost) natural contexts outside of school, as the study's data have shown. CLIL in a second national language, for instance, could provide a chance for students to discover the language through authentic content with less emphasis on grammar and literature and would allow them to choose among an even greater number of universities or job opportunities across all of Switzerland after graduation. This, in turn, requires trained teachers who can teach in a second national language and/or English, which again depends on teacher preparation and continuous training for in-service teachers. Importantly, CLIL is primarily a *bi*lingual teaching approach and is often associated with common languages in which study programs and teaching materials exist and, therefore, is seemingly incompatible with a *multi*lingual teaching mentality. That said, dedicating CLIL teaching to the national languages or English opens up time and resources to be allocated to HLs and language and culture classes, time which would otherwise not exist. This study, therefore, argues for the adoption of a transdisciplinary approach to teaching in which subjects are combined and taught based on students' desires and needs, and on logistical requirements, albeit to a lesser extent.

Additionally, given Switzerland's rather small size and good infrastructure, exchanges among the different language regions to experience the other languages and cultures firsthand and to learn together with peers in natural contexts should be promoted, institutionalized, and subsidized to a much more significant degree. Offers should further be expanded to include not only students, but also (pre- and in-service) teachers, and school leaders. Despite financial support through *Movetia*, for instance, some teachers reported that many educational institutions were reluctant to organize exchanges. A great deal of additional effort, energy, and time is needed (particularly from teachers) who deserve incentives for their tremendous work. Investing in such intercultural encounters can help to deconstruct existing prejudices and stereotypes and might inspire adolescents to learn about other languages and cultures so that they no longer feel like "they don't like us at all, they speak Swiss German, we can't understand anything [and] they won't understand us" (David, 171–172). Another implication can be derived from David's experience, to wit: how to deal with the dominant use of different Swiss German dialects in the German-speaking part of Switzerland when the French-and Italian-speaking parts learn standard German in school. Instead of adhering to 'standard-speech' ideologies, schools should teach languages in the way they occur naturally, especially if the objective is to increase communication and understanding among Switzerland's different language groups. Therefore, students from the French- and Italian-speaking regions could be trained to understand Swiss German and might learn about its cultural value and the (linguistic) differences among the various local dialects, SSG, and standard German. Again, such measures require language teachers with (receptive) competences in Swiss German, updated teaching material to guide teachers and provide students with authentic exposure, and finally concern the integration of such competencies in teacher preparation.

Finally, given the study's embeddedness in this transformative period, caused by the Covid-19 pandemic, further implications concern education's digital future. Given the increased opportunity and improved technological infrastructure in schools, minority and heritage language classes in particular could be made available to a wider audience via online learning tools. The lack of infrastructure or teachers in a specific language were commonly mentioned as reasons why schools do not offer LCO classes or teaching in minority/heritage languages. This was discussed with a Romansh teacher during an interview as a viable solution to reaching Romansh-speaking students in Zurich who would otherwise not receive any formal instruction in their L1. The same could be tested for students' other L1s. That being understood, the introduction of online learning opportunities for minority/heritage language-speaking students must not be seen as a replacement for learning experiences with other students in person. However, it can serve as an innovative, temporary, or bridging solution until schools are in a position to provide the necessary infrastructure and can recruit qualified teachers to also serve the interests and needs of *all* students and can stop promoting a linguistically restrictive education.

6.8 Future Research and Conclusion

The study strived to contribute to this change toward more equity and social justice and future research can further expand on this ambitious goal. This can be done by integrating individuals from linguistic and cultural backgrounds unaccounted for in this study, notably the Italian-speaking region. Given the uniqueness of every canton and its education system, including other cantons would also serve well as interesting research sites if urban centers were compared to more rural areas of Switzerland, for instance. Furthermore, migrant students with lower linguistic competences in the local school language are an essential inclusion, given the linguistic barriers and Switzerland's exclusive admission system to post-compulsory education. Including school leaders as important decision makers, regarding the implementation of students' HLs at an institutional level, is also recommended. Additionally, it would be interesting to draw a comparison among the different education levels (primary, secondary, tertiary) and to investigate the different challenges and successful practices of educational institutions regarding linguistic and cultural diversity. Future research could also analyze existing teacher preparation programs, curricula, and teaching material in order to determine whether the implications described here are practicable.

Although this study has come to an end, its purpose continues and becomes increasingly relevant every day. Switzerland's linguistic landscape is increasingly more diverse and complex with migration flows across Europe and different international policy changes impacting the Swiss job market for expats ruled by neo-capitalistic mechanisms. Languages, as one of the most crucial markers of one's identity and linguistic capital (Bourdieu, 1991), are caught between different societal forces that incorporate sameness or difference and either equity or injustice. Due to underlying hegemonic processes, not all speakers can employ their linguistic repertoires equally in social practices either because they are censored from official contexts or because of their perceived low self-esteem, which is in turn linked to linguistic insecurity. Others whose linguistic repertoires include the majority language and who fit into the socially constructed category of the legitimate 'native speaker' can benefit from it effortlessly to the disadvantage of the minoritized language speakers, however. Problematically, the education system partly reproduces and legitimizes these mechanisms by adhering to such ideologies and to the 'monolingual habitus.' Yet, if all of the actors involved can manage to deconstruct discriminatory policies and practices, regarding certain languages and/or groups of people, and can engage in the promotion of *true* linguistic and cultural diversity and structural change instead, then we are one step closer to equity and social justice. Only by further engaging with and advancing research on social diversity, and those processes that impede it, can we appreciate what makes us human and how we might learn from each other to succeed in our ever-changing society.

References

Abendroth-Timmer, D., & Fäcke, C. (2011). Migrationsbedingte Mehrsprachigkeit. In F.-J. Meißner, & U. Krämer (Eds.), *Spanischunterricht gestalten: Wege zu Mehrsprachigkeit und Mehrkulturalität* (pp. 16–48). Klett-Kallmeyer.

Abendroth-Timmer, D., & Hennig, E.-M. (2014). Introduction plurilingualism and multiliteracies: Identity construction in language education. In D. Abendroth-Timmer & E.-M. Hennig (Eds.), *Plurilingualism and multiliteracies: International research on identity construction in language education* (pp. 23–38). Peter Lang AG.

Aebeli, C. (2001). Englisch ab der ersten Klasse: Das Zürcher Experiment. In R. J. Watts, & H. Murray (Eds.), *Die fünfte Landessprache? Englisch in der Schweiz* (pp. 69–84). vdf Hochschulverlag.

Agha, A. (2005). Registers of language. In A. Duranti (Ed.), *A companion to linguistic anthropology* (pp. 23–45). Blackwell Publishing Ltd.

Altermatt, B. (2005). Die institutionelle Zweisprachigkeit der Stadt Fribourg-Freiburg: Geschichte, Zustand und Entwicklungstendenzen. *Bulletin suisse de linguistique appliquée 82*, 63–82.

Althusser, L. (1971). Ideology and ideological state apparatuses (Notes towards an investigation). In L. Althusser (Ed.), *Lenin and philosophy, and other essays* (pp. 127–188). Monthly Review Press.

Anchimbe, E. A. (2006). The native-speaker *fever* in English language teaching (ELT): Pitting pedagogical competence against historical origin. *Linguistik online 26*(1), 3–14.

Anderson, B. (2006). *Imagined communities: Reflections on the origin and spread of nationalism* (new ed.). Verso.

Anderson, J. (2018). Reimagining English language learners from a translingual perspective. *ELT Journal 72*(1), 26–37.

Apple, M. (1993). *Official knowledge*. Routledge.

Apple, M. (2012). *Education and power* (2nd ed.). Routledge.

Apple, M. (2019). *Ideology and curriculum* (4th ed.). Routledge.

Appadurai, A. (1996). *Modernity at large: Cultural dimensions of globalization*. University of Minnesota Press.

Austin, J. (1962). *How to do things with words* (2nd ed.). Oxford University Press.

Ayers, W., Kumashiro, K., Meiners, E., Quinn, T., & Stovall, D. (2017). *Teaching toward democracy: Educators as agents of change* (2nd ed.). Routledge.

Bakhtin, M. M. (1981) *The dialogic imagination*. University of Texas Press.

Baldauf, R. B., Jr. (2005). Language planning and policy research: An overview. In E. Hinkel (Ed.), *Handbook of research in second language teaching and learning* (pp. 953–970). Lawrence Erlbaum Associates.

Bale, J. (2015). Language policy and global political economy. In T. Ricento (Ed.), *Language policy and political economy: English in a global context* (pp. 72–96). Oxford University Press.

Bankston, C., & Zhou, M. (2002). Being well vs. doing well: Self-esteem and school performance among immigrant and nonimmigrant racial and ethnic groups. *The International Migration Review* 36(2), 389–415.

Barbour, R. (2007). *Doing focus groups*. SAGE Publications.

Bartlett, L. (2007). Literacy, speech and shame: The cultural politics of literacy and language in Brazil. *International Journal of Qualitative Studies in Education* 20(5), 547–563.

Bauman, R., & Briggs, C. L. (2000). Language philosophy as language ideology: John Locke and Johann Gottfried Herder. In P. V. Kroskrity (Ed.), *Regimes of language: Ideologies, polities, and identities* (pp. 139–204). School of American Research Press.

Beacco, J.-C. (2005). *Languages and language repertoires: Plurilingualism as a way of life in Europe: Guide for the development of language education policies in Europe: from linguistic diversity to plurilingual education*. Language Policy Division, Council of Europe, Strasbourg.

Becker, A. (2022). 'I'm also trying to figure out the identity of my students.' – Teachers' multilingual identity negotiation in the heritage language classroom. *International Journal of Multilingualism*. Ahead-of-print. https://doi.org/10.1080/14790718.2022.2078328

Becker, A. (2021). "I'm always in this conflict"-Students' struggle of plurilingual identity expression, linguistic insecurity, and assimilation in Switzerland's higher education. *European Education*. Advance online publication. https://doi.org/10.1080/10564934.2021.1971542

Becker, A., & Magno, C. S. (2022). Cognitive migration through language: Capturing linguistic movement and barriers in language portraits. In C. S. Magno, J. Lew, & S. Rodriguez (Eds.), *Innovative migration methodologies* (pp. 134–157). Brill.

Becker, A., & Knoll, A. (2021). Establishing multiple languages in early childhood: Heritage languages and language hierarchies in German-English daycare centers in Switzerland. *International Journal of bilingual education and bilingualism*. Advance online publication. https://doi.org/10.1080/13670050.2021.1932719

Benson, C. (2013). Towards adopting a multilingual habitus in educational development. In C. Benson, & Kosonen, K. (Eds.), *Language issues in comparative education:*

Inclusive teaching and learning in non-dominant languages and cultures (pp. 283–302). Sense Publishers.

Benteli, M. (2000, December 22). Diskussionen innerhalb der Kantonen und der EDK zum Thema Fremdsprache in der Schule. Retrieved June 30, 2021, from https://anneepolitique.swiss/prozesse/36691-englisch-als-erste-in-der-schule-unterrichtete-fremdsprache-zurich-appenzell-innerrhoden-setzte-erziehungsdirektorenkonferenz-entscheid-aus

Berthele, R. (2010). Dialekt als Problem oder Potenzial: Überlegungen zur Hochdeutschoffensive in der deutschen Schweiz aus Sicht der Mehrsprachigkeitsforschung. In F. Bitter Bättig, & A. Tanner (Eds.), *Sprachen lernen – Lernen durch Sprache* (pp. 37-52). Seismo Verlag.

Berthele, R. (2015). Language planning and standardization in a minority language context: A case study of Rumantsch Grischun in Switzerland. In W. Davies, & E. Ziegler (Eds.), *Language Planning and Microlinguistics: From policy to interaction and vice versa* (pp. 39–61). Palgrave Macmillan.

Berthele, R. (2020). The selective celebration of linguistic diversity: Evidence from the Swiss language policy discourse. *Journal of Multilingual and Multicultural Development.* https://doi.org/10.1080/01434632.2020.1715989

Berthele, R. & Lindt-Bangerter, B. (2011). *Evaluation des Projekts «Rumantsch Grischun in der Schule. Sprachstandserhebungen 3. Und 4. Klassen in den Fertigkeiten Leseverstehen, Schreiben und Sprechen».* Institut de Plurilinguisme.

Birra, R. (2017, May 15). Sprachenstreit: Zürich hat eine Schlüsselrolle. *Tagesanzeiger.* Retrieved June 30, 2021, from https://www.tagesanzeiger.ch/schweiz/standard/in-zuerich-entscheidet-sich-ob-der-bund-im-sprachenstreit-eingreifen-muss/story/26742201

Blackledge, A. (2010). The practice and politics of multilingualism. In U. Okulska, & P. Cap (Eds.), *Perspectives in politics and discourse* (pp. 301–326). John Benjamins.

Blackledge, A., & Creese, A. (2010). *Multilingualism: A critical perspective.* Continuum.

Blommaert, J. (1999). The debate is open. In: J. Blommaert (Ed.), *Language ideological debates* (pp. 3–38). Walter de Gruyter.

Blommaert, J. (2008). Language, asylum, and the national order. *Urban Language & Literacies 50*, 2–21.

Blommaert, J. (2010). *The sociolinguistics of globalization.* Cambridge University Press.

Bonilla-Silva, E. (2015). More than prejudice: Restatement, reflections, and new directions in critical race theory. *Sociology of Race and Ethnicity 1*(1), 75–89.

Bossart, M.-N. (2011). *Mehrsprachigkeit und Sprachenlernen aus Sicht von Schülerinnen und Schülern und deren Lehrpersonen. Eine qualitative Studie zur Situation vor und nach dem Stufenübertritt von der Primar- in die Sekundarstufe.* Université de Neuchâtel.

Bourdieu, P. (1991). *Language and symbolic power.* Polity Press.

Bourdieu, P. (1999). Understanding. In P. Bourdieu et al. (Eds.), *The weight of the world: Social suffering in contemporary society* (pp. 607–626). Stanford University Press.

Boylorn, R. M. (2008). Lived experience. In L. M. Given (Ed.), *The SAGE encyclopedia of qualitative research methods* (p. 490). SAGE Publications.

Braine, G. (2010). *Nonnative speaker English teachers: Research, pedagogy and professional growth*. Routledge.

Brown, K. D., Koreinik, K., & Siiner, M. (2017). Introductory chapter: Questioning borders. In M. Siiner, K. Koreinik, & K. D. Brown (Eds.), *Language policy beyond the state* (pp. 1–24). Springer.

Bruthiaux, P. (2003). Squaring the circles: Issues in modeling English worldwide. *International Journal of Applied Linguistics 13*(2), 159–178.

Bucholtz, M., & Hall, K. (2005a). Language and identity. In A. Duranti (Ed.), *A companion to linguistic anthropology* (pp. 369–394). Blackwell Publishing Ltd.

Bucholtz, M., & Hall, K. (2005b). Identity and interaction: A sociocultural linguistic approach. *Discourse studies 7*, 585–614.

Bucholtz, M., & Hall, K. (2008). Finding identity: Theory and data. *Multilingua – Journal of Cross-Cultural and Interlanguage Communication 27*(1–2), 151–163.

Busch, B. (2006). Language biographies for multilingual learning: Linguistic and educational considerations. *PRAESA Occasional Papers 24*, 5–18.

Busch, B. (2010). School language profiles: Valorizing linguistics resources in heteroglossic situations in South Africa. *Language and Education 24*(4), 283–294.

Busch, B. (2012). The linguistic repertoire revisited. *Applied Linguistics 33*(5), 503–523.

Busch, B. (2014). Building on heteroglossia and heterogeneity: The experience of a multilingual classroom. In A. Blackledge & A. Creese (Eds.), *Heteroglossia as practice and pedagogy* (pp. 21–40). Dodrecht: Springer Science+Business Media.

Busch, B. (2017a). Biographical approaches to research in multilingual settings: Exploring linguistic repertoires. In M. Martin-Jones, & D. Martin (Eds.), *Researching multilingualism: Critical and ethnographic perspectives* (pp. 47–59). Routledge.

Busch, B. (2017b). *Mehrsprachigkeit*. facultas.

Busch, B. (2017c). Expanding the notion of the linguistic repertoire: On the concept of *Spracherleben* – The lived experience of language. *Applied Linguistics 38*(3), 340–358.

Busch, B. (2018). The language portrait in multilingualism research: Theoretical and methodological considerations. *Working Papers in Urban Language & Literacies 236*, 1–13.

Butler, J. (1997). *Excitable speech: A politics of the performative*. Routledge.

Butler, J. (1999). *Gender trouble: Feminism and the subversion of identity*. Routledge.

Bylin, M. & Tingsell, S. (2021). The native speaker: A border marker of the standard, the nation, and variation. *Current Issues in Language Planning, Ahead-of-print*, 1–21. doi.org/10.1080/14664208.2021.1965741

Byram, M. (2009). Intercultural competence in foreign languages: Intercultural speaker and the pedagogy of foreign language education. In D. K. Deardorff

(Ed.), *The SAGE handbook of intercultural competence* (pp. 321–332). SAGE Publications.

Cambridge Assessment (2021). *C2 proficiency*. Retrieved June 30, 2021, from https://www.cambridgeenglish.org/exams-and-tests/proficiency/

Canagarajah, A. S. (1999). *Resisting linguistic imperialism in English teaching*. Oxford University Press.

Canagarajah, S. (2007). Lingua franca English, multilingual communities and language acquisition. *The Modern Language Journal 91*, 923–939.

Canagarajah, A. S. (2013). *Translingual practice: Global Englishes and cosmopolitan relations*. Routledge.

Candelier, M., Daryai-Hansen, P., & Schröder-Sura, A. (2012). The framework of reference for pluralistic approaches to languages and cultures – a complement to the CEFR to develop plurilingual intercultural competences. *Innovation in Language Learning and Teaching 6*(3), 243–257.

Carlucci, A. (2017). Language, education and European unification: Perceptions and reality of global English in Italy. In N. Pizzolato, & J. D. Holst (Eds.), *Antonio Gramsci: A pedagogy to change the world* (pp. 127–148). Springer.

Carney, S. (2009). Negotiating policy in an age of globalization: Exploring educational 'policyscapes' in Denmark, Nepal, and China. *Comparative Education Review 53*(1), 63–88.

Carney, S. (2011). Imagining globalization: Educational policyscapes. In G. Steiner-Khamsi, & F. Waldow (Eds.), *World yearbook of education 2012* (pp. 339–353). Routledge.

Chollet, A. (2011). Switzerland as a 'fractured nation.' *Nations and nationalism 17*(4), 783–755.

Chomsky, N. (1957). *Syntactic structures*. Mouton.

Chomsky, N. (1965). *Aspects of the theory of syntax*. MIT Press.

Chomsky, N. (1986). *Knowledge of language: Its nature, origin, and use*. Praeger.

Christensen, L. B., Johnson, R. B., & Turner, L. A. (2014). *Research methods, design, and analysis*. Pearson.

Clark, E., & Paran, A. (2007). The employability of non-native-speaker teachers of EFL: A UK survey. *System 35*(4), 407–430.

Cohen, D. K., Moffitt, S. L., & Goldin, S. (2007). Policy and practice: The dilemma. *American Journal of Education 113*(4), 515–548.

Conteh, J. & Meier, G. (2014) (Eds.). *The multilingual turn in languages education. Opportunities and challenges*. Multilingual Matters.

Cook, V. (2007). The goals of ELT: Reproducing native-speakers or promoting multi-competence among second language users? In J. Cummins, & C. Davison (Eds.), *International Handbook of English Language Teaching* (pp. 237–248). Springer.

Coray, R. (2001). Englisch in der Schweiz: Trojanisches Pferd oder Sprungbrett für die Zukunft? In R. J. Watts, & H. Murray (Eds.), *Die fünfte Landessprache? Englisch in der Schweiz* (pp. 161–182). vdf Hochschulverlag.

Coray, R. (2009). «Stai si, defenda, tiu code funczional!» Rumantsch Grischun im öffentlichen Diskurs. *Bündner Monatsblatt 1*, 3–24.

Coray, R., & Berthele, R. (2018). *L'allemand, langue officielle de la ville de Fribourg? État des lieux et analyse historique, juridique et sociolinguistique : Rapport à l'attention du Conseil communal de Fribourg*. Retrieved November 8, 2021, from https ://doc.rero.ch/record/323063

Coste, D., & Simon, D.-L. (2009). The plurilingual social actor. Language, citizenship and education. *International Journal of Multilingualism 6*(2), 168–185.

Coste, D., Moore, D., & Zarate, G. (2009). Plurilingual and pluricultural competence: Studies towards a Common European Framework of Reference for language learning and teaching. Retrieved 8 November, 2021, from https://rm.coe.int/168069d29b

Council of Europe (2001). Common European Framework of Reference. Retrieved June 30, 2021, from https://rm.coe.int/1680459f97

Council of Europe (2007). De la diversité linguistique à l'éducation plurilingue : Guide pour l'élaboration des politiques linguistiques éducatives en Europe. Retrieved June 30, 2021, from https ://rm.coe.int/16802fc3ab

Council of Europe (2019). Language repertoire. Retrieved June 30, 2021, from https://www.coe.int/en/web/lang-migrants/repertoire-language-

Council of Europe (2021). The CEFR Levels. Retrieved June 30, 2021, from https://www.coe.int/en/web/common-european-framework-reference-languages/level-descriptions

Creswell, J. W., & Poth, C. N. (2018). *Qualitative inquiry and research design: Choosing among five approaches*. 4th ed. SAGE Publications.

Crystal, D. (2003). *English as a global language* (2nd ed.). Cambridge University Press.

Cummins, J. (2000). *Language, power and pedagogy: Bilingual children in the crossfire*. Multilingual Matters.

Cummins, J. (2018). Urban multilingualism and educational achievement: Identifying and implementing evidence-based strategies for school improvement. In P. Avermaet, S. Slembrouck, K. Van Gorp, S. Sierens, & K. Maryns (Eds.), *The multilingual edge of education* (pp. 67–90). Palgrave Macmillan.

Cunningham, C. (2019). The inappropriateness of language: Discourses of power and control over *languages beyond English* in primary schools. *Language and Education 33*(4), 285–301.

Daryai-Hansen, P., Gerber, B., Lörincz, I., Haller, M., Ivanova, O., Krumm, H.-J., & Reich, H. H. (2015). Pluralistic approaches to languages in the curriculum: The case of French-speaking Switzerland, Spain and Austria. *International Journal of Multilingualism 12*(1), 109–127.

Davies, A. (2003). *The native speaker: Myth and reality*. Multilingual Matters.

Davis, A. (2003). Teachers' and students' beliefs regarding aspects of language learning. *Evaluation and research in education* 17(4), 207–222.

De Swaan, A. (2001). *Words of the world: The global language system*. Polity Press.

Delgado, R., & Stefancic, J. (2017). *Critical race theory: An introduction* (2nd ed.). New York University Press.

Delpit, L. (2006). *Other people's children: Cultural conflict in the classroom*. The New Press.

Demmerling, C., & Landweer, H. (2007). *Philosophie der Gefühle: Von Achtung bis Zorn*. J. B. Metzler.

Demont-Heinrich, C. (2005). Language and national identity in the era of globalization: The case of English in Switzerland. *Journal of Communication Inquiry* 29(1), 66–84.

Denzin, N. K. (1997). *Interpretative ethnography: Ethnographic practices for the 21st century*. SAGE Publications.

Denzin, N. K. & Lincoln, Y. S. (2017). Introduction: The discipline and practice of qualitative research. In N. K. Denzin & Y. S. Lincoln (Eds.), *The SAGE handbook of qualitative research*. 5th ed. SAGE Publications.

Derrida, J. (1996). *Le monolinguisme de l'autre : Ou la prothèse d'origine*. Galilée.

Duchêne, A., & Del Percio, A. (2014). Economic capitalization on linguistic diversity: Swiss multilingualism as a national profit? In J. Unger, M. Krzyzanowski, & R. Wodak (Eds.), *Multilingual encounters in Europe's institutional spaces* (pp. 75–101). Bloomsbury.

Dürscheid, C., & Sutter, P. (2014). Grammatische Helvetismen im Wörterbuch. *Zeitschrift für angewandte Linguistik* 60(1), 37–65.

EDK (2004). *Sprachenunterricht in der obligatorischen Schule: Strategie und Arbeitsplan für die gesamtschweizerische Koordination*. Retrieved June 30, 2021, from https://edudoc.ch/record/30008/files/Sprachen_d.pdf

EDK (2013). *Sprachenunterricht Sekundarstufe II*. Retrieved June 30, 2021, from http://www.edk.ch/dyn/12498.php

Edwards, J. (2009). *Language and identity*. Cambridge University Press.

Elmiger, D. (2021). *L'enseignement des langues étrangères en Suisse : Enjeux et tensions actuelles*. Livreo Alphil.

Erickson, F. (1996). Transformation and school success: The politics and culture of educational achievement. In E. Jacob, & C. Jordan (Eds.), *Minority Education: Anthropological perspectives* (pp. 27–52). Ablex.

Esteva, G., & Prakash, M. S. (2014). *Grassroots post-modernism: Remaking the soil of cultures*. Zed Books.

Fairclough, N. (2015). *Language and power*. Routledge.

Federal Department of Foreign Affairs (2021a). Languages and dialects. Retrieved November 8, 2021, from https://www.eda.admin.ch/aboutswitzerland/en/home/gesellschaft/sprachen/sprachen-und-dialekte.html

Federal Department of Home Affairs (2021b). Leichte Sprache. Retrieved June 30, 2021, from https://www.edi.admin.ch/edi/de/home/fachstellen/ebgb/themen-der-gleichstellung/e-accessibility-/communicationnumeriqueaccessible2/langue-facile-a-lire.html

Flyvbjerg, B. (1998). *Rationality and power: Democracy in practice*. University of Chicago Press.

Foucault, M. (1972). *The archaeology of knowledge and the discourse of language*. Pantheon Books.

Foucault, M. (1982). The subject and power. *Critical Inquiry 8*(4), 777–795.

Foucault, M. (1991). Governmentality. In G. Burchell, C. Gordon, & P. Miller (Eds.), *The Foucault effect: Studies in governmentality* (pp. 87–104). University of Chicago Press.

Foucault, M. (2007). What is critique? In S. Lotringer (Ed.), *The politics of truth* (pp. 41–81). Semiotext(e).

Fraser, N. (2003). Social justice in the age of identity politics: Redistribution, recognition, and participation. In N. Fraser, & A. Honneth (Eds.), *Redistribution or recognition? A political-philosophical exchange* (pp. 7–109). Verso.

Friedman, P. K. (2009). Ethical hegemony. *Rethinking Marxism 21*(3), 355–365.

FSO (2020). Bildungsabschlüsse. Retrieved November 16, 2021, from https://www.bfs.admin.ch/bfs/de/home/statistiken/bildung-wissenschaft/bildungsabschluesse.assetdetail.14836488.html

FSO (2021a). Languages. Retrieved September 23, 2021, from https://www.bfs.admin.ch/bfs/en/home/statistics/population/languages-religions/languages.html

FSO (2021b). Foreign population. Retrieved October 30, 2021 from https://www.bfs.admin.ch/bfs/en/home/statistics/population/migration-integration/foreign.html

Fuller, J. (2015). Language choices and ideologies in the bilingual classroom. In J. Cenoz, & D. Gorter (Eds.), *Multilingual education. Between language learning and translanguaging* (pp. 137–158). Cambridge University Press.

Gadamer, H.-G. (2004). *Truth and method*. Continuum.

Galloway, N., & Rose, H. (2015). *Introducing Global Englishes*. Routledge.

García, O. (2009). Educations, multilingualism and translanguaging in the 21st century. In T. Skutnabb-Kangas, R. Phillipson, A. K. Mohanty, & M. Panda (Eds.), *Social justice through multilingual education* (pp. 140–158). Multilingual Matters.

García, O. & Li, W. (2014). *Translanguaging: Language, bilingualism and education*. Palgrave Macmillan.

García, O., & Lin, A. M. Y. (2017). Extending understandings of bilingual and multilingual education. In O. García, A. M. Y. Lin, & S. May (Eds.), *Bilingual and Multilingual Education* (3rd ed.). Springer International Publishing AG.

Geeraerts, D. (2003). Cultural models of linguistic standardization. In R. Dirven, R. Frank, & M. Pütz (Eds.), *Cognitive models in language and thought. Ideology, metaphors and meanings* (pp. 25–68). Mouton de Gruyter.

Ghomeshi, J. (2010). Grammar matters: The social significance of how we use language. Arbeiter Ring Publishing.

Gigon, A. (2004, March 16). Zürich: Englisch ab der zweiten Primar-Klasse. *Swissinfo*. Retrieved June 30, 2021, from https://www.swissinfo.ch/ger/zuerich--englisch-ab-der-zweiten-primar-klasse/3816990

Gigon, A. (2014, August 26). Ist der "Sprachenfrieden" in der Schweiz bedroht? *Swissinfo*. Retrieved June 30, 2021, from m https://www.swissinfo.ch/ger/politik/franzoesisch-in-deutschschweizer-schulen-ruecklaeufig_ist-der--sprachenfrieden--in-der-schweiz-bedroht-/40570600

Giorgi, A. (2009). *The descriptive phenomenological method in psychology: A modified Husserlian approach*. Duquesne University Press.

Gogolin, I. (2002). Linguistic and cultural diversity in Europe: A challenge for educational research and practice. *European Educational Research Journal 1*(1), 123–138.

Gogolin, I. (2007). «Das ist doch kein gutes Deutsch!» – Über Vorstellungen von guter Sprache und ihren Einfluss auf Mehrsprachigkeit. In I. De Florio-Hansen, & A. Hu (Eds.), *Plurilingualität und Identität. Zur Selbst- und Fremdwahrnehmung mehrsprachiger Menschen* (pp. 59–71). Stauffenberg.

Gogolin, I. (2008). *Der monolinguale Habitus der multilingualen Schule* (2nd ed.). Waxmann-Verlag.

Graddol, D. (2006). *English next*. The English company for the British Council.

Gramsci, A. (1971). *Selections from the prison notebooks*. International Publishers.

Gramsci, A. (1985). *Selections from cultural writings*. Haymarket Books.

Green, A., Preston, J., & Janmaat, J. G. (2006). *Education, equality and social cohesion: A comparative analysis*. Palgrave Macmillan.

Grin, F. (2001). Der ökonomische Wert der englischen Sprache. In R. J. Watts, & H. Murray (Eds.), *Die fünfte Landessprache? Englisch in der Schweiz* (pp. 105–120). vdf Hochschulverlag.

Grin, F. (2006). Economic considerations in language policy. In T. Ricento (Ed.), *An introduction to language policy. Theory and method* (pp. 77–94). Blackwell Publishing.

Grin, F. (2015). The economics of English in Europe. In T. Ricento (Ed.), *Language policy & political economy: English in a global context* (pp. 119–144). Oxford University Press.

Grin, F. (2018). On some fashionable terms in multilingualism research: Critical assessment and implications for language policy. In F. Grin, & P. A. Kraus (Eds.), *The politics of multilingualism: Europeanisation, globalization and linguistic governance* (pp. 247–274). John Benjamins Publishing Company.

Grin, F., & Korth, B. (2005). On the reciprocal influence of language politics and language education: The case of English in Switzerland. *Language Policy 4*, 67–85.

Grin, F., Sfreddo, C., & Vaillancourt, F. (2010). *The economics of the multilingual workplace*. Routledge.

Grin, F., Vaillancourt, F., & Sfreddo, C. (2009). *Qu'en est-il des compétences en langues étrangères dans l'entreprise? Rapport final*. Programme national de recherche PNR 56.

Grosjean, F. (1985). The bilingual as a competent but specific speaker-hearer. *Journal of Multilingual and Multicultural Development 6*, 467–477.

Grünert, M. (2018). Multilingualism in Switzerland. In W. Ayres-Bennett, & J. Carruthers (Eds.), *Manual of Romance sociolinguistics* (pp. 526–548). De Gruyter.

Grünert, M., Picenoni, M., Cathomas, R., & Gadmer, T. (2008). *Das Funktionieren der Dreisprachigkeit im Kanton Graubünden*. Francke Verlag.

Grütz, D. (2018). Diglossie in der Deutschschweiz: Standardsprache versus Mundart – ein Problem in der Schule? In A. Ballis, & N. Hodaie (Eds.), *Perspektiven auf Mehrsprachigkeit: Individuum – Bildung – Gesellschaft* (pp. 113–132). De Gruyter Mouton.

Gumperz, J. J. (1964). Linguistic and social interaction in two communities. *American Anthropologist 66*(6), 137–153.

Haas, W. (2010). *Do you speak Swiss? Sprachenvielfalt und Sprachkompetenz in der Schweiz*. Nationales Forschungsprogramm NFP 56. Verlag Neue Zürcher Zeitung.

Hannerz, U. (2003). Being there ... and there ... and there! Reflections on multi-site ethnography. *Ethnography 4*(2), 201–216.

Hardt, M. & Negri, A. (2000). *Empire*. Harvard University Press.

Heidegger, M. (1962). *Being and time*. SCM Press.

Heinzmann, S. (2010). Hat die Einführung von 'Frühenglisch' in der Primarschule einen Einfluss auf die Motivation der Primarschulkinder Französisch zu lernen? *Bulletin suisse de linguistique appliquée 91*, 7–27.

Heller, M. (2006). *Linguistic minorities and modernity* (2nd ed.). Continuum.

Heller, M. (2007). Bilingualism as ideology and practice. In M. Heller (Ed.), *Bilingualism: A social approach* (pp. 1–21). Palgrave Macmillan.

Heller, M. (2008). Language and the nation-state: Challenges to sociolinguistic theory and practice. *Journal of Sociolinguistics 12*(4), 504–524.

Heller, M., & Duchêne, A. (2012). Pride and profit: Changing discourses of language, capital and nation-state. In A. Duchêne, & M. Heller (Eds.), *Language in late capitalism: Pride and profit* (pp. 1–21). Routledge.

Heller, M. & McElhinny, B. (2017). *Language, capitalism, colonialism: Toward a critical history*. University of Toronto Press.

Hélot, C. (2007). *Du bilinguisme en famille au plurilinguisme à l'école*. L'Harmattan.

Hickey, P. J. (2012). Unlearning to learn: Investigating the lived experience of learning English. *English Teaching: Practice and Critique 11*(2), 145–162.

Hilgendorf, S. K. (2007). English in Germany: Contact, spread and attitudes. *World Englishes 26*(2), 131–148.

Hobsbawm, E. J. (2012). *Nations and nationalism since 1780: Programme, myth, reality* (2nd ed.). Cambridge University Press.

Holliday, A. (2008). Standards of English and politics of inclusion. *Language Teaching* 41(1), 119–130.

Hornberger, N. H. (2006). Frameworks and models in language policy and planning. In T. Ricento (Ed.), *An introduction to language policy. Theory and method* (pp. 25–41). Blackwell Publishing.

Hornberger, N. H., & Johnson, D. C. (2010). The ethnography of language policy. In T. L. McCarty (Ed.), *Ethnography and language policy* (pp. 273–289). Routledge.

Hu, A. (2003a). *Schulischer Fremdsprachenunterricht und migrationsbedingte Mehrsprachigkeit*. Narr.

Hu, A. (2003b). Mehrsprachigkeit, Identitäts- und Kulturtheorie: Tendenzen der Konvergenz. In I. De Florio-Hansen & A. Hu (Eds.), *Plurilingualität und Identität. Zur Selbst- und Fremdwahrnehmung mehrsprachiger Menschen* (pp. 1–23). Stauffenberg.

Hua, Z., & Li, W. (2016) 'Where are you really from?': Nationality and ethnicity talk (NET) in everyday interactions. *Applied Linguistics Review* 7(4), 449–470. https://www.degruyter.com/document/doi/10.1515/applirev-2016-0020/html

Husserl, E. (1970). *The crisis of European sciences and transcendental phenomenology*. Northwestern University Press.

Hymes, D. H. (1973). Speech and language: On the origins and foundations of inequality among speakers. *Daedalus 102*, 59–80.

Hymes, D. H. (1980). Ethnographic monitoring. In D. H. Hymes (Ed.), *Language in education: Ethnolinguistic essays* (pp. 104–118). Center for Applied Linguistics.

Irvine, J. T., & Gal, S. (2000). Language ideology and linguistic differentiation. In P. V. Kroskrity (Ed.), *Regimes of language: Ideologies, polities, and identities* (pp. 35–83). School of American Research Press.

Ivanov, V. (2001). Heteroglossia. In A. Duranti (Ed.), *Key terms in language and culture* (pp. 95–97). Blackwell.

Ives, P. (1997). The grammar of hegemony. *Left History* 5(1), 85–103.

Ives, P. (2004a). *Language and hegemony in Gramsci*. Pluto Press.

Ives, P. (2004b). *Gramsci's politics of language: Engaging the Bakhtin Circle and the Frankfurt School*. University of Toronto Press.

Ives, P. (2006). 'Global English': Linguistic imperialism or practical lingua franca? *Studies in Language & Capitalism 1*, 121–141.

Ives, P. (2009). Global English, hegemony and education: Lessons from Gramsci. *Educational Philosophy and Theory 41* (6), 661–683.

Ives, P. (2015a) Global English and the limits of liberalism: Confronting global capitalism and challenges to the nation-state. In T. Ricento (Ed.), *Language policy and political economy: English in a global context* (pp. 48–71). Oxford University Press.

Ives, P. (2015b). Global English and inequality: The contested ground of linguistic power. In R. Tupas (Ed.), *Unequal Englishes: The politics of Englishes today* (pp. 74–91). Palgrave Macmillan.

Jackendoff, R., & Pinker, S. (2005). The nature of the language faculty and its implications for evolution of language. *Cognition* 97(2), 211–225.

Jakobson, R. (1960). Linguistics and poetics. In T. A. Sebeok (Ed.), *Style in Language* (pp. 350–377). Wiley.

Jenkins, J. (2007). *English as a lingua franca*. Oxford University Press.

Jenkins, J. (2009). English as a lingua franca: Interpretations and attitudes. *World Englishes* 28(2), 200–207.

Jenkins, J. (2015). *Global Englishes: A resource book for students*. Routledge.

Johnson, D. C. (2013). *Language policy*. Palgrave Macmillan.

Kachru, B. (1985). Standards, codification and sociolinguistic realism: The English language in the outer circle. In R. Quirk & H. G. Widdowson (Eds.), *English in the world: Teaching and learning the language and literatures* (pp. 11–30). Cambridge University Press.

Kachru, B. (1990). World Englishes and applied linguistics. *World Englishes* 9, 3–20.

Kachru, B. (1992). World Englishes: Approaches, issues and resources. *Language Teaching* 25(1), 1–14.

Kamm, C. (2016, April 4). Glücklich mit dem «Non». *Tagblatt*. Retrieved June 30, 2021, from https://www.tagblatt.ch/ostschweiz/gluecklich-mit-dem-non-ld.655437

Keller, R. (1994). *On language change: The invisible hand in language*. Routledge.

Kirova, A., & Emme, M. (2006). Using photography as a means of phenomenological seeing: "Doing phenomenology" with immigrant children. *Indo-Pacific Journal of Phenomenology* 6(1), 1–12.

Koven, M. (2001). Comparing bilinguals' quoted performances of self and others in tellings of the same experience in two languages. *Language in Society* 30, 513–558.

Kramsch, C. (1998). *Language and culture*. Oxford University Press.

Kramsch, C. (2009). *The multilingual subject: What foreign language learners say about their experience and why it matters*. Oxford University Press.

Kroskrity, P. V. (2000). Regimenting languages: Language ideological perspectives. In P. Kroskrity (Ed.), *Regimes of language: Ideologies, polities, and identities* (pp. 1–35). SAR Press.

Kroskrity, P. V. (2004). Language ideologies. In A. Duranti (Ed.), *A companion to linguistic anthropology* (pp. 496–517). Blackwell.

Krumm, H.-J., & Putzlar, V. (2008). *Tailoring language provision and requirements to the needs and capacities of adult migrants*. Retrieved June 30, 2021, from https://rm.coe.int/CoERMPublicCommonSearchServices/DisplayDCTMContent?documentId=09000016802fc1c8

Kubota, R. (2010). Critical multicultural education and second/foreign language teaching. In S. May, & C. E. Sleeter (Eds.), *Critical multiculturalism: Theory and praxis* (pp. 99–112). Routledge.

Kubota, R. (2015). Inequalities of Englishes, English speakers, and languages: A critical perspective on pluralist approaches to English. In R. Tupas (Ed.), *Unequal Englishes: The politics of Englishes today* (pp. 21–41). Palgrave Macmillan.

Kużelewska (2016). Language policy in Switzerland. *Studies in logic, grammar and rhetoric 45*(58), 125–140. https://doi.org/10.1515/slgr-2016-0020

Kvale, S. (2007). *Doing interviews*. SAGE Publications.

Kvale, S., & Brinkman, S. (2009). *InterViews: Learning the craft of qualitative research interviewing*. SAGE Publications.

Labov, W. (2006). *The social stratification of English in New York*. Cambridge University Press.

Ladegaard, H. J. (2000). Language attitudes and sociolinguistic behavior: Exploring attitude-behaviour relations in language. *Journal of Sociolinguistics 4*(2), 214–233.

Lahire, B. (2011). *The plural actor*. Polity Press.

Lambelet, A., & Berthele, R. (2015). *Age and foreign language learning in school*. Palgrave Macmillan.

Lamnek, S., & Krell, C. (2016). *Qualitative Sozialforschung*. Beltz.

Lefebvre, H. (1991). *The Production of Space*. Blackwell.

Levitt, P., & Jaworsky, N. (2007). Transnational migration studies: Past developments and future trends. *Annual Review of Sociology 33*(1), 129–156.

Lewis, G., Jones, B., & Baker, C. (2012). Translanguaging: Origins and development from school to street and beyond. *Educational Research and Evaluation 18*(7), 641–654.

Liebscher, G., & Dailey-O'Cain, J. (2013). Perceptions of the linguascape. In G. Liebscher, & J. Dailey-O'Cain (Eds.), *Language, space, and identity in migration* (pp. 35–88). Palgrave Macmillan.

Lippi-Green, R. (1997). *English with an accent: Language, ideology, and discrimination in the United States*. Routledge.

Little, D. (2012). *The linguistic integration of adult migrants and the 'common European framework of reference for languages.'* Retrieved June 30, 2021, from https://rm.coe.int/CoERMPublicCommonSearchServices/DisplayDCTMContent?documentId=09000016802fc1ca

Lob, G. (2016, August 27). Wird Italienisch im Sprachenstreit vergessen? *Neue Luzerner Zeitung*. Retrieved June 30, 2021, from https://m4.ti.ch/fileadmin/POTERI/DTCF/ITALIANITA/Wird_Italienisch_im_Sprachenstreit_vergessen_27_agosto_2016.pdf

Lok, I. M. C. (2012). World Englishes and postcolonialism: Reading Kachru and Said. *World Englishes 31*(4), 419–433.

Love, N. (2017). On languaging and languages. *Language Science 61*, 113–147.

Lüdi, G. (2010). Mehrsprachige Lehrlinge für eine mehrsprachige Arbeitswelt. *Babylonia. Zeitschrift für Sprachunterricht und Sprachenlernen. Kontinuität und Diskontinuität mehrsprachiger Praktiken N1*, 49–54.

Lüdi, G. (2016). English in the workplace in Switzerland between ideologies and practices. *Cahiers de l'ILSL 48*, 53–77.

Lüdi, G., & Py, B. (2009). To be or not to be ... a plurilingual speaker. *International Journal of Multilingualism 6*(2), 154–167.

Luhmann, N. (1995). *Die Realität der Massenmedien*. Springer VS.

Madison, D. S. (2012). *Critical ethnography: Methods, ethics, and performance*. SAGE Publications.

Magno, C. S. (2013). *Comparative perspectives on international school leadership: Policy, preparation, and practice*. Routledge.

Magno, C. S., Becker, A., & Imboden, M. (2022). Educational practice in Switzerland: Searching for diversity-engaged school leadership. *Educational Management Administration & Leadership*. https://doi.org/10.1177/17411432221086225

Mahboob, A., & Golden, R. (2013). Looking for native speakers of English: Discrimination in English language teaching job advertisements. *Voices in Asia Journal 1*(1), 72–81.

Makarova, E., & Birman, D. (2016). Minority students' psychological adjustment in the school context: An integrative review of qualitative research on acculturation. *Intercultural Education 27*(1), 1–21.

Makoni, S., & Pennycook, A. (2007). Disinventing and reconstituting languages. In S. Makoni, & A. Pennycook (Eds.), *Disinventing and reconstituting languages* (pp. 1–41). Multilingual Matters.

Marácz, L. (2018). Languages, norms and power in a globalized context. In F. Grin, & P. A. Kraus (Eds.), *The politics of multilingualism: Europeanisation, globalization and linguistic governance* (pp. 223–243). John Benjamins Publishing Company.

Marcus, G. A. (1995). Ethnography in/of the world system: The emergence of multi-sited ethnography. *Annual Review of Anthropology 24*, 95–117.

Mauranen, A., & Ranta, E. (Eds.) (2009). *English as a lingua franca: Studies and findings*. Cambridge Scholars Publishing.

Maurer, U. (2003, June 9): Secondos in der Schweiz. *Swissinfo*. Retrieved June 30, 2021, https://www.swissinfo.ch/ger/secondos-in-der-schweiz/3349984

Maxcy, S. J. (1995). *Democracy, chaos, and the new school order*. Corwin Press.

May, S. (2009). Critical multiculturalism and education. In J. A. Banks (Ed.), *The Routledge international companion to multicultural education* (pp. 33–48). Routledge.

May, S. (2012). *Language and minority rights*. Routledge.

May, S. (2014). *The multilingual turn: Implications for SLA, TESOL and bilingual education*. Routledge.

May, S., & Sleeter, C. (2010). Introduction: Critical multiculturalism: Theory and praxis. In S. May & C. Sleeter (Eds.), *Critical multiculturalism: Theory and praxis* (pp. 1–18). Routledge.

McClain, M. (2010). Parental agency in educational decision making: A Mexican American example. *Teachers College Record* 112(12), 3074–3101.

McKay, S. L. (2003). EIL curriculum development. *RELC 34*, 31–47.

McLellan, E., MacQueen, K. M., & Neidig, J. L. (2003). Beyond the qualitative interview: Data preparation and transcription. *Field Methods* 15(1), 63–84.

McNamara, T. (2011). Managing learning: Authority and language assessment. *Language Teaching* 44(4), 500–515.

Meier, G. S. (2017). The multilingual turn as a critical movement in education: assumptions, challenges and a need for reflection. *Applied Linguistics Review* 8(1), 131–161.

Meierkord, C. (2004). Syntactic variation in interactions across international Englishes. *English World-Wide* 25(1), 109–132.

Merleau-Ponty, M. (2014). *Phenomenology of perception*. Routledge.

Mero-Jaffe, I. (2011). 'Is that what I said?' Interview transcript approval by participants: An aspect of ethics in qualitative research. *International Journal of Qualitative Methods* 10(3), 231–247.

Merriam, S. B. (2015). *Qualitative research. A guide to design and implementation*. Jossey-Bass.

Milroy, J. (2001). Language ideologies and the consequences of standardization. *Journal of Sociolinguistics* 5(4), 530–555.

Milroy, J., & Milroy, L. (1999). *Authority in language: Investigating standard English* (3rd ed.). Routledge.

Mohanty, A. K. (2009). Multilingual education: A bridge too far? In T. Skutnabb-Kangas, R. Phillipson, A. K. Mohanty & M. Panda (Eds.), *Social justice through multilingual education* (pp. 3–18). Multilingual Matters.

Mollin, S. (2006). English as a lingua franca: A new variety in the new expanding circle? *Nordic Journal of English Studies* 5(2), 41–57.

Motha, S. (2014). *Race, empire, and English language teaching: Creating responsible and ethical anti-racist practice*. Teachers College Press.

Moussu, L., & Llurda, E. (2008). Non-native English-speaking English language teachers: History and research. *Language teaching* 41(3), 315–348.

Moustakas, C. (1994). *Phenomenological research methods*. SAGE Publications.

Moyer, M. G., & Martín Rojo, L. (2007). Language, migration and citizenship: New challenges in the regulation of bilingualism. In M. Heller (Ed.), *Bilingualism: A social approach* (pp. 137–160). Palgrave Macmillan.

Mukherjee, S. P., Sinha, B. K., & Chatterjee, A. (2018). *Statistical methods in science research*. Springer.

Myhill, J. (2003). The native speaker, identity, and the authenticity hierarchy. *Language Sciences* 25(1), 77–97.

Nash, R. (1990). Bourdieu on education and social and cultural reproduction. *British Journal of Sociology of Education* 11(4), 431–447.

Niedzielski, N. (2010). Linguistic security, ideology, and vowel perception. In D. R. Preston, & N. Niedzielski (Eds.), *A reader in sociophonetics* (pp. 253–264). Mouton de Gruyter.

Nieto, S., & Bode, P. (2018). *Affirming diversity: The sociopolitical context of multicultural education* (7th ed.). Pearson.

Nock, Y. (2017, July 20). Der Sprachenstreit hat Folgen: Französischlehrer sind Mangelware. *Aargauer* Zeitung. Retrieved June 30, 2021, from https://www.aargauerzeitung.ch/schweiz/der-sprachenstreit-hat-folgen-franzosischlehrer-sind-mangelware-ld.1440533

Noddings, N. (2013). *Education and democracy in the 21st century*. Teachers College Press.

Norton, B. & McKinney, C. (2011). An identity approach to second language acquisition. In D. Atkinson (Ed.), *Alternative approaches to second language acquisition* (pp. 73–94). Routledge.

Odegaard, E. E., & Pramling, N. (2013). Collaborative narrative as linguistic artifact and cultural tool for meaning making and learning. *Cultural-Historical Psychology* 9(2), 38–44.

Oliver, D. G., Serovich, J. M., & Mason, T. L. (2005). Constraints and opportunities with interview transcription: Towards reflection in qualitative research. *Social Forces* 84(2), 1273–1289.

Orelus, P. W. (2012). Unveiling the web of race, class, language, and gender oppression: Challenges for social justice educators. *Race, Gender & Class* 19(3–4), 35–51.

Ortega, L. (2019). SLA and the study of equitable multilingualism. *The Modern Language Journal* 103(1), 23–38.

Orwell, G. (1945). *Animal farm: A fairy story*. Secker and Warburg.

Otheguy, R., García, O., & Reid, W. (2015). Clarifying translanguaging and deconstructing named languages: A perspective from linguistics. *Applied Linguistics Review* 6(3), 281–307.

Park, J. S.-Y., & Wee, L. (2009). The three circles redux: A market-theoretic perspective on world Englishes. *Applied Linguistics* 30(3), 389–406.

Pavlenko, A. (2007). Autobiographic narratives as data in applied linguistics. *Applied Linguistics* 28, 163–188.

Pennycook, A. (1994). *The cultural politics of English as an international language*. Longman.

Pennycook, A. (2001). Lessons from colonial language policies. In R. D. González (Ed.), *Language ideologies: Critical perspectives on the official English movement, vol. 2:*

History, theory, and policy (pp. 198–220). National Council of Teachers of English. Lawrence Erlbaum Associates.

Pennycook, A. (2010). *Language as local practice*. Routledge.

Pennycook, A., & Otsuji, E. (2014). Metrolingual multitasking and spatial repertoires. 'Pizza mo two minutes coming'. *Journal of Sociolinguistics 18*(2), 161–184.

Petkova, M. (2016). *Multiples Code-Switching: Ein Sprachkontaktphänomen am Beispiel der Deutschschweiz*. Universitätsverlag Winter GmbH Heidelberg.

Pfenninger, S. E. (2016). All good things come in threes: early English learning, CLIL and motivation in Switzerland. *Cahiers de l'ILSL 48*, 119–147.

Phillipson, R. (1992). *Linguistic imperialism*. Oxford University Press.

Phillipson, R. (2003). *English only Europe*. Oxford University Press.

Phillipson, R. (2007). English in Europe: Threat or promise? In M. Craith (Ed.), *Language, power and identity politics* (pp. 65–82). New York: Palgrave Macmillan.

Phillipson, R. (2018). English, the *lingua nullius* of global hegemony. In F. Grin, & P. A. Kraus (Eds.), *The politics of multilingualism: Europeanisation, globalization and linguistic governance* (pp. 275–304). John Benjamins Publishing Company.

Pietkäinen, S., Alanen, R., Dufva, H., Kalaja, P., Leppänen, S., & Pitkänen-Huhta, A. (2008). Languaging in ultima Thule: Multilingualism in the life of a Sami boy. *International Journal of Multilingualism 5*, 79–99.

Piller, I. (2016). *Linguistic diversity and social justice: An introduction to applied sociolinguistics*. Oxford University Press.

Pogge, T. (2003). Accommodation rights for Hispanics in the United States. In W. Kymlicka, & A. Patten (Eds.), *Language rights and political theory* (pp. 105–122). Oxford University Press.

Polinsky, M. (2018). *Heritage languages and their speakers*. Cambridge University Press.

Pujolar, J. (2007). Bilingualism and the nation-state in the post-national era. In M. Heller (Ed.), *Bilingualism: A social approach* (pp. 71–95). Palgrave Macmillan.

Rai, L., & Deng, C. (2014). Globalisation and English language education in Chinese context. *Globalisation, Societies and Education 14*(1), 1–18.

Rajadurai, J. (2005). Revisiting the concentric circles: Conceptual and sociolinguistic considerations. *The Asian EFL Journal Quarterly 7*(4), 111–130.

Reichen, P. (2015, October 20). Der Sprachenstreit als erster Test für das neue Polit-Klima. *Der Bund*. https://www.derbund.ch/schweiz/standard/der-sprachenstreit-als-erster-test-fuer-das-neue-politklima/story/17678371

Ribeaud, J. (2010). *La Suisse plurilingue se déglingue : plaidoyer pour les quatres langues nationales suisses*. Delibreo.

Ricento, T. (2015a). Introduction: Language policy and political economy. In T. Ricento (Ed.), *Language policy and political economy: English in a global context* (pp. 1–26). Oxford University Press.

Ricento, T. (2015b) Political economy and English as a 'global' language. In T. Ricento (Ed.), *Language policy and political economy: English in a global context* (pp. 27–47). Oxford University Press.

Romaine, S. (1994). *Language in society: An introduction to sociolinguistics*. Oxford University Press.

Rudby, R. (2015). Unequal Englishes, the native speaker, and decolonization in TESOL. In R. Tupas (Ed.), *Unequal Englishes: The politics of Englishes today* (pp. 42–41). Palgrave Macmillan.

Rubin, H. J., & Rubin, I. (2005). *Qualitative interviewing: The art of hearing data*. SAGE Publications.

Said, E. W. (1978). *Orientalism*. Penguin.

Said, E. W. (1994). *Culture and imperialism*. Vintage Books.

Saraceni, M. (2009). Relocating English: Towards a new paradigm for English in the world. *Language and Intercultural Communication 9*(3), 175–186.

Schiffman, H. (2006). Language policy and linguistic culture. In T. Ricento (Ed.), *An introduction to language policy. Theory and method* (pp. 111–125). Blackwell.

Schneider, E. W. (2007). *Postcolonial English: Varieties around the world*. Cambridge University Press.

Schneider, E. W. (2011). *English around the world: An introduction*. Cambridge University Press.

Seidlhofer, B. (2004). Research perspectives on teaching English as a lingua franca. *Annual Review of Applied Linguistics 24*, 209–239.

Seidlhofer, B. (2005). English as a lingua franca. *ELT Journal 59*, 339–341.

Seidlhofer, B. (2011). *Understanding English as a lingua franca*. Oxford University Press.

Serra, C. (2007). Assessing CLIL at primary school: A longitudinal study. *International Journal of Bilingual Education and Bilingualism 10*(5), 582–602.

Shohamy, E. (2006). *Language policy: Hidden agendas and new approaches*. Routledge.

Siebenhaar, B., & Wyler, A. (1997). *Dialekt und Hochsprache in der deutschsprachigen Schweiz*. Pro Helvetia.

Sieber, P. (2013). Probleme und Chancen der Diglossie – Einstellungen zu Mundarten und Hochdeutsch in der Deutschschweiz. In B. Eriksson, M. Luginbühl, & N. Tuor (Eds.), *Sprechen und Zuhören – gefragte Kompetenzen? Überzeugungen zur Mündlichkeit in Schule und Beruf, Band 2* (pp. 106–136). hep verlag.

Skutnabb-Kangas, T. (2000). Linguistic human rights and teachers of English. In J. Hall, J. Kelly, & W. G. Eggington (Eds.), *The sociopolitics of English language teaching* (pp. 22–44). Multilingual Matters.

Skutnabb-Kangas, T. (2009). Multilingual education for global justice: Issues, approaches, opportunities. In T. Skutnabb-Kangas, R. Phillipson, A. K. Mohanty, & M. Panda (Eds.), *Social justice through multilingual education* (pp. 36–62). Multilingual Matters.

Speigelberg, H. (1960). *The phenomenological movement: A historical introduction.* Nijhoff.

Spies, T., & Tuider, E. (2017). Biographie und Diskurs – eine Einleitung. In T. Spies & E. Tuider (Eds.), *Biographie und Diskurs. Methodisches Vorgehen und Methodologische Verbindungen* (pp. 1–20). Springer.

Spivak, G. C. (1993). *Outside the teaching machine.* Routledge.

Spolsky, B. (2009). *Language management.* Cambridge University Press.

SRF (2016). Kantone wehren sich im Sprachenstreit. Retrieved June 30, 2021, https://www.srf.ch/news/schweiz/kantone-wehren-sich-im-sprachenstreit

SRF (2018). Sprachenstreit in Graubünden Retrieved June 30, 2021, https://www.srf.ch/news/schweiz/abstimmungen/abstimmungen/abstimmungen-gr/sprachenstreit-in-graubuenden-deutliches-nein-zur-fremdsprachen-initiative

Stewart, F. (2013). Approaches towards inequality and inequity: Concepts, measures and policies. *Office of Research Discussion Paper No. 2013–01*, UNICEF Office of Research, Florence.

Stotz, D. (2006). Breaching the peace: Struggles around multilingualism in Switzerland. *Language Policy 5*, 247–265.

Stotz, D. (2009). *Mehrsprachigkeit, Identität und Sprachenlernen in Schweizer Schulgemeinden. Schlussbericht. Sprachenvielfalt und Sprachkompetenz in der Schweiz.* Nationales Forschungsprogramm NFP 56.

Street, S. (2001). When politics becomes pedagogy: Oppositional discourse as policy in Mexican teachers' struggle for union democracy. In M. Sutton, & B. A. U. Levinson (Eds.), *Policy as practice: Toward a comparative sociocultural analysis of educational policy* (pp. 145–166). Ablex.

Sung, C. C. M. (2011). Race and native speakers in ELT: Parents' perspectives in Hong Kong. *English Today 27*(3), 25–29.

Swiss Education (2020). Upper secondary level. Retrieved November 16, 2021, from https://swisseducation.educa.ch/en/upper-secondary-level-0

Swissinfo (n.d.). State school system. Retrieved November 16, 2021, from https://www.swissinfo.ch/eng/state-school-system/29286538

Syrbe, M., & Rose, H. (2018). An evaluation of the global orientation of English textbooks in Germany. *Innovation in Language Learning and Teaching 12*(2), 152–163. https://doi.org/10.1080/17501229.2015.1120736

Tollefon, J. W. (1991). *Planning language, planning inequality: Language policy in the community.* Longman.

Tollefson, J. W. (2006). Critical theory in language policy. In T. Ricento (Ed.), *An introduction to language policy. Theory and method* (pp. 43–59). Blackwell.

Treichel, B. (2004). Suffering from one's own multilingualism: Biographical processes of suffering and their linguistic expression in narrative interviews with Welsh speakers of Welsh and English. In R. Franceschini & J. Miecznikowski

(Eds.), *Leben mit mehreren Sprachen. Vivre avec plusieurs langues. Sprachbiographien – Biographies langagières* (pp. 47–74). Peter Lang.

Tsui, A. B. M., & Tollefson, J. W. (2004). The centrality of medium-of-instruction policy in sociopolitical processes. In J. W. Tollfeson, & A. B. M. Tsui (Eds.), *Medium of instruction policies. Which agenda? Whose agenda?* (pp. 1–18). Lawrence Erlbaum Associates.

Tupas, R., & Rudby, R. (2015). Introduction: From world Englishes to unequal Englishes. In R. Tupas (Ed.), *Unequal Englishes: The politics of Englishes today* (pp. 1–17). Palgrave Macmillan.

Valdés, G. (2001). Heritage language students: Profiles and possibilities. In J. Kreeft Peyton, D. A. Ranard, & S. McGinnis (Eds.), *Heritage languages in America: Preserving a national resource* (pp. 37–77). Center for Applied Linguistics.

Valdés, G. (2017). From language maintenance and intergenerational transmission to language *survivance*: will "heritage language" education help or hinder? *International Journal of the Sociology of Language, 243,* 67–95.

van Manen, M. (1990). *Researching lived experience: Human science for an action sensitive pedagogy*. State University of New York Press.

van Manen, M. (2014). *Phenomenology of practice: Meaning-giving methods in phenomenological research and writing*. Left Coast Press.

van Manen, M. (2017). *Researching lived experience: Human science for an action sensitive pedagogy* (2nd ed.). Taylor & Francis Group.

Vertovec, S. (2007). Super-diversity and its implications. *Ethnic and Racial Studies* 30(6), 1024–1054.

Vygotskij, L. S. (1978). *Mind in society. The development of higher psychological processes*. Harvard University Press.

Watts, R. (1999). The ideology of dialect in Switzerland. In J. Blommaert (Ed.), *Language ideological debates* (pp. 67–103). Mouton de Gruyter.

Wenger, E. (1998). *Communities of practice: Learning, meaning, and identity*. Cambridge University Press.

Wiater, W. (2010). Mehrsprachigkeit als Herausforderung für die Schule in systematischer Perspektive. In F. Bitter Bättig & A. Tanner (Eds.), *Sprachen lerne – ernen durch Sprache* (pp. 332–342). Seismo.

Widdowson, H. (1997). EIL, ESL, EFL: Global issues and local interests. *World Englishes* 16(1), 135–146.

Widmer, K. (2008). *Entstehung der romanischen Idiome Graubündens*. Retrieved June 30, 2021, from https://www.drg.ch/customer/files/69/idiome_wi.pdf

Wierzbicka, A. (2014). *Imprisoned in English: The hazards of English as a default language*. Oxford University Press.

Williams, G. (2015). Language, hegemony, and economy. In T. Ricento (Ed.), *Language policy and political economy: English in a global context* (pp. 97–115). Oxford University Press.

Woolard, K. A., & Schieffelin, B. B. (1994). Language ideology. *Annual Review of Anthropology 23*, 55–82.

Yano, Y. (2009). The future of English: Beyond the Kachruvian three circle model? In K. Murata & J. Jenkins (Eds.), *Global Englishes in Asian contexts* (pp. 208–225). Palgrave Macmillan.

Zahavi, D. (2008). Phenomenology. In D. Moran (Ed.), *The Routledge companion to twentieth century philosophy* (pp. 661–692). Routledge.

Zakharia, Z. (2016). Language, conflict, and migration: Situating Arabic bilingual community education in the United States. *International Journal of the Sociology of Language 237*, 139–160.

Zimmermann, M. (2017). Researching student mobility in multilingual Switzerland: Reflections on multi-sited ethnography. In M. Martin-Jones & D. Martin (Eds.), *Researching multilingualism: Critical and ethnographic approaches* (pp. 73–86). Routledge.

Zünd, C. (2017, May 19). L'enseignement des langues, éternel alibi. *Le Temps*. Retrieved June 30, 2021, from https ://www.letemps.ch/suisse/lenseignement-langues-eternel-alibi

Appendix A

Questionnaire "Multilingual Switzerland"

(The original online version can be accessed at https://forms.gle/XGdfs6QmqkQRQgda8)

Welcome to the questionnaire of my dissertation project about multilingual education in Switzerland. First of all, thank you very much for your participation! Please remember that your name will only be used by me to get in touch with you for the interview. If you wish not to share a certain information, feel free to leave the answer blank. In case you have any further questions or comments, please write an email to anna.becker@unifr.ch or leave a comment in the comment section below the questions. The questionnaire should take approximately 15 minutes.

Your personal information

1. First and last name
2. What best describes your gender?
    a. Female
    b. Male
    c. Prefer not to say
    d. Other
3. Year and country of birth
4. Nationality/ies (by passport/s). Please separate them by pressing enter.
5. If you were not born in Switzerland, how old were you when you came here?

Languages and country of origin

1. What language(s) did you learn first? If you learned several languages as a child, list them all in the order you learned them using 1), 2), ... or 1), 1) if you learned them simultaneously.
2. What language(s) do you speak at home?

3. If the language(s) you learned first is/are not the same as the school language, when and with whom do you use it or them?
4. If you have two or more mother tongues: How well can you read and write them? (Language 1)
5. If you have two or more mother tongues: How well can you read and write them? (Language 2)

Languages at school

If you learn other languages at school which are not mentioned in the table, please add the language(s), how much you like it or them and your report mark(s) for this year in the comment section.

1. Which language(s) have you learned at school and how much do you like them?
2. What are your report marks for the current school year?

Language use

Refer to the following explanations of your language level when answering the questions:

1= I can introduce myself, understand and use familiar everyday expressions, e.g., where do you live?
2= I can exchange and ask for personal and family information, talk about shopping, local geography, and work.
3= I can express myself on familiar topics of personal interest (school, work, hobbies) and talk about experiences, events, dreams and hopes.
4= I can discuss the main ideas of a complex text in language and argue a particular point of view with some fluency.
5= I can use language flexibly and communicate in detail and in a well-structured manner on complex topics.
6= I can use the language for virtually anything in unfamiliar situations.

1. What other language(s) do you use that is/are NOT your native language(s)?
2. How well can you speak them? Differentiate from 1–6 depending for each language (see table).
3. Where/with whom/how did you learn them? Please provide one response for each language.
4. Where/with whom/how do you use it now? Please provide one response for each language.

Language preferences

Here you can classify the languages, dialects or other ways of speaking you use or would like to learn into two rankings. Which languages are important for you personally (family, friends, free time, heritage, identity) and which ones do you consider relevant for educational and professional reasons (traveling, studying abroad, working in international companies)? You can name the same languages in both rankings.

1	2
personal	professional
1) …	1) …
2) …	2) …
3) …	3) …
…	…

1. Please create ranking 1 (personal) and classify the languages accordingly.
2. Please create ranking 2 (professional) and classify the languages accordingly.
3. How satisfied are you with the teaching of foreign languages at school?
4. Would you rather learn English before French or German (depending on where you live in Switzerland)? Please explain why.
5. If you have a mother tongue which is not used in school, would you like to include it more actively into school or class? If so, how and why? If not, why not?
6. If you could choose, would you get rid of languages that you learn in school and introduce/intensify others? Please give examples and explain why.
7. More time in class should be spent on English than on other languages spoken in Switzerland.
8. When I learn a language, I want to speak it like native speakers.
9. When I learn a language, I want teachers to correct my mistakes in grammar and pronunciation.
10. I prefer learning American or British English to "Swiss English" (English with Swiss features in pronunciation and grammar).
11. Swiss German should be taught in school instead of Standard German.
12. English is a neutral language that should be used for communication between the different Swiss language regions.
13. There is no reason why English should be prioritized in the curriculum.
14. Other students' first languages should all be integrated in class.

15. We should debate more about the cultures and languages we have in our class.

Semi-structured interview guide for students

1. When and where do you use the languages you speak?

   - Are there places where you cannot use a specific language? Examples? Stories? Are there times when you have tried? What happened?
   - Are there times when you would like to use a specific language but cannot? Are there times when you have tried? What happened? Examples? Stories?
   - Are there any situations in which you use (your) language as a "secret language"?

2. Please explain why you [insert answer from questionnaire, e.g., don't like] [insert language, e.g., French].
3. Do you have a favorite language? Why?
4. Which additional language would you like to learn that is not offered at school? Why? In what way is this (im)possible?
5. What do you think about teaching approaches in which the subject, e.g., history, is taught in a foreign language?
6. What is your experience with English (school, movies, music, internet, friends)? What do you like about it? What do you think about how English is used in national and international communication, that is, between speakers of different first languages? Should everyone try to speak it as 'native-like' as possible or is understanding more important despite 'mistakes' and 'wrong pronunciation'? What about other languages, i.e., French, German/Swiss German?
7. Explain your rankings of the languages you created in the questionnaire for personal and professional opportunities.
8. To what extent do you agree with the following sentences?

   - I like learning languages so that I can learn about other cultures, communicate with people from other countries and travel.
   - I like learning languages so that I can use it for my future job.
   - Languages are important because I can express who I am and how I feel.

9. To what extent are proficient English language skills responsible for better personal and professional opportunities? What exactly does this mean for your future? Can you give an example?
10. To what extent can/should English be a neutral mediator among the Swiss language regions?

Semi-structured interview guide for teachers

Introduce, briefly explain project, anonymity, ask for permission to record with cell phone, anonymity, all answers are voluntary

1. What languages do you use regularly (at home, at work, etc.)?
2. How would you describe the relationship between languages and identity?
3. How would you describe the relationship between languages and economic opportunities?
4. Under the current conditions, can you teach your lessons in the way you want?

   - In what way does the curriculum influence the way you choose and teach content?
   - In what way does the curriculum influence the teaching approaches you use in class?
   - In what way does the curriculum influence your teaching philosophy?

5. Are you familiar with the Swiss "Language Law"? (If so, what do you think? If not, show an excerpt and have it commented) Which position do you take? How is it discussed at school and by whom?
6. Are you familiar with the EDK's 2020 language strategy? (If so, what do you think? If not, show an excerpt and have it commented) Which position do you take? How is it discussed at school and by whom?
7. What do you think about the Swiss debate on national languages vs. English? (Although debates on language teaching in the multilingual Swiss society have been a constant phenomenon since the early days of its foundation, the decision taken by a couple of German-speaking cantons to introduce English before French has created nation-wide tensions.)
8. What language are used at school? Are there any languages present in school that are neither a national language nor English nor other foreign languages taught? How do you handle the situation? How about heritage languages such as Portuguese or Tigrinya? Can you give me an example how you would integrate it in your own class/why you wouldn't do it? What kind of support would you like/need from the school?
9. What do you think about how English is used in national and international communication, that is, between speakers of different first languages? Should everyone try to speak English as 'native-like' as possible or is understanding more important despite 'mistakes' and 'wrong pronunciation?' What about other languages, i.e., French, German, Swiss German?
10. Do you speak and teach as native-like as possible or do you prefer your "personal language variety"?

11. To what extent are proficient English, French or German language skills responsible for better personal and professional opportunities for students? To what extent do you think it is important that it is a 'prestigious'/standard variety? Can you give an example?
12. If you were a policy maker or curriculum designer, how would you arrange the order of languages to be learned at school?
13. Should the teaching of foreign languages change in the future?

Appendix B

Transcription

Transcription conventions were adapted from Lamnek & Krell (2016).

(-)	Very short breaks
(--)	Long breaks
CAPITAL LETTERS	Emphasis
( )	Unclear
(Example?)	Assumed wording
(Laughs)	Nonverbal behavior
[Phone rings]	Surrounding
Hmm	Hmm (+) affirmative
Hmm	Hmm (-) negative
Hmm	Hmm (=) filler
Uh, etc.	Uh
<Name>	Anonymize

Appendix C

Descriptive statistics

Student questionnaire answers by mean and standard deviation divided by canton

Item	ZH	FR	GR
Liking English (6= a lot)	4.7 0.63 SD	5.3 1.37 SD	5 0.75 SD
Grading English (6= best)	4.8 0.64 SD	4.7 1.1 SD	4.8 0.69 SD
Self-evaluation English (6= best)	5.2 0.74 SD	4.5 1.2 SD	4.4 0.91 SD
Liking French (6= a lot)	4.1 1.18 SD	N/A	4.5 (13 students)[1]
Liking German (6= a lot)	N/A	3.9 1.46 SD	N/A
Grading French (6= best)	4.5 0.6 SD	N/A	4.4 (5 students)
Grading German (6= best)	N/A	4.4 1.2 SD	N/A
Self-evaluation French (6= best)	3.3 1.08	N/A	2 (6 students)
Self-evaluation German (6= best)	N/A	3 0.95 SD	N/A

---

[1] The number in parentheses indicate that not all the sample is accounted for here since only a minority of Grisons students take French classes.

Satisfied with language teaching (1= very)	2.2 0.79 SD	2.9 0.96 SD	2.3 1.0 SD
More time for English in classes than other languages in CH (1= strongly agree)	1.9 0.87 SD	3.1 1.27 SD	3.4 1.0 SD
Aiming at native-like competence (1= strongly agree)	1.9 0.98 SD	2 1.05 SD	1.9 0.97 SD
Want teachers to correct grammatical mistakes & pronunciation (1=strongly agree)	1.7 0.68 SD	1.4 0.66 SD	1.6 0.78 SD
Preferring AE/BE over "Swiss English" (1= strongly agree)	1.5 0.79 SD	1.3 0.71 SD	1.4 0.78 SD
Teaching Swiss German instead of German (1=strongly agree)	3.7 1.39 SD	4.3 1.13 SD	3.9 1.5 SD
English for communication among language regions (1= strongly agree)	2.9 1.6 SD	3.5 1.47 SD	4.3 0.8 SD
English priority in curriculum (1=strongly agree)	1.8 0.75 SD	2.6 1.24 SD	2.8 1.1 SD
Include all L1s in class (1=strongly agree)	4.4 0.89 SD	4.1 1.1 SD	2.9 1.2 SD
Discuss more about languages & cultures (1= strongly agree)	2.8 1.2 SD	2.6 1.24 SD	2.2 1.0 SD

Appendix D

Pseudonym	Student (S), teacher (T)	Cantons Fribourg (FR), Grisons (GR), Zurich (ZH)
Adya	S	ZH
Anastasia	S	GR
André	S	GR
Arthur	S	ZH
Carmen	T	ZH
Christine	S	GR
David	T	FR
Eleonore	T	ZH
Elisabeth	T	ZH
Enzo	S	GR
Etienne	T	FR
Gita	T	GR
Hanna	S	GR

Henri	T	GR
Jana	S	GR
Jeanne	T	FR
Jessica	S	GR
Jovin	S	GR
Julia	S	FR
Julien	T	FR
Leonie	S	GR
Linda	S	GR
Lucien	S	FR
Luisa	T	FR
Marco	S	ZH
Maria	T	ZH
Marie	S	FR
Martin	T	GR
Melissa	S	GR
Mia	S	ZH
Mona	S	FR
Nesrin	T	ZH

Nicolas	S	ZH
Nicole	T	GR
Patrick	T	ZH
Peter	S	ZH
Philipp	S	ZH
Ricardo	S	FR
Roberto	T	GR
Sabine	T	ZH
Samira	S	ZH
Sebastian	S	GR
Sonja	T	ZH
Timo	S	GR
Tina	T	ZH
Tobias	S	ZH
Tom	S	ZH
Victoria	T	FR
Yasmin	S	ZH

CPSIA information can be obtained
at www.ICGtesting.com
Printed in the USA
LVHW051726170523
747260LV00024B/247